JOURNEY TO FINLAND

JOURNEY TO FINLAND

DIANA ASHCROFT

Illustrated with photographs

LONDON
FREDERICK MULLER LTD
Earls Court Gardens, S.W.5

FIRST PUBLISHED BY FREDERICK MULLER LTD.
IN 1952

PRINTED IN GREAT BRITAIN BY
THE CAMELOT PRESS LTD.
LONDON AND SOUTHAMPTON

To

The Finnish British Society of Kajaani

Contents

Illustrations

Glossary of Names

THROUGHOUT this book, where Finnish and Swedish place-names exist side by side, the Finnish names are the ones used. An exception, however, has been made in the case of the Åland Islands because to refer to them as Ahvenanmaa would be needlessly confusing. The same, of course, applies to the word "Finland," which is in Finnish "Suomi". A list of the places mentioned that have dual names follows:

Finnish	*Swedish*
Ahvenanmaa	Åland
Hamina	Fredrikshamn
Hanko	Hangö
Helsinki	Helsingfors
Hämeenlinna	Tavastehus
Kajaani	Kajana
Karesuanto	Karesuando
Laatokka	Ladoga
Maarianhamina	Mariehamn
Oulu	Uleåborg
Pori	Björneborg
Savonlinna	Nyslott
Tornio	Tornea
Turku	Åbo
Uusikaarlebyy	Nykarleby
Viipuri	Viborg

As geographical terms are frequently found in the form of suffixes attached to Finnish place names, a list of those in common use is given below:

Arctic Fell	Tunturi
Bay or Gulf	Lahti
Beach	Ranta
Cape	Niemi

Castle	Linna
Fell	Vaara
Hamlet	Kylä
Hill	Mäki
Island	Saari
Lake	Järvi
Mountain	Vuori
Rapid	Koski
Ridge	Harju
River	Joki
Road or street	Katu
Shore	Ranta
Sound	Salmi
Water	Vesi

Preface

S*UOMI: Finland*—to-day these words, and all that they stand for, have become so vivid a part of my experience that I find it hard to realise how shadowy a picture they conjured up that morning in October, 1946 when it was first suggested that I might go there. Yet the fact is that at the time I had never met a Finn and I knew little or nothing about their country. Nor was I a great deal wiser when I left for Finland five months later. My efforts to remedy the situation had not proved very successful; information—other than text-book information—had been difficult to come by. As a result, it was left to me to discover Finland, to learn for myself that although the Finnish forest might stretch interminably and no hill south of Lapland rise above 1,200 feet, though one lake might be very like another, island resemble island and swamp swamp, the Finnish countryside was far from monotonous. It has an elusive, mysterious beauty of its own—a beauty not quite of this world; a beauty of light rather than form, of expression rather than feature; a transient, intangible beauty as different from that of any other country as are the Finns from any other race in Europe.

And what of these people? For the moment all that I wish to say is that it is because I spent a very happy year among them that I have written this book. Such as it is, it is a token of my gratitude for the many kindnesses they showered upon me; for there is nothing more noticeable in Finland to-day than the ardent desire of most Finns for the friendship and understanding of the British people. Indeed, so potent is this desire that there are now sixty-five flourishing Anglophil societies in the country; whereas, in July, 1945, only fourteen were in existence.

It was as secretary to one of these societies that I went to Finland in April, 1947. I stayed until the following April and in July, 1949 returned for five weeks. Thus, while making occasional reference to the summer of 1949, what I have written is mainly concerned with the year 1947/48.

At that time life was far from easy for the Finnish people. The energy which should have been devoted to post-war reconstruction was being expended on reparations for the

Soviet Union, and the crying needs of countless refugees were taxing the nation's already meagre resources to the utmost. Shortages of all kinds were acute and casual intercourse with the outside world virtually at a standstill. Fear of Communism was widespread and a deep sense of isolation prevailed. To be isolated is, however, no novelty for the Finnish people. It is a chronic condition that is basically the outcome of Finland's geographical situation and that varies only in intensity. Nevertheless, apart altogether from considerations of security, the people have never been wholly resigned to it. To them isolation is, by its very nature, galling, for they are a friendly people with a veritable passion for being up-to-date. In fact, one of the most remarkable consequences of Finland's isolation has been that it has produced a nation, steeped as are no other European people in their own peculiar, cultural tradition, who are at one and the same time, extremely progressive in their outlook and modern in their taste.

Happily, many of the conditions I have described are already a thing of the past. By 1949 the standard of living in Finland had improved out of all recognition. To-day it is even better, although the housing shortage is still very severe. Furthermore, the Russian debt has been almost paid off and foreign travel, which in the years immediately following the war was all but completely banned, is now, within slowly widening limits, open to the Finnish people.

But although, little by little, the Finns are emerging from their northern fastness and re-establishing contact with the world at large, this contact can never be achieved unless they themselves take the initiative. In the matter of language it is always they who must meet the foreigner, as the Finnish language is an exceptionally difficult one and of so little use beyond the borders of Finland that the outsider who speaks it is very rare indeed. This has led to most educated Finns speaking not only Finnish and Swedish, but also more or less fluent English or German and sometimes both; and partly, at any rate, as a result of this fluency I myself made small headway with their language. I was not encouraged to try. In the first place, my friends always wanted to talk English; and, in the second, they were unanimously of the opinion that for me the game was not worth the candle and very soon my early efforts to learn it petered out. I little dreamed that I was going to write a book about Finland and so gave no thought to the various sources of information I should have to consult. But, even if I had, I doubt if it would have made much difference. I have no flair for languages and could never have absorbed enough to enable me to do my own devilling. In January, 1949, I started writing. By the following summer the gaps in my knowledge were yawning wide. I took the line of least resistance, returned to Finland and peppered my friends with questions. But even this was not enough. I had not been back in England long before I was once more in need of help. There was nothing for it but to have recourse to the post and, here and now, I would like to thank all those of my Finnish friends who, throughout the last two years, have so painstakingly dealt with my numberless inquiries. Very few Finns enjoy writing letters, yet their replies poured in in such profusion that I was rarely at a loss for the information which I needed. To the writers of these letters I can only say that I am deeply grateful, and that it is my fondest hope that the fruit of their combined labours will meet with their approval.

But it is not only to my Finnish friends that I am profoundly indebted. I wish also to acknowledge with gratitude the assistance of Edith Eccles, Peggy Jacobson and Mary Thompson; and, in particular, I have to thank my friend Robert Merlin for the unfailing help and encouragement which he gave me, help so invaluable that all thanks must be inadequate. Step by step we went through the text together; pulling it to pieces—arguing hotly, albeit amicably—and then putting it together again. His interest was unfailing; his criticism constructive; his opinion of my spelling unprintable and his enthusiasm the tonic that I most needed. In short, it was Bob who first suggested I should write this book and Bob who saw to it that it was written.

D. M. A.

January, 1952.

Part I

Spring in Kajaani

EARLY FORM OF SNOWSHOES

from *Historia de Gentibus Septentrionalibus* by Olaus Magnus (published in 1555).

See p. 80.

Part I

Spring in Kajaani

"HOW would you like to go to Finland? The Finns and the Turks are the same race, you know."

Obsolete as this theory now is and much as the Finns dislike it, here was a member of the British Council cheerfully putting it forward as a reason for my going to Finland; and here was I, equally cheerfully and just as ignorantly, taking his word for it and savouring all kinds of new and exciting possibilities. True, I was not very interested in the racial origins of the Finns, and Finland itself was a far cry from any country to which I had visualised going, but there was a novelty about the idea that was not without appeal. I had applied for work in the eastern Mediterranean area, but it was abundantly clear that there was none going there. If Turkey suggested Finland to even one member of the British Council's staff, so much the better for me.

Full of curiosity, I asked what the prospects of my getting work in Finland were, but all that my informant knew for certain was that jobs were in the wind—not jobs with the Council, but jobs in which the Council were prepared to take a great interest. It appeared that there was a wealth of good pro-British feeling in Finland; that Anglophil societies were springing up all over the country and that some of these societies were thinking of employing British secretaries. As yet, however, no one in the London office knew which societies proposed employing them, what they were to do, how they were to live or what they were to be paid. If the conditions offered turned out to be satisfactory, the Council would do all in their power to find suitable people for the posts. If not, the matter would end there. As far as I was concerned, there was nothing that I could do but go home and await developments.

It was nearly three months before the Council wrote and told me that secretaries were to be sent to Kajaani and Normarkku to help organise the activities of the local Anglophil societies and give a few English conversation classes. Their initial contracts were to be for one year and the pay and holidays offered them were virtually identical, but nothing at all was said on the all-important subject of the places themselves. The vacancies were to be filled shortly and a selection board was imminent.

Kajaani or Normarkku? Neither name rang a bell of any sort. Where were they? What were they like? No one that I asked seemed to have the faintest idea—least of all the Council. Before committing myself, I had somehow or other to find out.

One glance at the map of Finland in the *Times Atlas* sufficed to locate Kajaani—a small black dot between two lakes that looked horribly near to the Arctic Circle—but Normarkku was not to be seen on this, nor any other map to which I had access. Wise after the event, I suppose that the most sensible thing I could have done would have been to visit the Royal Geographical Society, but I never thought of it. Instead, I set off down the Charing Cross Road to hunt for books about Finland. I found exactly three: Agnes Rothery's *Finland*, which contained abundant general information but no reference to either Kajaani or Normarkku; E. R. Burnham's *Who are the Finns?*, which was an abstruse study in pre-history—hardly applicable to my needs, although both I and my friend in the Council might have been the wiser for reading it—and Mrs. Alec Tweedie's *Through Finland in Carts*, a book which was published as early as 1897. Yet Mrs. Tweedie was the only one of the three to mention Kajaani, where, judging from her account, she and her friends had spent one highly uncomfortable night.[1] But although she passed from a description of the hotel where she had stayed to one of the tar-boats that braved the rapids and plied up and down the river past the town, she contented herself with disposing of Kajaani in a mere half-sentence: "Iisalmi is nothing—hardly possesses an hotel, in fact—and Kajana is not much better although the rapids make it of great interest."

This being little enough to go on I decided to visit the offices of the Political Representative of Finland in London[2] in the

[1] "We were worn out and weary when we reached Kajana, where we were the only visitors in the hotel, and, as the beds very rapidly proved impossible, we women-folk confiscated the large—and I suppose only—sitting-room as our bedchamber. A horsehair sofa, of a hard old-fashioned type, formed a downy couch for one; the dining-table, covered by one of the travelling-rugs, answered as a bed for number two; and the old-fashioned spinet, standing against the wall, furnished sleeping accommodation for number three!"

[2] The Finnish Embassy in London was not reinstated until after the ratification of the Peace Treaty in September, 1947.

hope of adding to it. There, the Swedish Finn, with whom I discussed my project, urged me whole-heartedly to apply for one of the jobs. It did not appear to worry him in the least that he had never set foot in either Kajaani or Normarkku. He was perfectly prepared to vouch for them both and, getting out a detailed map of Finland, he pointed to the south-west corner and remarked, "There's Normarkku. It's very small; just a mushroom growth of streamline factories."

Described in those terms, Normarkku did not appeal to me much but Kajaani sounded rather more promising. It boasted a population of 9,000, an old ruined castle, a modern teachers' seminary and a large paper mill.

"What about the rapids and the tar boats?" I asked, remembering Mrs. Tweedie.

"The tar boats don't run any more," he replied, "and the rapids have been spoilt by two large power stations."

This was rather a blow and, because I had almost made up my mind to go and preferred to harbour some romantic illusions, I deliberately refrained from asking any questions about the castle. Changing the subject, I inquired what post-war living conditions were like in Finland.

The answer I got was scarcely compatible with the enthusiastic encouragement I was receiving. Conditions were hard, shortages numerous and, if I went, I would do well to take all that I should need for a year with me, sheets, blankets, soap, tooth-paste—everything.

Visualising a mountain of over-weight luggage, I turned to the all-important topic of clothes and very soon I had elicited the information that small-town dwellers in Finland had old-fashioned views about women in trousers. No matter how cold the weather, trousers were only countenanced for ski-ing. Not being the right shape for trousers, I resolved quite happily to swim with the tide, but when I was told that every Finnish woman had one black dress for parties it was a totally different matter. I had not got a black dress and I had no intention of buying one; I look muddy in black.

I came away from this interview undeterred. If the British Council would send me to Finland, to Finland I would go. In reality I doubt if I had ever been in two minds about it, but I was none the less horribly afraid that the Selection Board might prove less single-minded. After all, I had never been a secretary nor had I ever taught anybody anything. I took a deep breath, attended the Board and awaited results.

It was three weeks before I heard anything more, but the news, when it came, was good—the Finnish British Society of Kajaani would be glad to have me. I wrote a formal acceptance and started shopping. What a job it was! It was February, 1947, and the power cuts were at their height. Nobody knew how long any order would take to complete and selection by candlelight was extremely difficult. With the fifty supplementary clothing coupons I had been given, I made one abortive attempt to buy a new fur coat. By the light of a pocket torch, I scanned the stock of a big London store and then carried my selection into the street. There, in front of a long glass that flanked one side of the doorway, I tried on coat after coat. The daylight was poor and it was all hopelessly unsatisfactory. Giving it up as a bad job, I determined to have my old white lambskin altered. This went sorely against the grain, for it was a well-made swagger coat which really did fit me, but, alas, it let in all the draughts. Regretfully, I took it to a furrier and asked if it could be made to envelop me completely.

"We only deal in fur here," she said. "That's wool."

Considerably abashed, I took it elsewhere.

The final result was warm and cosy. But my fears for my coat had been all too well founded; it was no longer what it had been. In it I looked exactly like Shelley's moon—"A white and shapeless mass."

The question of headgear came next. Providentially, this was solved for me by the unearthing of a sealskin cap that had been worn by my paternal grandfather on a visit to Russia many years before I was born. It did not fit, it was, in fact, several sizes too small—but with a gusset let in the back it became, if not chic, at least serviceable and on a par with my coat.

Having dealt with my top clothes, it remained to procure an adequate supply of woollen underwear and stockings. This was far from easy. Rebuffed here, rebuffed there, I tried first one shop and then another. In each I heard the same story: quotas were small and the weather was phenomenally cold; all their woollen goods had been sold out the day they came in. Yet, by dint of persevering, I did in the end manage to obtain almost everything that I needed and, on the morning of March 25th, I left London for Kajaani accompanied by Sylvia, who was bound for Normarkku.

* * *

Travelling by way of Denmark, Sylvia and I spent two nights and one damp, foggy day in Copenhagen and finally reached Stockholm on the evening of March 28th. Here our tickets gave out and our instructions were to report to the Council to find out how to proceed.

The following morning, therefore, we went straight to their offices and as they were at some distance from our hotel we took the tram; a beautiful, bright blue, streamlined tram that bore the awful warning "Fast Konductor" placarded outside it. As a notice we thought it altogether too good to be true, and were still smiling inwardly at the picture which it conjured up, when, safe and sound, we reached our destination. Here our spirits were soon dashed; the Council staff were gloomy beyond belief. They obviously thought us crazy to be going to Finland, where, they assured us repeatedly, living conditions were very bad indeed. Did we realise how much of their valuable time was spent in sending food parcels to their staff in Helsinki and Turku? This was an altogether new aspect of the matter and one to which we had not given a thought. Nevertheless, now that our attention had been drawn to it, we found it encouraging rather than discouraging, for might not their services be extended to us also. So we listened attentively to all that they had to say and accepted gratefully when our hopes were fulfilled and they offered, on deposit of some of our precious crowns, to send monthly food parcels to us also—an offer that I fear they lived to regret as the Swedish regulations grew increasingly stringent.

* * *

We left Sweden in the late afternoon of April 1st on board the S.S. *Bore*, a Finnish ship in which every berth had long since been taken. The Council having been relatively late in making our reservations, Sylvia and I were allotted the Chief Engineer's cabin. We thought this rather hard on him, but he took it remarkably well, beamed on us and assured us that it made no difference to him as he never used his cabin while at sea. Although we did not then realise it, this was our first experience of the good-natured way in which the Finns as a whole have adapted themselves to overcrowding.

Sylvia and I settled ourselves in gratefully. There was not much room and what there was was cluttered up with the Chief's gear, but we had at least somewhere to sleep and for this, as we looked about us, we knew that we had every reason to be thankful. There must have been at least twice as many passengers on board as berths to accommodate them and, when night came, they dossed down all over the place. Below decks every passage was strewn with recumbent forms and all movement was severely hampered.

Standing on deck, we talked for a while with a friendly American who was on his way to join the Quaker Relief Unit in North Finland and, as we talked, Stockholm vanished into the mist. Around us the waters of the Saltsjön lay hidden beneath a smooth sheet of snow-clad ice that must have been quite three feet thick. It stretched the whole way across the Baltic, its surface unbroken except by the streak of coal-black water no wider than Piccadilly that the ice-breaker had left in its wake.

There was something very strange and exciting about the way in which we steamed slowly and deliberately down this narrow channel with the recently shattered ice boulders clanking against the ship's side and the distance shrouded in mist. There was about it an overwhelming sense of adventure; a sense of moving, slowly and deliberately, into the unknown. Yet fascinating as it all was, it was no weather for standing about, or even for pacing the deck, and we had not been under way long before the cold forced us to go below. It was then that, too late, we thought to reserve our places for supper. There were no seats to be had before the fourth and last service, which did not start till 11 p.m. This meant a weary wait of some five hours, but it was a meal worth waiting for. In the centre of the dining-saloon was a table piled high with delectable dishes to which everyone helped themselves and all did full justice.

Tired and replete, we turned in immediately afterwards. The crossing was scheduled to take fourteen hours and we expected to dock first thing in the morning.

I woke early, caught a glimpse of land through the port-hole and promptly assumed that we were arriving. Leaping out of bed, I roused Sylvia and started hurriedly dressing. Once ready, I put on my coat and went out on deck. I need not have hurried; I might well have left Sylvia to sleep in peace; far from arriving, we were among the outer Åland Islands.

As we drew alongside the wharf at Maarianhamina the engines ceased to throb and a pall of silence descended. It was the frozen stillness of the Arctic and as such it was something that I had never before experienced. Hitherto I had always thought of silence as alive and pregnant with sound, but this northern quietude was muffled and dead. It was almost impossible to believe that life could ever quicken beneath the snow and ice. Even the sea—and I smiled as I thought of the anti-seasick tablets tucked away in my bag—lay motionless, imprisoned as in a sheath of ice embossed with small rocky islands. Stunted trees stood out stark against the skyline. It was a study in black and white as devoid of colour as an etching.

We did not stop long at Maarianhamina, the home of Gustaf Erikson's famous and fast-dwindling fleet of sailing ships,[1] but were soon once more ploughing our way through the ice; soon, too, the fog-horn was moaning. The crowd sat huddled below decks, where it was hot, airless and smoky, and Sylvia and I were more than glad to curl ourselves up on the worn red velvet settee in the Chief Engineer's cabin.

We docked at Turku at about 7 p.m.—almost exactly twelve hours late. The formalities that followed seemed endless. It must have been fully an hour before we got ashore and we felt very sorry for the two members of the Council's staff who had come to meet us and who were waiting on the chilly dock.

Actually the process of disembarking in Finland is not so much difficult as prolonged, and in this connection a story is told of the recent arrival in Turku of a number of bishops. The occasion was a conference in celebration of the fourth centenary of the translation of the New Testament into Finnish by Michael Agricola, and the bishops had come from many parts. From the outset everything possible was done to make them welcome and in order that they might be free to go ashore immediately a man was detailed to meet the ship and see to all the donkey work for them. This man was nothing if not enterprising. Having dealt with their passports and collected their ration cards, he had a brainwave. Knowing that spirits were only sold to foreigners on production of a passport, he proceeded straight from the ship to the Government wine store and when, later that evening, the episcopal passports were returned to their owners, each one was accompanied by a bottle of schnapps.

After spending one night in the hotel where the Council's staff themselves were staying, we devoted the morning to

[1] Before the war Gustaf Erikson operated a fleet of thirteen large sailing vessels. This number has now been reduced to five.

cashing cheques and clearing our big luggage—the quest for money coming first, because Finnish money had not been obtainable outside Finland and we were penniless. We were a long time in the bank and even longer in the Customs, and when at last our trunks had been released and registered to our final destinations, we had only just time to snatch a hasty meal before catching the train to Helsinki. Of Turku we saw next to nothing.

I fell in love with the little, wood-burning Finnish engines at first sight, for there is something very endearing about them. They are so fussy and slow and their funnels, which are bedecked with spark-catchers, have an ingenuously pioneering look. Busy is perhaps the adjective which best describes them; busy and voracious, for every Finnish journey is prolonged in time by the constantly-recurring need to take fresh logs on board.

Beyond their engines, however, there is little that is lovable about Finnish trains. They tend to be overheated and in midwinter their windows are almost always so thickly coated with frost that it is impossible to see through them. Moreover, most Finnish rolling stock is shoddy in the extreme, but as the Soviet Union has appropriated all their best coaches this is scarcely surprising.

Our journey was scheduled to take six hours, a considerable increase on the pre-war time because of the enforced detour round the Russian Base at Porkkala, but even so the total distance was only 170 miles. We shared a compartment with two Finnish women, one of whom spoke fluent German and soon she and Sylvia were chatting away together. My German being of the bed, bath and railway station variety, I left them to it and sat gazing out of the window at a flat snow-clad landscape made drab and dismal by a partial thaw.

At Helsinki we were once again met by members of the Council's staff and taken to a hotel. Later they gave us each a typewritten programme for the following day. These, on perusal, we found to be identical and to include a drive round Helsinki, a visit to the Finnish British Society and a succession of meals with different members of the Council's staff, beginning with lunch with the Representative himself. The day in question was Good Friday—a grey day, bleak and cold. Museums, shops, cinemas, restaurants, everything was closed and there were few people in the streets. Wherever we looked, shop windows were almost empty and everything looked inexpressively sad.

By contrast, lunch was a cheerful meal during which we were given our first lesson in Finnish etiquette, the gist of which was: never drink, even at table, before either your host or hostess has caught your eye, and never leave the dining-room until you have shaken your hostess by the hand and thanked her for her hospitality. This is a matter of common politeness and in no way denotes that you are leaving. We were also given this piece of advice—advice that it was not humanly possible to follow—never talk politics.

That evening the Assistant Representative and Sylvia saw me off on the night train for Kajaani. Sylvia was not leaving until the next day for Normarkku. I was tired and as it was already dark I got into my sleeper almost immediately. It was supplied with a paper undersheet which crackled every time I moved, and I did not sleep a great deal. Why, oh why, was the train so overheated? I tossed and turned, reduced my undersheet to ribbons and wished whole-heartedly that the Finnish language were not so utterly alien to me. I would have liked to be able to talk to my companion. It would have set my mind at rest if I could have found out at what time the train arrived at Iisalmi—that place of which Mrs. Tweedie thought so poorly—because I knew that on arrival there the sleepers were detached and that, before this happened, I had to dress and walk down the train. I had visions of being detached with the sleepers and waking up in a siding and, combined with the excessive heat, this rather horrifying thought was keeping me awake. I need not have worried; at about 7.30 a.m. there was a commotion outside my door and I heard my name spoken very distinctly. It was Maarit Hyyrylainen, a Kajaani girl, who was on her way home for Easter from Helsinki University. Her mother, so she told me, had rung her up just before she left and asked her to find me and look after me, and she had now run me to earth and was anxious to help me transfer my belongings down the train. This was an operation which left us chilled and windswept, as the coaches were not linked together by any covered way.

Maarit's flow of English was encouraging. Everything, even the date seemed auspicious. It was April 5th, and April 5th, now that I came to think of it, was the name of almost the only Derby winner that I had ever backed with success. With all my heart I hoped my new venture would prove as successful.

From Iisalmi to Kajaani is a bare fifty miles. Apprehensive and impatient by turns, I glanced from my watch to the endless vista of forest that stretched on either side of the line and then back again. The hands of my watch moved steadily forward, but outside there was no sign of a break in the trees—nothing to indicate that we should be arriving at any moment. Then, quite suddenly, the trees parted and a tall red brick fire-tower came into view. A minute later and we were running into Kajaani Station, and there, lined up like sentinels on the platform, were Aili Parviainen, Gretel Eberling and Kalle Frey. They stood stiffly in a row, looking very correct and, as they extended their hands in greeting, one after the other they enunciated their surnames very distinctly. Parviainen—Eberling—Frey; flustered as I was, their names went straight in at one ear and out of the other, but I was none the less very properly impressed by the performance.

My registered luggage, which had arrived before me, was quickly collected and strapped on to the back of a waiting car. Then, with all my belongings safely accounted for, we four piled inside. It was Easter Saturday morning and the time was about 10.30.

Leaving the station, we drove the whole length of the main street, dropped Kalle Frey at the hospital, where he was the assistant surgeon, and continued on beyond the outskirts of the town until we reached the large paper mill that provides most of Kajaani's inhabitants with employment. Opposite was the factory club, a low white building where business visitors were put up and entertained and where those of the firm's personnel who wished to do so could have their meals. Here, for the time being, I was to live.

As we entered we were met by the housekeeper, an elderly grey-haired woman who at once showed me to my room. She knew no more English than I Finnish, but her smile was warm and friendly and I felt at once that I was in good hands when Aili and Gretel committed me to her care, promising, as they did so, to return later and fetch me for lunch. I was glad of the respite; it gave me a chance to do a little unpacking and, as I set about getting myself straight, I wondered for the hundredth time when I should meet the Society for whom I had come to work and what its members would turn out to be like.

I was soon to find out. No sooner had Aili and Gretel

returned than they told me that we were going to the Maakunta Hotel, where the Society was giving a lunch for me. Now that the moment had come, I suddenly felt most horribly and unreasonably nervous.

But not for long. Although the assembled company was obviously on its best behaviour, and if anything more diffident than I was, there was no doubt at all about the underlying warmth of the welcome they were giving me. I could feel that beneath their native shyness they were genuinely glad to have me there, and this feeling put new heart into me.

There must have been about a dozen people gathered in the Maakunta's private room and beginning with Yrjö Tähtinen, the Society's President, I was formally introduced to each one in turn. This done, we all sat down to lunch.

The main dish was pike—a never-to-be-forgotten pike, full of unexpected threadlike bones that made the business of dissecting it an all-engrossing matter. I, who had never eaten pike before, had no idea how to set about it. What if I swallowed a bone and choked? The very thought appalled me. I can think of no dish less conducive to polite conversation and the making of a good impression, yet, in a way, it was not ill-chosen, as from legendary times onwards the pike has always been the most Finnish of fishes.[1]

But whatever the impression I myself created, I know that by the time the meal was over, the one that I had formed was pleasant. Although the general conversation was somewhat halting, for many of the company were handicapped by having to grope for English words, it was clear that a little practice would soon remedy this and, because I knew that in the fluency of all lay my main guarantee against loneliness, I was overjoyed.

As we were finishing a reporter arrived from the local newspaper. She was very young and, it soon became apparent, very inexperienced. Furthermore, she spoke very little English. A concerted effort was made to help us both and I found myself bombarded with questions—questions about my journey, questions about the fuel crisis at home and questions about my still inchoate impressions of Finland.

As soon as she had gone, the party broke up, and I went with Yrjö Tähtinen to the post office to send a cable home. This

[1] The legendary hero Väinämöinen fashioned his famous *kantele*, or Finnish harp, out of the jaws of a monster pike (*Kalevala*, Runo XL).

done, I returned to the club to complete, at my leisure, the process of settling in.

* * *

Easter Morning—and all around the countryside lay buried beneath a carpet of snow. At first sight it might have been Christmas, yet only at first sight, for the sky overhead was a cloudless blue and the sun was shining brightly with a promise of warmth to come.

I set out to explore, feeling strangely light-hearted and nostalgic by turns, for, snow or no snow, spring was in the air. A late spring, as I subsequently discovered, as it is quite usual for the snow to be gone by April. This year, however, the thaw had not yet reached Kajaani. The world on which I gazed was still a white one and only the bare trees bore witness that no fresh snow had fallen for some time past.

Turning my back on the road leading from the factory to Kajaani and leaving behind me the club and the saw-mill, I followed a track that led across the frozen river, through a trim settlement of workmen's dwellings, over some open country and on into the outskirts of the forest. Not many people were about. The few that I passed I greeted. But I might as well have saved my breath as all that I ever got in return was a stony stare. Clearly, I mused, I should have to learn the local salutation and see if it were possible to do better.

But, however dour the farm-hands, the sun smiled and its broken light rippled like laughter among the pines and spruce, throwing a warm glow on to their stems and causing deep blue shadows on the snow. It was a peculiarly neat forest; neat and well cared-for, the outcome of years of labour and the backbone of Finnish economy. "Finland's Green Gold" the people call it and it could not be more aptly named.

I did not walk far as I was afraid of getting lost, and of one thing I was certain: I was utterly incapable of asking my way. Nor did the unresponsiveness I had met with embolden me to try. Moreover, as if to add to my difficulties, very few of the peasants whom I had met had been on foot. The majority had been riding on sleds; a fact which made them doubly unapproachable in my eyes. This, however, was unreasonable, as the stocky little chestnuts, that were drawing their sleds, were obviously in no hurry. Horses and men alike moved with a slow deliberation that, I was to learn later, is characteristic of the nation as a whole. In fact, to this day I can hardly ever recall seeing a Finn who was noticeably pressed for time—that is with the exception of the drivers of motor vehicles on ice-bound roads, whose business is apt to appear terrifyingly urgent. But they are the exception and *more haste less speed* the rule. How so much is achieved at so slow a tempo is something at which I have never ceased to marvel.

* * *

The club in which I was housed had been built by the Kajaani O.Y.[1] beside their factory about a mile and a half west of the town in the suburb of Tihisenniemi. Like Kajaani, this suburb overlooks the river that links the waters of the Sotkamojärvi with those of the Oulujärvi and, like Kajaani, it is out of sight of both. Unreasonably, I felt that the maps I had consulted in London had misled me on this score. Kajaani was no miniature Interlaken, complete with dual waterfront. The only water to be seen from the town was that of the river, which flowed past wide and deep between two large power stations. For here the once-famous rapids had been harnessed to provide motive power for the factory and electricity for the town.

The club-house was a relatively new addition to the factory; a small white wooden building that was dwarfed into insignificance by the dominating red-brick mass of the works. One story high, the back looked out over the river, while two wings projected from the front towards the mill. One of these wings was devoted to guest-rooms, the other to the operatives' canteen, and linking the two together was the staff's combined dining-room and library. This was a large room that was to become very familiar to me, as in it the Finnish British Society generally met. It was lined with bookshelves and filled with small tables and hard wooden chairs. Devoid of carpet and curtains, not even the three armchairs which, together with a grand piano, were tucked away in an alcove, could save it from being cheerless and utilitarian in the extreme. Nevertheless, it was much in demand for social functions, and could, on occasions, be made to look quite festive.

My bedroom was in the guest wing and faced the sulphite mill, a circumstance that it was not easy to ignore, as a pungent odour of sulphur was wafted in at my window whenever the

[1] The letters O.Y. stand for *Osake Yhtio*, or Limited Liability Company, and the name Kajaani O.Y. is the full title of the firm, despite the fact that it indicates nothing of its business.

wind was southerly. But, the odour apart, there was little of which anyone could complain. The room, though small, was centrally heated, comfortably furnished and supplied with cold running water. Furthermore, it had a telephone; a temperamental instrument that I viewed from the start with misgivings and that was, indeed, to prove most unaccountably addicted to pealing in sympathy with every other extension in the building.

In all I think what struck me most forcibly about my surroundings was their complete lack of homeliness. The shining linoleum on the floor, the pale, highly varnished, birchwood furniture and above all the view from my bedroom window were all so very impersonal. Last thing at night and first thing in the morning I would watch from my bed an endless stream of cellulose being carried by an overhead railway from one end of the factory to the other. It was packed and ready for export, and as each carrier dumped its load it returned empty along a parallel cable On and on they went, back and forth, full and empty. As the summer wore on and the darkness ceased to hide them even at midnight, I watched as one hypnotised, my range of vision limited to the centre of the track and my mind concentrated on betting with myself as to whether the next empty carrier would appear before the last full one had vanished.

All this, however, was unimportant. Everyone had been at great pains to explain that my living at the club was a temporary expedient, and only intended to last until more suitable accommodation could be found. They all realised that as an arrangement it was far from ideal, not only because the club was inconveniently far from the town, but also because the company could ill afford to be one guest-room short. All being well—that is, provided that we liked the look of each other—after the summer holidays I was to move to the Freys. By then the student from the Teachers' Seminary, who was occupying their spare room, would have graduated and left Kajaani.

Accommodation was, and still is, the Finns' greatest problem, for since the loss of Karelia the country has been flooded by refugees. Some idea of the immense size of this problem can be obtained by remembering that the total population of Finland is rather under 4,000,000, and that when the Soviet Union annexed the area to which the Finns always refer as Karelia, they offered the inhabitants the choice between leaving the

Finnish Engine taking on fuel

Kajaani, O.Y.

Kajaani River in winter

Kajaani River in summer

country empty-handed or staying and keeping their homes and possessions. Of 420,000 people—that is, approximately one-eighth of the whole of Finland's population—only 1,000 stayed. The result has been an enormous influx of people into the urban areas and the passing of temporary laws which lay down that no one person may have more than one room, and that, for the purposes of reckoning, a kitchen counts as a room if it is of any size at all. This means that for the time being many people are suffering from an almost total lack of privacy, as any town-dweller with a sizeable house or flat has it automatically filled with strangers. Moreover, these strangers, even with the best will in the world, must often find it hard to keep themselves to themselves, because of the way in which Finnish architects habitually dispense with passages and landings in favour of communicating rooms. Proud as the nation is of the mass loyalty of the Karelian people, there was many a familiar ring about the current evacuee stories.

Karelia—it was a subject from which there was no escape, and so merits a word or two in passing. The Finns talk about Karelia and East Karelia. This is confusing, for by Karelia they mean the area to the south-east which borders on the north-western half of Lake Laatokka and which was recently ceded to the Soviet Union, while they use the term East Karelia to indicate the province that lies north of Lake Laatokka and extends along Finland's eastern border as far north as the Kola Peninsula, and through which runs the Leningrad-Murmansk railway. In East Karelia live 140,000 Finns who have long been under Russian domination. They are a relatively backward people unlinked to Finland by any living memory. The Karelians proper are very different. Although their country has been an almost constant battleground, they have always been Finns first and last. Many of my new friends had been born and brought up in Karelia, and all spoke of it with deep yearning. To them it had been the most beautiful part of Finland; Viipuri had been the finest of all Finnish cities and the Karelian people the most vivacious and lovable of all Finns. And so the words "in Karelia" were to recur constantly, and always with pathos.

* * *

I arrived back from my walk to find lunch in full swing at the club. This was puzzling, because it was barely half-past eleven.

It became even more bewildering when I heard it referred to as "breakfast," as I had begun the day with a Continental breakfast that had appeared on a tray by my bedside at about 8.30. I had, moreover, been profoundly impressed by my breakfast, because lording it over the tray had been a monster tea-pot, the like of which I had never seen before. It resembled a cottage loaf and was, in reality, two tea-pots, a large and a small. The large one had contained hot water, the small one tea, and the one sat snugly on top of the other in place of a lid. To my surprise, I was told that all these pots were made in England and there was general incredulity when I confessed that I had never seen one before—let alone used one. Nor would I, if an alternative pot were available, as I cannot but feel that the Finnish system of pouring one mouthful of very strong tea into a cup and then filling it up with hot water is a mistaken one. Yet in their shape these pots have a definite appeal; they cry aloud to be animated—to be allowed to figure in a children's story book or come to life in a Disney cartoon.

A few inquiries brought to light the fact that "breakfast" was "lunch," but not the reason why. The simple truth is that, for some obscure reason, the Finns, when speaking English, always refer to "lunch" as "breakfast" and to "breakfast" as "coffee" or "porridge" or whatever they may happen to consume first thing in the morning. I, however, have no intention of following suit. The normal Finnish lunch hour is 11.30 and it is usual for people to dine between 4.30 and 6 p.m. But on Sundays—and this was Easter Sunday—most families have only one major meal, and that is known as "dinner" and eaten in the early afternoon.

Had the club followed the same routine as private individuals, I should not, at the outset, have found Finnish mealtimes so mystifying, but this was not possible. The mill was working non-stop night and day on reparations. Sunday or weekday, holiday or no holiday, some members of the staff had to be on duty and, being on duty, to be fed as usual. Thus, when still virtually ignorant of what to expect, I was faced by a conflict of hours. On the one hand, the club housekeeper was encouraging me to eat at 11.30—at least, that is what I took her gestures to mean—and on the other I had been invited to lunch at one by the Freys. That the club lunch should be called "breakfast" was just one more item designed to fox me. Wisely, I decided to give it the go-by and save myself for the Freys' Sunday dinner.

Punctually at the hour arranged, Kalle Frey and his six-year-old son, Harri, arrived to fetch me and together the three of us walked back towards Kajaani. It was not a long walk, at most a mile, for the Freys' house was close to the hospital on the edge of the town nearest to the mill. Nor did it seem long, as all the way there Kalle chatted quite unshyly in English that was both ambitious and colloquial—English that has never ceased to give me pleasure, for the element of surprise is never absent from it for long. In fact, only recently, I had a letter from Kalle that, to use his own words, was *a real gallimaufry*, a lapse into the archaic that sent me flying to my dictionary.

But now he was busily talking about Harri, who, dressed in a navy-blue siren suit, was running round us in circles. He was, it appeared, already in his second year at school, although Finnish children do not normally go until they are seven. For this Harri himself was responsible. The headmaster of the elementary school which was run in conjunction with the Teachers' Seminary was a family friend, and one day in his presence Harri had clamoured to be allowed to start school. "Let him come," had been the response. "He won't stay more than a couple of days and then you can take him away again." But Harri was firm as the Rock of Gibraltar. He had gone to stay.

On arrival I was greeted by Kalle's wife, Sirkka, whom I had already met the previous day at lunch at the Maakunta. "Welcome," she said with a beaming smile, "welcome to our house."

Number 5 Seminaarinkatu was the house in which I was destined to spend the following winter, and right from the start I knew that I should be happy there. For a Finnish house it was spacious and homely and the people of Kajaani always referred to it as English-type. Just why I could never make out. Perhaps it was because it was less formal than most; perhaps because it was reputed to be cold. I only know that it never seemed to me to be typically English, or for that matter Finnish. Neither did I find it cold, although I did sometimes find other houses uncomfortably hot.

Sirkka, although she understood almost everything that I said, did not express herself in English with the same ease as Kalle. But this did not prevent her from struggling along valiantly. Leading me into the sitting-room, she introduced me to their other guest, Inger Pajari, a Norwegian by birth, the widow of a Finnish doctor and the mother of twin daughters whom I never succeeded in telling apart.

In a short while Harri disappeared and we sat down to lunch. Finnish children, I was soon to realise, are little in evidence when their parents are entertaining. In fact, I had been over two months in Kajaani before I ever sat down to table with a child of any age, as when visitors are present they are almost always banished to the kitchen to eat.

Both the room and the table were decorated with small witches made of straw. Easter Witches the Finns call them, because tradition has it that on Easter night they sail through the darkness on their broomsticks. But, when I asked what they were up to, everyone present seemed rather vague. Beyond agreeing that it was only natural for the powers of darkness to be disturbed at Eastertide, no one seemed to know what they were about. Further inquiries have, however, brought three alternative theories to light. The most original asserts that on Easter night the witches gather at the old windmills, taking with them the wool that they have collected during the year, and that those who have failed to amass their quota spend the night scouring the country in search of sheep to shear—a superstition that can scarcely be Finnish in origin, as windmills are rare in Finland and few sheep are out of doors by Easter. Others say that on this night the witches assemble at Kyöpelinvuori,[1] a hill haunted by spinsters atoning for their unmarried state, while a more commonplace supposition is that they go to feast with the devil. It does not matter except in so far as the tradition serves to illustrate the strange blend of Christianity and paganism that was current everywhere in the Middle Ages and which has always made a very special appeal to the Finns.

This combination is to be found at its most charming in the works of Zachris Topelius,[2] who is called by many the Hans Andersen of Finland. His children's stories are as beautiful as they are simple and in them he mixes angels and trolls with delightful impunity. Unfortunately, I believe that the Finnish children of to-day have largely ceased to read them; at any rate, I remember, on one occasion, hearing Kalle remark somewhat wistfully, "Only the grown-ups read Topelius nowadays. The children must have tales of aeroplanes and atom bombs."

[1] Kyöpelinvuori—Ghost Hill. [2] Zachris Topelius, 1818–98.

But to return to the matter of traditional decorations; at Easter straw witches predominate, but the use of straw for ornamental purposes does not stop short at Easter, it plays an amazingly large part in decoration generally. This always surprised me, because straw has never seemed to me to have many decorative qualities. Yet to the Finns it must have some, as it reappears at Christmas, this time in the form of angels and peculiar hanging ornaments[1] that are slightly Oriental in effect and strongly reminiscent of Mecca cafés.

Kalle was a great talker. In this he was not a typical Finn, but then his ancestry had been very varied. He was, so he told me, of Huguenot extraction, and his forebears, like many others, had been forced to leave France at the time of the persecution. Their first refuge had been Switzerland, and there, in honour of their new-found freedom, they had taken the name of Frey. What followed I do not know, but within the next 200 years branches of the family must have spread out all over Europe, as Kalle appeared to have relations everywhere, and try as I might I could never get them properly sorted out.

Throughout an excellent lunch conversation never flagged and not for a moment was I allowed to feel that I was being appraised in the way it would have been only natural to appraise a prospective lodger. Far from it; everyone seemed bent on making me feel at home. Sirkka was a first-class cook and I ate much too much. This was partly because I was greedy and partly because I had still no idea what to expect. In fact, right at the start I was taken in by the *hors d'œuvres*, both hot and cold, which were so good and so plentiful that I mistook them for the main part of the meal and ate accordingly. As a result, when a steaming dish of succulent pork made its appearance I was somewhat nonplussed. Nevertheless, as a dish, it was a highly significant one. It was all that remained of the Frey's pig; meat had just come off the ration; things were getting easier and they would not need to keep another. Thus it betokened, if not the end of the lean days, the turning of the tide. The traditional Easter dish, *mammi*,[2] brought the meal to an end and, surfeited though I was, I still managed to find it delicious.

Lunch over, with the lesson in etiquette that Sylvia and I had been given in Helsinki fresh in my mind, I shook Sirkka warmly

[1] These ornaments are known as *himmeli*.

[2] *Mammi* is a concoction of rye flour, grated orange peel and malt.

by the hand before moving out on to the glass veranda, where, sitting in the sunshine, we drank coffee and a very good liqueur that is made from the Arctic bramble and called *mesimarja.* It was the colour of a *vin rosé* and its taste reminded me of passion fruit. The actual berry from which it is distilled has little but its shape in common with a blackberry, as the plant on which it grows is quite different. Devoid of thorns, it grows low on the ground, its starlike flowers a deep pink and its leaves almost indistinguishable from those of a wild strawberry.

We lingered a long time on the veranda drinking our coffee and savouring the delicate flavour of the *mesimarja*, and very pleasant it was sitting there and trying to get a slant on these people among whom I had come to live, and very soon it was borne in upon me that social gatherings, like everything else Finnish, can in no way be hurried. As good manners dictate that you drink only when either your host or hostess has caught your eye, they hold the whip hand. So long as your glass is prematurely replenished, so long you must stay; there can be no casual drinking up and saying goodbye.

Conversation ranged over a variety of topics and the ball rolled smoothly and pleasantly back and forth until a diversion was created by Petra, the youngest of the three Frey children, who toddled in to pay us a visit. Petra was almost completely round and her very fair hair encircled her head in two tight little plaits that ended in cherry-coloured bows. These plaits were woven with considerable skill out of hair that was nowhere more than four inches long. In effect, they were enchanting, but how Petra was persuaded to sit still while they were made was more than I could ever understand, for Petra was clearly no more addicted to sitting still than her namesake, the reindeer —Petra being the Lapp word for a reindeer and not to be confused with Peter the Rock.

After a while we all moved towards the nursery, where three-and-a-half-year-old Torsti was in bed with some childish ailment. From the glimpse I had of him, he did not seem to be very ill, but it was only a fleeting glimpse, as the sight of me—or perhaps the sound of English—was altogether too much for him. He disappeared under the bedclothes giggling merrily and could not be prevailed on to come out.

The party broke up at about four and I strolled back to the club reflecting as I went what a pity it was that there were no longer any Easter eggs for the children. I arrived just as the dinner gong began to sound—and this in a country that I knew to be short of food! Taking no notice, I whiled away the next hour or two writing letters.

* * *

That evening I had been invited to a party at the Eberlings, who lived with their three children on the other side of the river at a place called Karolineburg. With characteristic thoughtfulness, one of the factory's cars was sent to fetch me, as I should never have found my way alone.

Ilmari Eberling was the head of the forestry department of the Kajaani O.Y. and as such was a very important man indeed, for the company owned a great deal of forest land not only locally, but scattered over the length and breadth of the country. Unfortunately, I never really got to know him, as we spoke no common language. I always regretted this, because he had a quiet humorous expression that invariably made me feel that I was missing something worthwhile. Gretel Eberling, however, spoke excellent English. She was a dentist, and a very good one too, but I shall come to that later. She was also reputed to be the best-dressed woman in Kajaani.

The settlement of Karolineburg consisted of four houses built round a square, in the centre of which rose a tall white flag-pole. In the old and spacious dwelling on the south side lived the Eberlings and the Parviainens, the Eberlings on the ground floor and the Parviainens on the first. The house stood high above the river and commanded a pleasant long-distance view.

I arrived to find quite a large gathering of people, some of whom I had already met, others as yet strangers. Outdoor clothes were abandoned in the front hall and, as one after the other the female guests peeled off their fur coats, I noted with some amusement that the greater number of them were wearing coloured frocks. After all, it seemed, I was not to be the exception. Not even in the matter of language was I to be allowed to feel the odd man out, for the whole company was speaking English. It was a gesture that I shall always remember with gratitude.

But although both men and women were united in speaking English, it was clearly the women who were doing most of the talking as, before many minutes had passed, the majority of the men had managed to segregate themselves and were standing about in detached and relatively silent groups. Although I was still too green to know it, there was nothing at all unusual in this. Finnish men rarely talk much in mixed company and if given half a chance will disappear altogether into a room apart to smoke and—though they may not admit it—to gossip with each other. Not that there is any ban on smoking—or gossiping—in mixed society; it is simply that Finnish men as a whole are far more at ease with their own sex.

Once all the guests were known to have arrived, a shining copper coffee kettle was carried in and put at the end of the dining-room table. Then turn and turn about, first the women and then the men went into the dining-room where, armed with a plate and a fork, each one helped himself or herself from a central table that was loaded with biscuits, cake and a kind of sweet white bread known as *pulla*. It appeared to be the done thing to sample everything; almost rude, in fact, to leave anything out, so it was with plates piled high that each guest collected a cup of coffee and returned to the drawing-room.

The refreshments over there was music supplied by the guests themselves, two of whom played the violin and one the piano. I cannot honestly say that I remember what they played, or even how the performers acquitted themselves, but I know that I was relieved to be spared the onus of making conversation, and that I sat back with pleasure to listen.

Parties in Finland, I reflected, had something slightly Victorian about them. Everyone was so very polite, and the conversation among the women seemed to flutter. Everywhere I was conscious of a strong sense of the proprieties. All the men were addressed by professional titles. Their names were prefixed by engineer, forester, lawyer, doctor, or whatever they might happen to be. Professional women, too, were addressed in this way, though among them there was a tendency to use the simpler forms *Ruova*[1] or *Neiti*[2]. It seemed that among adults the use of titles was irrefutably fixed by convention. This is difficult for foreigners, who anyway cannot distinguish a name from a title, and apparently it is also too much for the Finnish children. They have reduced the status of practically all grown-ups, with the exception of their parents and grandparents, to that of uncle and aunt. To this mode of address Christian names are prefixed. Thus by rights I should have been known to the youth of Kajaani as *Dianatäti*, but the lamentable truth is that before

[1] Mrs. [2] Miss.

I was aware of what was happening I had been labelled *Missitäti*. All my remonstrances went for nothing. "Missi," I was told, was such a nice name; so easy for the children, why it might even be Finnish! There was nothing to do but grin and bear it. But there was worse to follow. I have recently acquired a Finnish goddaughter who, I understand, is expected to call me *Gummi*—an epithet that makes me feel remarkably like an india-rubber. But all this was of little consequence; what really concerned me was that I found the adult world so loath to use my first name. Naturally, I did not expect it at once and was resigned to waiting a little, but I never thought it would take as long as it did. However, in retrospect, I feel sure that a mutual wish not to do the wrong thing led us all to keep up the formalities longer than usual.

Sitting listening to the music, I looked about me. In one corner was a grandfather clock which fascinated me. It was one of two in the Eberlings' flat, both of which were quite unlike any that I had ever seen and, in my imagination, they appeared highly anthropomorphic—and palpably female at that, for their faces were small and round and their bodies curved and waisted. One was tall and slim and painted with a floral design that suggested a ball dress of pink-and-white brocade; the other, an undoubted duenna, was short, plump, and far more soberly clad. I pulled myself together with a jerk and focused my attention elsewhere. It had suddenly dawned on me that clock-watching on my part might be misconstrued.

* * *

Easter Monday was another beautiful day. It was also another holiday and, as nobody seemed to expect me to start work before the following Wednesday, I decided to occupy myself by taking a good look at the town, which hitherto I had only seen from a car.

I think the first thing that struck me was the enormous area it covered; I had never imagined it would be nearly so extensive; but when I remarked upon this I was told that it was reputed to cover more ground than almost any other town in Finland, and certainly far more than any other of comparable population. But this expansion is only of recent date, the result of the growth of five largely residential suburbs. The old town is relatively compact and goes back in history nearly 400 years to the time of Per Brahe.

Per Brahe, the first Swedish Governor-General of Finland, is chiefly renowned as the founder of the country's oldest university, that of Turku, which he established in 1640. But his claim to fame does not rest on this alone. While in office he founded ten new towns, of which Kajaani is one, as well as reforming the administration of the whole country. The year 1651 is the date given for the founding of Kajaani, but some form of settlement undoubtedly existed before this time, as Kajaani Castle was built between 1604 and 1619.

Little, however, remains of this early military outpost for, ten years after the birth of the city, its original wooden fortifications were replaced by stone ones. At this time the northern frontier of Finland was not very different from that of to-day, so that on first glancing at the map it seems strange that anyone should have bothered to build so massive a fortress in so remote a spot; but it was, in fact, a place of major strategical importance because it commanded the two great rapids which formed the principal obstacle in the lake system that linked northern Russia with the Baltic. Without roads, there was no other way through the forest by which an advancing army could move, nor could a water-borne invasion avoid the hindrance of bypassing the rapids. A castle so situated commanded the only possible defensive position between Russia and the relatively densely-populated coastal area. Nevertheless, in spite of its situation, the life of both the town and the Castle was shortlived, for this was the period of the Swedish-Russian wars—wars of which Finland, not Sweden or Russia, bore the brunt. The Great Wrath swept over the country, and in 1712 the Russians sacked Kajaani. The Castle held out against the soldiers of Peter the Great for four years longer than the town, but in the end it too was forced to yield. Then, contrary to the terms of the surrender, the Russian soldiers gave vent to their anger at discovering that only a handful of men had been holding them at bay by blowing up the Castle.

It was never rebuilt, nor did the town begin to recover until the latter part of the nineteenth century. Between 1833 and 1853—those years now famous in the annals of Kajaani, when Lönnrot, the acknowledged father of Finnish literature, lived and worked there—it was still a village of barely 400 inhabitants. Ultimately, however, revival of trade put the town once more on its feet, and by 1938 the population had risen to 7,700, to which must now be added well over 1,000 refugees.

Walking down the road to the Castle, I must confess to a bitter disappointment, for it would be hard to conceive of a grosser piece of vandalism than that to which the ruins have been subjected. They stand upon an island in midstream, and in so far as is possible they have been restored. Had those responsible stopped there all would have been well, but these walls, now reinforced by concrete, carry the main road to the north right over the top of the Castle. Small wonder that with this bridge the erstwhile charm of the ruins has vanished.

I never saw a picture of the Castle in its heyday, but without doubt it was a formidable bastion; all that remains is the ruin of a rectangular building from which the base of a great round tower bulges at either end. This building, whose walls are quite three feet thick, must have been a very primitive one, more especially when compared with contemporary buildings in the more southerly parts of Europe. But what it lacked in comfort it made up in security, for in those days both above and below the great rapids swirled unchecked.

I turned and retraced my steps, and as I climbed up the hill from the bridge there, facing the Castle, and looking almost as disapproving as I felt, was the statue of Lönnrot—a monstrous black figure several times larger than life. Here, in Kajaani, he had spent twenty years working as a country doctor, and here too he had compiled that great national epic, *The Kalevala*. Stiff and rigid, he sits staring into space, dressed in a frock coat and high collar, and looking every inch a puritan. How misleading that statue must be, I felt, how washed and brushed-up for Sunday. For what little I had read of Lönnrot had described him as a true son of the people; a man clad in home-spun who wandered through the length and breadth of the country, a flute in his hand and a gun on his back, amassing the great wealth of folklore that he afterwards incorporated in the *Kalevala*. This he did from his youth upwards, and even the fact that he became a doctor by profession did not deter him. He would leave his practice to a *locum tenens* and disappear for weeks together into the backwoods.

It would be difficult to exaggerate the importance which most Finns attach to Lönnrot's epic, because, quite apart from its intrinsic merit, at the time of its publication—that is, in 1835—it filled a deep psychological need. Little more than a quarter of a century had elapsed since the Tzar Alexander I had annexed the country, and the Russian yoke was no more popular than the Swedish had been. Nationalism was rife and the slogan "Swedes we are no more; Russians we can never be, therefore we must become Finns" was the cry of the people. Yet in spite of this, written Finnish was still, to all intents and purposes, limited to the Bible and Luther's Hymn-book, and all learning and education were still the prerogative of the Swedish-speaking minority. To the vast majority of Finns the *Kalevala* was a gift straight from Heaven, the epic of the Finnish people written in their own language. It was in a very real sense their own creation and it promptly became—that which it has remained ever since—the focal point of Finnish nationalism.

And thus it is that still to-day no one can go to Finland without immediately becoming aware of its influence for the people continue to look to it for inspiration in all forms of creative activity. Though several attempts have been made to translate it into English, none is wholly satisfactory; largely because the metre in which it is written—that of *The Song of Hiawatha*—is so tiresome to our ear. Yet hard though the going may be, no student of Finland can afford to ignore it, because it contains the key to so much that is Finnish. In it are to be found the creation myth and the heroic legends of the Finns, as well as a wealth of detail as to their everyday life, customs, rites and festivals. In it, too, are all the early Shamanistic beliefs of the people, the essence of whose early religion was belief in the power of "The Word (or Words) of Origin," to know which was to be all-powerful. These words were hidden in riddles and incantations which in their turn were interwoven with the heroic ballads and handed down from one generation to another in the form of runes—runes which through the ages were subjected to the inventive genius of the rune-singers, who chanted them to the accompaniment of the *kantele*, or five-stringed Finnish harp.

It is, moreover, interesting to note that true to the democratic tradition of to-day, as J. Hampden Jackson says, "The heroes of the poem are really popular heroes, fishers, smiths, 'medicine-men' or wizards; exaggerated shadows of the people pursuing on an heroic scale not war, but the common daily business of primitive but peaceful man."

* * *

A few paces further brought me to the Market Square, and here the term "Market Square" is rather confusing. "The Old

Market Square" would be a better name, for the actual market takes place at the other end of the town on an open space by the river. On the old Market Square stands the Court House, once the Town Hall and, unquestionably, the most charming building in Kajaani. It was erected in 1831 and designed by Carl Ludwig Engel, the German architect who is famous as the man responsible for all the finest architecture in Helsinki that dates from its inauguration as capital of Finland.

Turning left, I walked slowly down the Kauppakatu. Every Finnish town has a "Kauppakatu"; it means quite literally "Shop Street" and is the exact counterpart of our "High Street." There, jumbled together, were small wooden houses one story high and new concrete blocks. The effect was so unbalanced that it impressed me as unfinished, only half-built, a town in the making; with the snow and the horse-drawn sleds and the dearth of motor traffic, it held for me something of the character of a Western film set. But this was a feeling that did not bear closer investigation, and which was probably rooted in a consciousness of the enterprise and vitality that lay behind the recent developments rather than in any actual affinity of which there was little evidence.

I strolled along looking in the shop windows. Their contents were pitiable. There did not seem to be anything to buy that was not made either of paper or wood. Only the book-shops had anything worth while on show, and they appeared to have a very impressive selection of books, although they were of little use to me, being exclusively written in Finnish or Swedish.

I did not know then what an all-important part books play in Finnish life, and with what great veneration they are treated. But since then I have heard it contended that this is because the written word still holds for the mass of the people something of the magic of the "Word of Origin."

Whether or not this theory is true, the book-shops throughout the country appear to bear it out, for no town, however small, is without one of first-class calibre. Kajaani, being a sizable place, had two, and staring through the window of one of them I was struck by the very high percentage of books that were translations from other languages.

At the far end of the Kauppakatu I came upon the market, which at that late hour was a mere collection of booths, all of which, I was surprised to find, sold exactly the same things:

brushes of all kinds, baskets, wooden buttons, bootlaces, cheap-jack kitchen utensils, and garden implements; there was not a halfpennyworth of difference between the stalls, nor was there a single article of decent quality to be seen. Yet year in year out, in summer and winter, no matter how low the thermometer falls, these vendors ply their trade unprotected from the elements except by a strip of canvas overhead, and in really bad weather another strip which is unrolled from above and pegged down to windward.

* * *

That afternoon Yrjö looked in on me. He wanted to find out if I had all I needed, and also to tell me that the firm were expecting a guest from England, a Mr. Leigh.

"We think," he said with a charming smile, "that it would be so nice for him if you would eat your meals with him while he is here."

Hoping that Mr. Leigh would share this view, I agreed. Yrjö then undertook to make all the necessary arrangements with the housekeeper, which was just as well, as I myself was incapable of making her understand any but my simplest needs.

Eating with Mr. Leigh, I soon discovered, meant eating very well; it also meant sitting in state in the private dining-room at the club. Looking back upon it all, I now realise just how misleading my introduction to Finland really was; for during the first three days that I spent in Kajaani I lived on the fat of the land, on food the like of which had not been seen in England since before the war, and then only rarely. I did not know then how deep-rooted was the Finnish tradition of hospitality, nor yet what great importance is attached to keeping up appearances, and in retrospect I have often wondered whether it is, in fact, as admirable as it appears at first sight. For why should the casual traveller be given a completely erroneous picture of the true state of affairs? How can he, in the circumstances, appreciate the gulf that exists between the way the people live and the way they entertain? What real value has this pride and generosity? Personally, I cannot but feel that it must hinder understanding abroad and that, at home, it militated against casual social intercourse and resulted in an abnormally large number of lonely people.

Mr. Leigh arrived that evening, and the next day at lunch we were entertained by Arvo Milán, an endearing, elderly employee of the Companys', who afterwards became one of my pupils. Though what he hoped to learn from me was hard to understand, as his flow of English was as good as it was picturesque. Having served in a windjammer on the Australian run and lived for many years, as a young man, in England and the United States, he really knew the language, and the only fault I had to find was with his indistinct diction. For Arvo Milán, who looked as if he ought by rights to be in Holy Orders, would, from time to time, come out with such a remarkable mixture of nautical terms, up-to-date business jargon and pre-1914 English and American slang that I often found it hard to believe that I had heard aright.

After lunch he took us round the factory, which was turning out newsprint, cellulose, pre-fabricated houses and, as a by-product, wood alcohol. Just how much we saw I cannot remember, but I know that I understood very little of what was going on. This was due in part to the noise of the machinery, which effectively drowned all explanation, and in part to the fact that we did not begin at the beginning of any process. This, of course, did not matter to Mr. Leigh; he understood what it was all about, but to me it was all very confusing. Looking back, I suspect that it was a purely business trip, and that we went systematically from point to point in which Mr. Leigh was interested, but the only part I found coherent was the section where the pre-fabricated houses were made.

In that shop a great many women were employed, and I have rarely seen any who looked tougher. They worked methodically, putting great force behind each action. With the great dearth of housing in Finland, it was heartrending to think that everything that was being turned out was destined as reparations for Soviet Russia.

* * *

That evening had been set aside for the enrolment of my pupils, and at about seven-thirty the majority of those who wished to learn English came out to the club. Most of them were members of the Finnish British Society, but outsiders were not excluded, for my salary had to be met, and funds were all important. I think all the Society's officers were present: Yrjö Tähtinen, the President, Gretel Eberling, the Vice-President, Kalle Frey, the Treasurer, and Aili Parviainen and Toini Simola, the Secretaries. Aili wasted no time in handing over to me her share of the secretarial work which, before my arrival, she and Toini had divided between them. Now her responsibilities were at an end, as the English correspondence had been her job. For Toini it was very different, because all arrangements that had to be made in Finnish devolved on her, and my complete ignorance of the language augmented, rather than detracted, from her duties, as nurse-maiding me was added to them.

After a little Kalle became extremely businesslike, and settled himself at a table in front of a shining black cash-box and a pile of receipt forms. Thereupon Aili sat down beside him and opened a file full of lists. It was obvious that everything had been organised, for there, already divided into twelve groups, were the names of sixty-five people who wished to learn English. I watched Kalle, and as I did so I felt not a little apprehensive. Here was I surrounded by people each of whom was paying 1,000 marks (540 marks=£1) for the benefit of learning English from me twice a week for the next ten weeks, and I had never given a lesson in my life. It was clear that all my ideas about life in Kajaani would have to be revised. I had thought of myself primarily as a secretary who would be willing to give a few conversation classes, but with every minute that passed it was becoming more and more apparent that teaching was to be my main occupation. In front of me lay a timetable. It told me that I was expected to teach daily at the factory between the hours of twelve and one; that every afternoon in somebody's home I must give classes to the womenfolk, and that every evening, in the Lyceum,[1] I had to teach relays of daily-breaders through three consecutive hours. Twice a week, however, I came off lightly; I had only one class on Saturdays and two on Wednesdays. This was not because of any traditional mid-week half-holiday, but because school on Wednesday evenings would have interfered with the fortnightly club meetings, and this, of course, was out of the question. The Finnish British Society was, by the way, always referred to as the English Club.

Next day I was scheduled to begin teaching in the lunch hour, and a group of engineers from the factory was detailed to be the guinea-pigs. Later that afternoon I was to go to the Ehos. It was a Wednesday, so I was being let down easily.

When all had been arranged, I asked if someone would teach

[1] The Lyceum was the name commonly given to the secondary school.

Kajaani Castle

Lönnrot's Statue, Kajaani

Kajaani Market

The Court House, Kajaani

me Finnish. One and all seemed to think that this was the Finnish Secretary's responsibility, and Toini, when consulted, smilingly acquiesced, and promised to give me a lesson every Tuesday and Friday morning.

At last the party broke up and I was left alone. I could hardly remember a single name, far less could I fit any name to any face. How would it all work out? Were the groups in fact properly divided? I had a strong feeling that they had been organised more on the basis of "Who would I like to learn with?" than "Who knows about as much as I do?" But in this I was proved quite wrong; with very few exceptions, it had been admirably done, and both birds had been killed by the same stone. I was glad that nobody had objected when I had refused to teach complete beginners, as even without them I felt it would be uphill work. Nevertheless, in the main I was not downhearted; to be so would have been almost ungrateful, for everybody seemed bent on making my life as easy and pleasant as possible; and if I had come to Finland under a slight misapprehension that was probably my own fault. Furthermore, I knew that even had the main stress been laid on teaching I would still have come—more than that, I was glad that I had come.

* * *

Next day, punctually at twelve o'clock, four of the younger engineers presented themselves to me at the club-house, but this was the only occasion on which we used the club for lessons. Subsequently, we always sat in the technical library in the engineer's wing of the factory because it was quiet there, and we were undisturbed except by the throb of the machinery next door. The effect of this was to make the library vibrate continuously like a ship at sea—at sea, that is, on a calm day. Actually, the whole setting was in tune with this illusion, as like many an inside cabin or saloon the room was windowless, and lit exclusively from overhead. In fact, so vivid was this impression, that on the rare occasions when the machines stopped, I automatically felt that we were coming into port.

But on the first day Gunnar Enwald, Aarne Enroth, Ville Nurminen, Uolevi Suominen and I sat in the corner of the staff dining-room.

"What," I hazarded, "do you want to do?"

"Talk," they replied unanimously.

Silence followed, a prolonged silence during which I looked

from one to the other and wondered what on earth one talked about to Finnish engineers, most of whom looked very young, and whose English, I feared groundlessly, was as negligible as my own knowledge of engineering. I could think of nothing more original than their relations. Pulling myself together, I focused on Ville Nurminen, who was sitting nearest to me, and asked him if he had a family.

"One wife and two children," he replied proudly. I gave a start of surprise, for the expression "one wife" seemed momentarily to postulate the possibility of two or even more, until on further reflection I concluded that the Finns probably did not differentiate between "a" and "one." I was almost disappointed.

"Boys or girls?"

I catechised this class for a whole hour, and found it a very long one. All the same, as time went on lessons became progressively easier. The first real step forward was taken when they produced *Brush Up Your English*, a book that was immensely popular in Kajaani.

Brush Up was a godsend; there was no end to the number of topics it suggested for conversation. What the hero and heroine, Charles and Mary Smith, did not do was not worth doing, and what they did we did with them. They went sight-seeing and shopping, that was child's play; they went to the bank and they played bridge, that was a little more complicated; worst of all, they went on a motor tour. The trouble they had with their carburettor and sparking plugs was as nothing to the trouble they gave me.

"What is a carburettor?" I was asked. "And what are sparking plugs?"

How was I to describe them? At best I knew that a carburettor was flooded and that sparking plugs sparked. In despair, I turned to my English-Finnish dictionary and looked up sparking plugs.

"What are they?" I looked from the circle of expectant faces to the book. The word which confronted me was *Sytystystulppa*!

But all this took place much later and happened at a time long after the ice had been broken. Actually the process was not one of ice-breaking, but of a gradual thaw, which I finally eralised was complete when one day, as I entered the library, they all four sprang to their feet and saluted smartly. Needless to say, I was completely taken aback.

"All captains," they said grinning, "all captains together." Then seeing my puzzled expression someone added, "We were all captains in the war and so were you. We read about you in the newspaper."

Dumbfounded, I had to confess that I had never risen to dizzier heights than those of a W.A.A.F. Section Officer. The whole idea seemed to amuse them immensely. It was not the thought of having women in the armed forces that was new to them, it was the idea of giving them officer status that they considered strange. This in itself is curious, because Finnish women are among the most emancipated in the world, and are to be found competing on an equal footing with men in every sphere except those of the Church and the armed forces. Even so, there was an organisation that functioned during the war known as the *Lotta Swärd*, so called after the heroine of one of Runeberg's patriotic ballads.

The original Lotta—no one seems certain whether she was a purely fictitious character or not—was a camp sutler who made her mark during the Swedish-Russian War which ended in 1809, when Finland became a Grand Duchy under the Tzars. A stout-hearted sergeant's widow, she had a weakness for mothering brave boys and a courageous habit of pitching her "rickety tent" in the battle zone. According to Runeberg, she was never seen again after "Oravais' bloody day."[1]

As for the poet Runeberg,[2] I shall come back to him later. At present I am only concerned with Lotta Swärd and the organisation to which she gave her name. Nevertheless, I should like to say in passing that the last stanza of Runeberg's poem appears to me to be in some way a measure of his work—in all fairness, be it said, in translation:

"For a pearl on the pathway of war was she,
And a pearl all genuine, too;
Though sometimes laughable she might be,
More oft was honour her due."

The modern Lottas were officially founded in 1919, although in reality they had sprung into being a year earlier during the Finnish War of Independence. Since then they have been all our women's services rolled into one, their main function varying with the stress of the moment. Thus between the wars

[1] September 14th, 1808.

[2] Johan Ludwig Runeberg, 1804–87, was the first Finnish author of patriotic verse, which he wrote in the Swedish language.

their activities were largely devoted to social service. In those peaceful days they were an unpaid and entirely voluntary organisation, 72,000 strong, who had much in common with the W.V.S., but with the outbreak of war, while remaining a voluntary organisation, they were paid as soldiers and controlled by the Civil Guard. Then they quickly reverted to their original character and resumed the duties they had performed in 1918; duties that had in the interim become infinitely more complex. Their numbers swelled rapidly to 200,000 who were employed as nurses, cooks, military clerks, A.R.P. workers, radio and telephone operators, and observers.

Nearly all my women friends had been Lottas of one kind or another, and they often used to tell me of their doings, and I know that they did a great job. One has only to consider what the manning of an observation post at 40° below zero[1] means, for the post was probably the top of a fire-tower or ski-jump in the forest, on which they were exposed to the wind and weather for hours on end.

Field-Marshal Mannerheim, in his last Order of the Day, which he wrote on March 14th, 1940, pays them this tribute:

"With joy and pride, my thoughts dwell on the Lottas of Finland—their spirit of self sacrifice and untiring work in many fields, work which has liberated thousands of men for the fighting line. Their noble spirit has spurred on and supported the army, whose undivided gratitude and respect they have achieved."

At the instigation of Moscow, the Lottas were abolished on November 23rd, 1944.

* * *

Later in the afternoon I found my next victims congregated at the Ehos', whose home was a small white house near the Post Office. Never in my life have I known a house of such elastic capacity. In addition to accommodating Aili and Eero and their two small children, it had recently been stretched to take in three orphaned cousins of Aili, two of whom were still of school age. How Aili succeeded in squeezing them all in I could never make out, but she managed it somehow, and even contrived to have her consulting-room in the house, for she, like Gretel, was a dentist.

Certainly Aili and Eero are among the kindest people I have

[1] −40° C.=−40° F.

ever met. They were also amongst my first real friends in Kajaani and from first to last I enjoyed my visits to their home. Their interests were so wide and they went to so much trouble to help me to understand the Finns and to see the country. Moreover, as I got to know them better, it struck me that their outlook was in much better perspective than that of most of their fellow countrymen. Together we had many amusing discussions and many a good laugh. They both spoke English easily and invariably shared each other's idiosyncrasies of speech, the most striking being the use of the word *this* on any and every occasion. It was "This our house is rather too small for us," "This our car has broken down," "I have not learned this my lesson." There was no end to it, and with the best will in the world I failed to put a stop to it.

The group who learned with them was composed of Irmeli Virkkunen, Aune Perttunen and Daisy Franti.

Irmeli was to prove another very good friend to me. She was married to a man who combined a passion for salmon fishing with the management of the bank, above which they lived in a flat whose living-room looked out on to an open space where before the war their home had stood; that was before the Soviet bombers came to Kajaani. With Irmeli I was always sure of a warm welcome, because she really enjoyed being dropped in on, a custom that disconcerts most Finns. As a result, I dropped in frequently for a friendly chat and many were the pleasant hours we spent together, in the course of which she kept me up-to-date with the local news, which she invariably referred to as the "gossips."

Aune was the wife of the only male dentist in Kajaani, and she lived with her husband and three children in a flat in the Kauppakatu. She was a great talker; nothing really stopped her, and language difficulties meant nothing to her at all. They were swept away by the flow of her words like the foam of a river in spate. In common with the majority of Finnish women, she was preoccupied with her home and her family, but, unlike many, she appeared to be perfectly content to devote herself to domesticity. At any rate her conversation was regularly punctuated by the two phrases, "I am always so busy" and "I am always so happy." Late for every appointment, she sailed through life talking volubly, and the last letter which I had from her was signed with characteristic exuberance, "With sunny and vernal greetings."

Daisy Franti I knew far less well than the others because after the summer I hardly saw her. A third baby was on the way, and she decided that having it was not compatible with learning English.

On introduction to this group I think one of the things that impressed me most was the number of dentists by whom I seemed to be surrounded. Already, directly or indirectly, I had come across three, but I know there was at least one more in the town. In so small a place as Kajaani it seemed a great many, but there was plenty of work to keep them busy. Later on I was to be struck by the amazingly high standard of their work. I even went so far as to bring home a new front tooth of which I am inordinately proud, and which I defy any casual observer to identify. How long Finnish dentistry has been at this peak I have no idea, but not long ago, while reading a book about Sibelius, I came across the following quotation from an old Scottish ballad,

"A Finn cam ower fra Norroway
Fir ta pit töthache away."

Unhappily, I have not been able to trace the ballad, because it would be amusing to know if the "Finn fra Norroway" was successful. All that I know is that the author of the book uses the quotation to illustrate the reputation that Finns had for wizardry in the Middle Ages. But where the relief of toothache is concerned surely the end justifies the means and perhaps, who knows, the Finns always have had a way with tccth.

But to return to my English class: with this group, from the word "go," there was no tension at all. They wanted to talk and they talked. Furthermore, they had had the forethought to provide themselves with *The Amazing Adventures of Mr. Ernest Bliss*, by E. Phillips Oppenheim, in an especially abridged edition with a vocabulary at the back. We read a little, drank coffee, and ate doughnuts. Nothing, from my point of view, could have been pleasanter, and I returned to the club considerably heartened.

* * *

That evening there was no club meeting, so that when Aune invited me to go to her I was free to accept. At her flat I found a gathering of about eight women, most of whom I had already met. It was all very friendly and informal, and stands out in my mind as being the occasion on which I first met Heljä Hovi.

She came into the room like a breath of ozone, talking as only Karelians do talk, and in fluent English. Heljä's home, now that her family has been forced to leave Karelia, is in the south, at Hamina, but she was then settled in Kajaani teaching in the Lyceum. There, although she had been engaged to teach German, she found herself taking many English classes, as there was a great dearth of English teachers in the school. This state of affairs exists almost everywhere in the country and is the outcome of the switch-over from German to English that followed the war. At present no foreign languages are taught in the elementary schools, but on entering the secondary ones the children begin at once to learn Swedish or, should it be a Swedish school, Finnish. In their second year they start English, German or Russian. In the past it was usual for them to make German their second language, and to start English or French only in their sixth year, but now the balance has shifted, and it is German, and not English, that has been relegated, with French, to the last three years The teaching of Russian has not made much progress because the children will only learn under coercion, and in any case few schools have Russian teachers. In Kajaani there were none at all, and not enough English ones to meet the demands made on them, with the result that some divisions were compelled to learn German, whether they liked it or not. But in any case everything was, and still is, in a state of transition, for the new régime only affects the younger children who have entered the school since its inauguration.

Heljä had set out to take her degree at Helsinki University in both English and German, but she had only succeeded in taking the highest honours in German when war broke out and she left to join the Lottas. She was therefore not, strictly speaking, qualified to teach English; but now at the very moment I am writing she is deep in her final examinations, for she left Kajaani when I did to complete her degree. Her last letter tells me that she has passed her English essay, which she had to write about Virginia Woolf. Poor Heljä, I never have understood why, with so much to choose from, the Finnish professors have such a tremendous penchant for the difficult works of Virginia Woolf and James Joyce.

Another of Aune's guests on this occasion was Anna Ekström,

an unusually tall woman for a Finn who had large hazel eyes—a colour rare in Finland, where blue predominates and where very dark brown is the usual alternative. With Anna I felt instantly at home, for there was something very familiar about her—familiar, yet hard to define. So difficult, in fact, that when, not long ago, I was trying to describe her to a friend, I let slip the flagrant contradiction in terms, "If she were English, she would be Scotch"—a statement to which my friend replied in all seriousness:

"I know exactly what you mean, but I do think you ought to say Scots!"

Anna had two daughters. Our conversation centred round the elder because she was in the throes of her final school examinations—student exams as they are called, because they are all that is needed to enter the university. These exams are the invariable climax of eight years' schooling; eight years which can in no circumstances be shortened, for the Finnish educational system is very rigid.

Anna's daughter, in common with all the other candidates, had spent the day writing an essay; six hours was the allotted time, and those sitting for the exam went armed with sandwiches. Naturally, the subjects came under discussion. I thought them dull and lacking in scope, but academically the Finns do not seem to set much store by originality.

Surprisingly enough "What can I do for my country?" was the most popular subject set, and was one which the candidates attacked without self-consciousness, for the Finns, who are far and away the most undemonstrative people I have ever come across, became quite overwhelmingly lyrical and patriotic the moment that they put pen to paper. Then they say all the things which, however much we may think them, we never put into words. This is the more remarkable because in ordinary conversation emotion is even more taboo than it is in England, while undemonstrativeness is the hall-mark of the Finn. One of my friends even went so far as to tell me, smiling, that at the moment when she accepted her husband he warned her solemnly that he would never kiss her at a railway station; while another once remarked: "Oh yes, we have a word for 'darling,' but we *never* use it." And while on this subject, I was very amused by a young friend whom I managed to place as a mother's help with an English family. When I asked her if she was happy, she replied without a minute's hesitation: "Yes, they lovely family. Do you know that every morning when he goes out Mr. X kisses Mrs. X and says, 'Goodbye, darling.' No Finnish husband do that. I think perhaps I marry Englishman."

But to return to Aune's party; it was something in the nature of a sewing bee and most people had brought knitting or darning with them. I alone seemed empty-handed. There was no dearth of talk and it was all carried on in English. After a while coffee was served with *pulla* and cakes. Everything that Aune offered was superlative of its kind, and proved that, without doubt, she was a very good cook; most Finnish women are, although how this comes about I am at a loss to know, for the young, especially if given to their books, appear to do next to nothing in their own homes, and certainly their schooling does take up most of their time. One of the results of this seems to be that those who, like my young protégée, have managed to come to this country in a domestic capacity, are generally found to know practically nothing about their job on arrival. But of course it must be borne in mind that the majority of these are students whose primary object is to learn English, and whose lives in Finland have been devoted to study. Nevertheless, it is amazing what domestic efficiency seems to come with marriage, which even the *Kalevala* considers a radical change:

"Brilliant is the day in summer,
But a maiden's lot is brighter.
And the frost makes cold the iron,
Yet the new bride's lot is colder.
In her father's house a maiden
Lives like strawberry in the garden,
But a bride in house of husband
Lives like house-dog tightly fettered.
To a slave comes rarely pleasure;
To a wedded damsel never."

But if Finnish girls took the *Kalevala* to heart none of them would ever marry.

This domestic issue really brings me to the question of foreign travel, because at the time of which I am writing, at any rate as far as Great Britain was concerned, the taking of domestic work by Finnish women was practically the only way into the country or, for that matter, out of Finland. The Finns themselves had put almost insurmountable barriers in the way of all travelling for pleasure, and formalities over passports and currency[1] were legion, even for those with the best possible reasons for going abroad. The result of this was, inevitably, to make the Finns feel very cut off from the outside world, more especially as foreign visitors to their country were few and far between. Such visitors as came did so on business. In 1947 the country as a whole was in no position to cope with tourists. There was little food and less accommodation. Conditions that were bad in the south were even worse in the north, where the fleeing Germans had left a trail of destruction in their wake. Visits to see the midnight sun at Petsamo were no longer possible and such foreigners as drove up and down the Arctic Highway were almost all employed on relief work.

But there was one loop-hole by which a few Finns could escape for a short while to England. The Bank of Finland allowed a small amount of money to students going on the British Council's recognised courses. I discovered this the day after Aune's sewing bee. I had gone as usual to the mill to take my midday class—Yrjö Tähtinen, Olli Parviainen and Paavo Kivi—when Yrjö, who was the first to arrive, asked me if I would help Gretel Eberling to get to Exeter University, where, it transpired, there was to be a course for the officers of Finnish Anglophil societies in June. Application has already been made for Gretel to go on this course and the morning's post had produced the inevitable form to complete, together with a request for a personal recommendation from the President. Confronted with this task, Yrjö smiled appealingly at me and begged me to write the necessary recommendation for her.

"But," I argued, "I haven't been here a week. I scarcely know her."

"Say just what you think best," he pleaded. "You will do it so much better than I can, and you know it is good for the club if she goes."

After a while I acquiesced on condition that he took full responsibility for anything I might say; a stipulation to which he agreed without demur. The class once over, I spent the remainder of the afternoon concocting the document.

The following six weeks were largely punctuated by difficulties arising out of Gretel's journey. It was then that I began to

[1] The first relaxation of the currency regulations came in the summer of 1949, when 10,000 marks worth of foreign currency was granted to those wishing to visit Norway, Sweden or Denmark.

appreciate fully what a tiresome business travelling preliminaries were for the Finns and at the same time to realise just how they abhorred answering letters and loved long-distance telephone calls. All arrangements took an eternity to put through and right up to the last minute were clouded by uncertainty. For quick results it appeared to be practically essential to go to Helsinki in person.

* * *

Next morning I was due to have my first Finnish lesson, so as soon as I had had my breakfast I went round to Toini's flat. She and her husband, Pauli, and her eighteen-months-old daughter, Paula, lived in a new block belonging to the Kajaani O.Y. Their flat was small, but it possessed one priceless asset, a bathroom, which Toini promptly put at my disposal. As the club had neither a bath nor a *sauna*,[1] this made all the difference to my life and many was the time I took advantage of Toini's offer, and many was the Finnish lesson cut off in the interests of cleanliness. But this morning there were more important things to do than bathing and studying Finnish; if I was to continue to eat, I must obtain ration cards, and in order to do this I must first register with the State Police.

This organisation, I was told, was in an entirely different category from that of the regular police force and, in fact, it was a long time before I succeeded in discovering anything at all about it. The Finns themselves were very chary of mentioning their State Police. Occasionally someone would murmur, "Our Gestapo," and shrug, but it rarely went further than that. Actually, their position was completely anomalous, for they had been inaugurated in 1918 at the end of the Civil War expressly to keep an eye on the Reds, but in 1945 the Communists had taken them over and completely reversed their functions.

They it was who issued me with a permit to work and, later in the summer, with one to travel to Lapland and that, but for one visit that they paid me the following autumn, was the beginning and end of our relationship.

I remember the afternoon of their visit well. I had by then been living a few weeks with the Freys, and was sitting in my room writing a letter. Suddenly my peace was shattered by Martta, the cook-general, who burst in on me talking nineteen to the dozen. I, of course, could not follow her words, but I

[1] *Sauna* is the word used by the Finns both for their own particular type of steam bath and for the room or outhouse in which they have it.

followed her person, as that seemed what she expected of me, to the kitchen. There I was confronted by two total strangers whom I promptly took to be would-be pupils, though why they were in the kitchen and why they did not take off their hats I could not make out. All that I knew was that it behoved me in the Society's interest to be polite to prospective pupils, so I wrung them each warmly by the hand while I debated with myself whether to take them into the sitting-room and offer them coffee. I was only saved from this excess of hospitality in the nick of time by the arrival of Sirkka, who explained that all they wanted was to see my papers. State policemen—in a flash I understood their lack of manners, their squash hats, their belted mackintoshes, the whole aura of the Hollywood thriller so untypical of the country. But why the back door? That even Sirkka did not understand.

The State Police have now ceased to exist. Forewarned by events in Czechoslovakia, a special commission was set up some time after I left to inquire into their activities. This proved them to be nefarious beyond doubt, and led to their dissolution in December, 1948, and to the creation in their place of a new body, the Security Police. Compared with those of the State Police, the powers of this new force are definitely restricted; furthermore, and this is of primary importance, they are without political bias.

The functions of the regular police were a very different matter, being much the same as those of similar bodies the world over—the control of traffic and the enforcement of the law. In Kajaani, a small law-abiding town where there was no traffic to speak of, they were not much in evidence. All the same, I did once have a slight contretemps with one of them, and all because they suddenly, and quite unaccountably, embarked on a traffic week. It was a lovely spring morning and, as I sauntered down the Kauppakatu, nothing could have been further from my thoughts than a safety first campaign. I little dreamed that overnight a square of parallel white lines had been painted round the cross-roads by the market place for the benefit of pedestrians. I approached them unwarily, and as I did so an impulse as simple as the proverbial chicken's set me off on a diagonal crossing. The only car within sight was a taxi drawn up on the market square and waiting for a fare. A moment later there was a shout behind me. Oblivious of the fact that it was aimed at me, I took no notice whatsoever.

Another yell followed, but I disdained that also; it never occurred to me that it was any concern of mine until a second later I found myself gripped firmly by the arm and the object of an angry tirade from an irate policeman. I stammered something in English. The flood of his eloquence faltered and stopped, and as light dawned a slow smile spread over his face. With a friendly gesture, he tucked his arm in mine and walked with me solemnly round the entire square. Back at our starting-point he freed himself and, using both hands to lend weight to his words, said emphatically something which I took to mean, "Next time don't you dare forget." What, I wondered as I went on my way, happens when the lanes are under snow? But we never had a traffic week in winter. It was all as inconsequential as a race game where a chance throw of the dice might land you on a marked square and the rules in the lid read: "Failure to cross between the white lines, miss a turn while pacifying policeman."

But all this long post-dates the April morning when Toini and I, with the Food Office as our final objective, pushed Paula in her pram—a squat conveyance on minute wheels—round to the Police Station. By all the rules of the game, Paula should have been asleep; but Paula was not playing. I cannot altogether say I blamed her, because the roads were rough, and Finnish perambulators are practically unsprung, a combination guaranteed to keep any child awake. But however bumpy, Paula seemed to enjoy the motion, and it was not until we had to abandon her outside the Police Station that we had any trouble. There she started to bawl, and having a good pair of lungs kept it up until the police were through with me. Actually, although exasperatingly off-hand, they did not keep us long, and after examining my passport rang up the Food Office and instructed them to issue me with ration cards. I was also informed that I must apply to Helsinki for a permit to work, and that my visa would have to be renewed in three months' time. All this was greatly simplified for me by Harri Attila, the Kajaani Company's lawyer, who lived in the same block as Toini and was a wizard with forms. He, in fact, did everything that had to be done for me.

To my surprise, at the Food Office I was issued with double ration cards for everything except clothing, and I left clutching a sheaf of cards of all colours and sizes, enough to last me for six months.

"Why," I asked, frankly puzzled, "do I get so many?"

"I think perhaps it is because you are a foreigner," Toini replied tentatively. "You see, you can't be expected to know your way about the black market. Anyway, don't worry. If you were a Russian, you would get three of each, not two."

I must admit I found this state of affairs somewhat perplexing, because, if true, it seemed such a curious action on the part of a law-abiding nation, so I was less surprised than I might have been when I discovered that it was a diplomatic privilege extended to me by courtesy. In this I was fortunate, for although it was a favour invariably accorded to the British Council staff, it was by no means always granted to teacher secretaries.

The possession of this dual set of ration cards was a real boon. It saved me all the bother of having to go to the club housekeeper for my cards every time that I wanted to eat out, for in restaurants coupons had invariably to be surrendered for all rationed food.

Rations were issued on a monthly basis, and the cards covered bread, fats, milk, clothing and sundries, under which heading came sugar, coffee, soap, jam, tobacco and, on rare occasions, a very small quantity of cocoa or tea.

On the whole, I came to the conclusion the Finns were more dependent on their rations that we are on ours, simply because they were harder to supplement. Had all things been equal, it would probably be true to say that in quantity they compared not unfavourably with ours, but all things were not equal, and the life of the Finnish housewife was far from easy, as the unrationed food that was apparently plentiful came only within the scope of the well-to-do.

The monthly allowance of bread and flour—if my arithmetic is correct; the Finns use the metric system—was 13¾ lb., but only a small proportion of it was white. Not that that was a great hardship, as most Finns prefer rye bread, and the white flour, what there was of it, was *white*. To obtain cakes or biscuits from the baker it was necessary to supply him with all the ingredients.

The butter ration was unreliable. In theory it was 1 lb. 10 oz. a month, but periodically there were butterless months when margarine, always nauseous in Finland, was substituted. These months came at irregular intervals, and there were three between April and December. Apart from the actual butter there was a monthly allowance of $8\frac{3}{4}$ oz. of margarine or cooking fat; alternatively, for those who preferred it, double that weight in cheese.

The sugar ration was bound up with the tobacco one, and varied with the amount you smoked. Non-smokers drew the maximum sugar, about 1 lb. 10 oz. Heavy smokers drew the maximum tobacco ration of 300 cigarettes and only the minimum of sugar. Between these two grades was an intermediate one with less tobacco and correspondingly more sugar. The only available cigarettes were Finnish ones; these were poor in quality, being very dry, and foreign cigarettes were always popular.

I think of all rationed commodities milk gave the most trouble because the quantity was so small and you had to fetch it daily. In actual fact all talk of rationed milk is misleading, for, in the province of Kainuu at any rate, there was no milk for adults, nor was the children's ration always honoured, although while I was in Finland the situation steadily improved. Grown-up people did, however, receive one-tenth of a pint of thin cream daily provided that they went to fetch it and took their own bottle. But meagre as this ration was, there was no getting round the daily pilgrimage to the dairy. Although cold storage through the winter months presented no problem at all, much as they might wish it, even single people could not collect for more than one day at a time and, as a result, many who lived alone could not be bothered and went without for days on end.

Milk, however, was only one of many things that had to be fetched. Only letters and newspapers came to the house; there was no parcel post delivery. All you got was a card from the Post Office announcing that a parcel addressed to you was awaiting collection. As a system it had distinct drawbacks. A kind American friend once sent me a bulky food parcel festooned with metal bands, the weight of which was 14 lb. Mercifully, this figure was mentioned on the card. I took my rucksack with me to the Post Office and unpacked it on the spot. In its original form I should have made very heavy weather of lugging it—as I should have had to lug it—practically the whole length of the town.

But to return to Finnish rations; I cannot leave the subject without a word about coffee, because the Finns are a nation of coffee-drinkers and their ration was of major importance to them. They had three issues in the year: at Christmas, Easter and midsummer, and each was of about half a pound. This was eked out by an *ersatz* variety made of roasted cereal and a certain amount of black-market coffee that was smuggled into the country from Sweden via Lapland. As to a large extent the Swedish authorities turned a blind eye to this smuggling, it became in Finland a very profitable racket; so profitable that the necessity for keeping it within bounds was one of the reasons why it was necessary to have a police permit to travel to Lapland.

Soap was of pretty poor quality and most people made their own; while as for clothing, it was a heartbreak! The already meagre cards with which everyone was issued were of little use without friends in the trade, and for new shoes a special permit had to be obtained from the Police Station.

* * *

After leaving the Food Office, I parted from Toini and spent the best part of the afternoon writing my name and address and the date of my birth half a dozen times on each sheet of ration cards—each sheet being issued half-yearly and divided into six. This gave me a total of fifty-four cards to fill in.

As for my Finnish lessons which should have begun that morning, I started them a few days later. Poor Toini, she had an uphill job with me. I have no natural aptitude for languages and Finnish is an extremely difficult one. It belongs to a group called Finno-Ugrian and is utterly remote from all other European languages except Esthonian, which it resembles very closely, and early Magyar, to which it is distantly related. Thus, while Finns and Esthonians can fraternise without difficulty, there is no truth in the popular belief that Finns and Hungarians can also understand one another. In fact, I had one pupil, a soldier, who had a pen-friend in Hungary with whom he always corresponded in English, and his English was of the most elementary kind.

The Finnish language has no gutturals and is pleasant to listen to, though inclined to be singsong. For the child learning to read and write it presents few difficulties as it is invariably written as it sounds; no word ever begins with a double consonant and the accent is always on the first syllable. So far so good, I felt when Toini explained this to me, and went on to say that there were no articles, definite or indefinite; that no distinction was made between "he" and "she," and that, most wonderful of all, there were no irregular verbs. Already I felt I was halfway to having learnt it, but round the corner lay my Waterloo. There were no prepositions; instead, there were fifteen cases for nouns, pronouns and adjectives. Nor were these cases merely differentiated by suffixes; root modifications were disconcertingly addicted to disguising the original word beyond recognition.

Matters were scarcely helped by my grammar. The only one I could find was written in German for Germans, and neither Toini nor I were very good at German. Laboriously we deciphered the first few lessons. It was "confusion worse confounded"—they were devoted to word order, which, as everybody knows who has tried to learn German, is what is commonly known as "the end." "*O weh, O weh,* what a waste of effort," I murmured to Toini as with mental anguish we twisted Finnish into German and then German into English, only to discover that the German alone complicated the issue and that the Finnish order was not so very different from the English one.

"You must say '*Voi, voi,*' " Toini admonished me, "if you want to say 'Oh dear, oh dear' in Finnish." And how often that was just what I did want to say!

Then there was Paula, a friendly, strong-willed child who enjoyed attention. She can scarcely have been said to help, for, beyond the somewhat doubtful service of teaching me an assortment of words that I later discovered to be of the bow-wow, gee-gee variety, she gave us little uninterrupted peace.

But I suppose the real reason that I made so little headway was that Toini was far too gentle and did not bully me half enough. I never studied my lessons. I had so much other work to do, because, being unused to teaching, I spent hours with my English grammar preparing my classes and trying to find simple explanations for the inexplicable. If only Toini had looked angrily at me and accused me of wasting her time, I might have been galvanised into giving my Finnish more attention, but as it was she was sweet and understanding, and my lessons degenerated into a pleasant social chat which was usually followed by a bath.

Nevertheless, I did progress beyond the stage of saying "*Voi, voi!*" so far as to learn to count with a modicum of success. That is to say, I could get a number on the telephone if no one was about to do it for me, and I could buy stamps, a feat that was always a gamble, because I never could tell whether I should leave the Post Office with fifteen ten-mark stamps or ten fifteen-mark ones. And last, but not least, there was my cheque-book; just when I thought I was becoming adept at filling in cheques the bank clerk, noting my wrapt concentration, offered to accept them in English. What a come-down this was, as Finnish numbers, when written in full, are truly impressive, for they roll them all into one word and, as far as I could see, only the size of my salary stood between me and writing a cheque for:

"ninehundredandninetyninethousandandninehundredand ninetynine" marks or more!

* * *

On Saturday evening Kalle took me to a concert in the Town Hall. Sirkka was not with us; she was away on a visit to her mother in Turku. The Town Hall, which was built of wood, was a great barrack-like building that overlooked the market and sadly needed a coat of paint. Inside was a large rectangular auditorium that no one had made the least effort to brighten. A grimy green wash covered the walls, and hard wooden chairs filled two-thirds of the floor space. It was a dismal background for music or entertainment of any kind and one that I found hard to ignore, probably because I am not really musical. But most Finns have music in their blood; they rose above their surroundings without difficulty.

The concert was being given by a male choir. They sang unaccompanied and they struck me as good—amazingly good for so small a town—and what surprised me very much was that they all wore evening dress. Where, I wondered, had they raised so many dinner jackets, for the clothing shortage was still very severe, and many of the singers must have been far too young to have owned them in '39. Yet there they were, forcing me to wage war on the word "smoking".

The number of choirs in Kajaani never failed to astonish me. There were no fewer than five that gave concerts at frequent intervals. These recitals were always of a high standard and were generally well attended, both because the Finns love music and because Kajaani has not much alternative entertainment to offer. On this particular Saturday two of my pupils were taking part and many more were among the audience. It was all very encouraging; here, in the concert hall, exactly one week after my arrival, I seemed to be surrounded by friends, three of whom had had the thoughtfulness to ring me up and invite me to come with them.

And what of Finnish music? It is a subject on which I am not qualified to speak. I found it preponderantly brooding and sad. Suffused with the magic of the Northern Lights, there yet seemed about it a great sameness, and, listening to it, I had the feeling that it was largely based on folk-music—the folk-music of a people once obsessed by the occult. Be that as it may, Finnish music is to me essentially an expression of environment. Its temper is that of the countryside; an endless expanse of woods and water, the monotony of which is rarely monotonous because of the light which lends to it an infinite variety of colour. I believe that, consciously or sub-consciously, the early Finns acknowledged this affinity between music and nature in the very name they gave their hero Väinämöinen. For Väinämöinen, who takes pride of place among all the heroes of the *Kalevala*, was first and foremost a musician:

> "Outside the *sauna* . . . restlessly roaming
> The wind rose up, half sighing and half moaning:
> 'Väinämöinen . . . Väinämöinen.' "[1]

The very sound is of the wind soughing in the trees.

But if I am to stick to hard facts all that I really know about Finnish music is that its main development has taken place within the last 120 years, that during this period its evolution was rapid, and that to-day all Finns point proudly to Sibelius as the foremost composer of the age.

I cannot remember what was sung on the evening of which I am writing. I wish now that I had kept all my programmes, because the recitals that I heard in Kajaani have tended to become one in my mind: a single recital pre-eminently Finnish in character, for the Finns, at any rate in the provinces, share with the French the habit of concentrating almost exclusively on their own music.

During the evening there were three intervals, in each of which the conductor was given flowers. For the first time I began to realise just what flowers mean in Finnish life, where they have a scarcity value throughout most of the year that is hard for us to appreciate. Once the short summer is over they

[1] *Sauna*, by James Bramwell.

are cultivated indoors with assiduous care. They are the Finns' natural expression of gratitude; their instinctive way of saying "Thank you." Yet they are so scarce that three, two or even one bloom is enough. At first, I must admit, it surprised me to see a rather gawky lad advancing towards the conductor with two roses. I was even more surprised when another equally awkward-looking youth shambled up in the second interval with a few more blooms, to be followed by yet another in the third. It was a gauche performance; the people seemed as oblivious to the way they gave their flowers as to the background they gave their music. This was a pity, because the presentation had neither artistic finish nor natural spontaneity, and so robbed itself of its rightful charm and became faintly embarrassing.

* * *

Almost before I could turn round it was Wednesday—the alternate Wednesday when the club met. What, I asked myself, were we to do? The question was altogether too pertinent. Already several people had asked me what the programme was to be, and I had not been able to enlighten them. The time had come when I could no longer afford to sit back and wait for inspiration to come to me. I had to be ready with something, so I set about racking my brains for ideas, and in so doing called to mind the visit that Sylvia and I had paid to the Finnish British Society in Helsinki. "Games," their Secretary had said, "the Finns love playing games." Games it would have to be for at least half of the evening if only I could remember enough.

But what of the other half? It was then that I bethought myself of Lady Constance Malleson. During the past week so many of my pupils had asked me if I knew her.

"No," I had replied with some curiosity, for Lady Constance appeared to have made a profound impression on Kajaani. "I've never met her. What was she like?"

In the descriptions that followed, the phrase "A very strange woman" recurred again and again, and I was left with the picture of a highly theatrical individual reading Yeats to a wide-eyed audience, many of whom understood very little of the poetry, but all of whom were vastly intrigued by the performance.

Well, at least it was an idea; if Lady Constance read poetry, so would I. The only problem was what should I read? I turned the matter over in my mind and eventually decided on *The Pied Piper* as, being a narrative poem, it is a relatively easy one for a foreigner to follow.

The gathering was held in the big room at the factory club, so I, at least, was on my home ground. Not that this filled me with any degree of self-confidence; I longed to have the evening behind me. Was I to run the whole meeting or only to lend a helping hand? On this point everyone whom I had asked had been maddeningly non-committal. There was nothing for it but for me to feel my way.

Towards seven-thirty the first arrivals began to drift in and stand around silent and expectant. Meanwhile, I hovered from one to another of them feeling horribly self-conscious. Then, when a dozen or so members had assembled and it was abundantly clear that they intended to sit back and leave everything to me, I began hopefully to pin the names of famous people on their backs. "You must find out who you are," I told them, "but only answer yes or no to all questions." Luckily this set the ball rolling and proved a good opening gambit, because there was no great reason why the game should have any particular beginning or end, and so could be kept up until everybody arrived. It was as absurdly inconsequential as the Caucus-race, and I felt a fellow feeling for the Dodo:

"There was no 'One, two, three, and away,' but they began running when they liked, and left off when they liked, so that it was not easy to know when the race was over. However, when they had been running half an hour or so, and were quite dry again, the Dodo suddenly called out 'The race is over!' and they all crowded round it, panting, and asking 'But who has won?'

"This question the Dodo could not answer without a great deal of thought, and it sat for a long time with one finger pressed against its forehead (the position in which you usually see Shakespeare, in the pictures of him), while the rest waited in silence. At last the Dodo said, '*Everybody* has won, and all must have prizes!' "

Luckily for me, members were not interested in either winning or prizes! In the end about twenty-five to thirty people turned up, a very average attendance, for though the club was over seventy strong, quite a few were sleeping members. The people who came to the meetings were generally the regulars, noticeable among whom were Elli Hyyrylainen and Samuli Koponen.

Elli was a great friend of Lady Constance, and is described by her in her book, *In the North*, as the most Irish Finn she had ever met, and, being Irish herself, she should know. Certainly alone among the Finns with whom I came in contact Elli never appeared to care a rap about appearances. As Lady Constance says, "She didn't care two hoots whether her hat sat on the back of her head or on her nose. Wherever it sat, you could be quite certain it was where nobody else's hat sat." It was Elli who met me in the street one day and asked me how her younger daughter and her friend were getting on with their English. Laughingly, I said something about their learning a little more if they worked a little harder; at which she looked me in the eye and said, "Oh but they don't come to learn; they come for their amusement." In view of the fact that this conversation took place nearly a year after my arrival, and that all this time they had been coming to my classes regularly twice a week, this remark gave me food for considerable thought.

Samuli Koponen was equally regular. He was a dear old man, how old I do not know, but he had white hair and a rubicund, smiling face. All his life he had read English, but he had rarely had the chance to speak or listen to it. Though I judged him well past seventy, he came as unfailingly to my lessons as to the club meetings, which was the more remarkable because the Lyceum where I taught in the evenings was far from comfortable, and going there must have entailed for him no small effort. Tired as he must have been, on two evenings a week he would sit at a hard wooden desk with his hand behind his ear; and this no matter how cold the night, and after a day spent teaching in the seminary. I often wondered sadly what benefit he reaped from it all, as his hearing was very bad—so bad that the replies that I got to my questions often had about them an irrelevancy that out-Tchekoved Tchekov. Not long after I left he had a stroke and died; club meetings, I am afraid, will never be quite the same again.

After a while everyone settled down to play paper games. Conversation became animated. Kalle and Aili Parviainen, amid peals of laughter, collaborated flagrantly in a corner; all remonstrances ran off them like water off a duck's back, but what did it matter? Nobody cared who won, anyway. All that mattered was that everybody should be happy and amused and talking English, and this they all seemed to be doing.

About nine tea and buns arrived, and everyone stopped to eat and drink.

After the tea interval I volunteered tentatively to read aloud, and they were all much too polite to say "No." In absolute silence they listened to *The Pied Piper* and to what little I could tell them about Browning. Most people, I think, understood the gist of the poem, but only two had heard it before. I am pretty sure that the majority of them preferred Belloc's *Cautionary Tales*, with which I wound up the evening. But there was always a difference of opinion between the men and women on literary matters. This was most noticeable when alternative programmes were submitted by visiting lecturers; the more advanced women were all highbrow, the men for the most part scouted literary subjects.

About ten-thirty everyone went home, and with a sigh of relief I said "Good-night"—relief not so much because the meeting was over, but because, rather to my surprise, I had enjoyed it.

* * *

I believe the next landmark in my life was Niilo Kanto's fiftieth birthday. In the ordinary way Finns do not take much notice of birthdays; name-days are what they celebrate, and the variety of Finnish names is enormous. Each one is supposed to have a different day, but as there are well over 365 many are forced to share. Yet over and above name-day celebrations, every tenth year birthdays are kept, and marked by increasing ceremonial. If you look at any picture paper you will find pages devoted to the photographs of prominent Finns who have just achieved another decade.

So it came about that, being the head of the Kajaani Company, Niilo Kanto's fiftieth birthday was the signal for great celebrations. The first I heard of it was from Yrjö, who came and asked me if I would mind moving into the hotel for a few nights, as the rooms in the club were wanted for guests. I need not, he told me, pack up everything, but there he and the club staff did not see eye to eye, and before I could collect myself all my belongings were being deposited in washing-baskets and carted off to the attic.

What actually happened on the great day I only heard

indirectly. I had not met Niilo Kanto and naturally enough was not invited, but I understand that all day long, surrounded by his family, he kept open house and that throughout the day friends and acquaintances poured in to congratulate him. The evening was reserved for the more important guests; then it was a question of white ties and evening dresses.

It was an invaluable topic of conversation. "What did so-and-so wear at the Kanto's party?" The men were unobservant almost to a man. Only Yrjö knew what his wife had worn, and that was because he himself had given her the material for her dress, a present from the United States, where he had been on business.

The women, on the other hand, showed a profound interest in clothes ("clo-thees," as they would persist in calling them), and it really was remarkable how well they were dressed considering the enormous difficulty there was in getting clothes of any sort. Doubtless with money there were ways and means, but most of them were very good needlewomen and made the utmost of everything.

It was at this time that I first met Airi Uoti, one of the most entertaining women in Kajaani. She had been away on a visit and had only returned in time for the festivities. Dear Airi, she was so attractive, and she made me laugh more than any other of my pupils. She had a delightful sense of humour and the most casual observation made in her presence would often call forth the most absurd anecdote. A shameless embroiderer with an infinite capacity for laughing at herself, she was wonderfully good company. But of all her stories I preferred those of her childhood, of the years when she had lived in Hanko with her grandmother, an old lady of character, who had had mirrors fixed on both sides of her windows so that she might miss nothing that happened in the street.

* * *

The Maakunta Hotel, where I spent the three or four days of Niilo Kanto's birthday celebrations, was in no way remarkable. It was like a hundred and one other such places, as throughout Finland there is a great sameness in hotel accommodation. With few exceptions, hotels are places where travellers may pass a night or two, but they are not designed to live in. Bedrooms, restaurant and *sauna* are provided, but nowhere to sit or lounge. Dining-rooms are for the most part to be found on the first floor, failing that, right at the top of the building. The service is always very slow and eating takes an unconscionable time. This is partly, but not wholly, because most food is served *à la carte*. Set meals, as I knew them, were largely composed of very dull concoctions made out of left-overs. But for this the managements were scarcely to blame, as most food was terribly expensive.

By now I was in a far better position to judge what the people were up against. This was because, since the departure of Mr. Leigh, I had been eating with the factory staff who regularly ate at the club, which meant subsisting on rations eked out by what was cheap to buy. The result was a diet of raw salt fish, potatoes and porridge. At lunch-time the potatoes were always boiled in their skins and the porridge—rye, oatmeal or barley—was eaten with berry juice when, as frequently happened, the milk from the Company's farm gave out. Added to this there was a little fresh meat or fish at the evening meal; vegetables were exclusively beetroot or carrots. It was a lucky thing for me that I liked potatoes and porridge, because I do not take at all kindly to raw salt fish.

Food was certainly monotonous, but even so the arrangements that I had at the club were very satisfactory. Room and service were laid at my feet; the cost of my food averaged about 10*s*. a week. This meant that when the summer holidays came and I wanted to travel I had saved enough to make all my projects possible. It had all been worth while, and in any case I could have asked for extras—I know I should have been given them—but one hesitates to be different, more especially when language difficulties make one dependent for getting what one wants upon the help of others—others who, for the most part, cannot afford extras. Besides, I wanted to know what it felt like to be a Finn. But in that I think I overdid it, for most of my companions had at least one major meal a day at home, and that probably of a rather higher grade. All the same, the cost of living was appalling. Meat was the equivalent of 12*s*. and upwards a pound and eggs anything from 1*s*. to 1*s*. 8*d*. each. Most people reckoned on spending three-quarters of their income on food, which swallowed it up in no time at all.

As in post-war Britain, so in post-war Finland food was a constant topic of conversation—food, and the dearth of domestic help—but as far I was concerned food was the greater trouble. For the first time it was borne in on me that to teach a language one must be a walking encyclopædia. Reading *Brush Up* with Yrjö Tähtinen, Paavo Kivi and Olli Parviainen, we chanced one day on a reference to a suet pudding.

"What," said Paavo Kivi, "is suet?"

"Fat," said I.

"What kind of fat?"

"I don't know. Wait a minute and I'll look it up in the dictionary."

Silence ensued while I found it.

"Kidney fat."

"Is the pudding sweet?"

"Yes; we generally eat it with treacle; it's called rolypoly."

"You can't make a sweet pudding out of kidney fat."

"Oh, yes, you can. We always do."

"It must be nasty. How is it done?"

"We steam it."

"What else do you put in it?"

"Mr. Kivi," I said, "I've never made a suet pudding in my life. I really don't know." There and then I registered a resolve to write home for a cookery book. Luckily, he was the only one of my pupils to evince great interest in cookery, though they all wanted to know what food was available in England, and what was rationed and controlled.

Soon after this episode Yrjö went for a few days to Helsinki. He returned clutching four copies of *Stalky and Co.*, which he thought would be interesting for us to read. It was one of a series of well-known books selected by an enterprising individual in Copenhagen who had taken the originals and tried, with the minimum of textual alteration, to reduce the total vocabulary employed in them to 1,500 words. This series gloried in the perfect misnomer, *Easy Readers*, for the result was not only totally ungrammatical; it was also completely incomprehensible. However, I corrected the book as we went along. All went well till we reached the part where the dead cat is hidden under the next-door dormitory floor. Here I could not make head or tail of the text and, after an hour spent by my pupils demonstrating with pencil and paper all the possible ways and means of clandestinely inserting cats beneath floor boards, we gave up. The original was not available and none of us could say with any certainty just what Kipling had meant. For the rest, all that stands out in my mind about the story was the recurrence of the word "Bush"—which both Paavo Kivi and Olli Parviainen had a chronic tendency to make rhyme with "Hush"—that, and a reference to an angel.

"What," I asked, "is an angel?"

Both Paavo Kivi's arms began to flap up and down vigorously.

"That's no good," I remonstrated. "I want you to tell me."

At that he stopped, reconsidered the matter, and then said with a broad grin: "An angel is a common person in Heaven."

* * *

Paavo Kivi and his very pretty wife, Kirsti, lived in a house next door to the club. They had three small boys, of whom the second, Pekka, was already a friend of mine, because while I lived in the club he and two little friends, both boys, spent a large part of their time in the surrounding grounds.

The first time I saw them they were playing in the snow outside my windows. It was then that I remembered the kilo of caramels I had brought from Sweden. I opened the window and gave them some. "*Kiitos, kiitos* (thank-you, thank-you)," they said, and made off beaming from ear to ear. That was the beginning of a somewhat inarticulate friendship. They played daily nearer and nearer to my window, through which, it being on the ground floor, they could see quite clearly; there was never any question of my being "not at home." If I took no notice of them, first one and then another would say, "*Paivää.*" (The whole expression is *Hyvää paivää* and means "Good day," but nobody bothers much about the *Hyvää* in the same way as we drop the "good" before "morning.") If I still failed to respond, they would shout it all together in an increasing crescendo until I relented. Then off came their caps and down went their heads until they almost hit the ground. This happened every day, but to their great credit be it said they never once asked for sweets; if they had, I should have understood—as a word, *karamelli* is self-explanatory—and this in a country where the only sweets children ever got were small packets of boiled ones resembling those that we used to get out of penny-in-the-slot machines. These were the reward given by the Government for each ten kilos of waste paper salvaged. Needless to say, when I had sweets the little boys generally got them, but either way they smiled.

Then, when summer came, Pekka had a brain-wave—flowers. I know it was his idea, for I saw it all happen. From my window I watched the children denude the lower branches of a flowering tree that was covered with a sweet-scented white blossom; then they all went into a huddle. Presently they hid the blossom behind their backs and advanced towards my window, the greenery sticking out like fantails, and their eyes dancing. "*Paivää*," they chanted in unison; of course the manœuvre, if manœuvre it was, met with success; they were in luck, supplies were good. From that day onwards every receptacle down to my tooth-glass was always full, not only of wild flowers, but also, I am afraid, of the cowslips that the gardeners were doing their best to grow in the flower-beds round the house. They were the most endearing trio, two very fair and one dark. I loved their wide and somewhat toothless grins, and if I have given the impression that their attentions were all cupboard love, that is wrong; several times when I returned late to my room I found wilting bunches of wild flowers left on my writing table, bunches that bore the indelible stamp of small, hot hands, and this in defiance of the fact that they certainly were not allowed to penetrate the precincts of the club.

It was strange, I felt, that flowers should play such a part in Finnish life, for their season is so short. Probably that is the reason. After all, the ancient Greeks glorified every stream, no matter how insignificant, simply because they were few and far between. But the case is not quite parallel, because when the Finns do have flowers they have them in abundance. In their short summer season everything matures at a phenomenal rate because there is perpetual light and the plants never stop growing. So for a brief spell the flower markets are a blaze of colour. Nevertheless, it is not the summer flowers that are peculiarly Finnish; it is the indoor plants that fill the houses through the winter months which are so characteristic of the country. Along the window-sills of most living-rooms are rows of pots where, in the warmth, all kinds of exotic blooms flourish. And warm it undoubtedly is, for the tiled stoves on which most people depend are very efficient, and to make assurance doubly sure all houses are fitted with double windows whose frames are sealed to prevent draughts—all, that is, but a bare minimum which is needed for airing purposes.

The plants vary from almost tropical ones to ivy, of which the Finns are curiously fond. They train it up their window-frames, across the lintels of their doors, up specially-made trellis-work—

up anything, in fact, which is a fixture and to which it will cling. Cacti, too, are much in evidence, and I saw many that I had never seen before in bloom. Sometimes, even, you will find plants hanging from the ceiling in vessels suggestive of incense-burners or lamps, and against which I came near to braining myself on more than one occasion.

But though flowers were the invariable attribute of all houses, in the main the more peculiarly Finnish types of floral decoration were not to be found in the homes of the comparatively well-to-do, whose taste tends to be more cosmopolitan.

I had been in Kajaani about three weeks, when one evening in the Lyceum I was handed a beautiful pink primula in a pot. Attached to the plant was a card bearing the legend, "This is for you. Now you see how we educate flowers in Finland." It cheered my room for many weeks to come, and brightened for one evening the large, whitewashed class-room in which I was teaching—and brightening was just what it needed. It was all too apparent that the Lyceum was purely utilitarian in concept, and I could not help feeling a little sorry for the school-children because I do not believe that austerity promotes imagination, even if necessity does father inventive genius. This feeling was to recur on more than one occasion, and as time went on my conviction grew that the young in Finland suffer from lack of mental stimulant. Yet most parents are almost painfully interested in the progress their offspring are making at school; but progress to them means absorbing facts, because facts are what the examination system demands.

I remember one day, when Irmeli and Aili Eho were discussing their children's recent marks, that in the course of the conversation one of them remarked to me: "This evening they have their Swedish exercises."

"I expect they'll enjoy that," I replied glibly. "Most children do."

"Oh, no," came the prompt rejoinder. "They find them very difficult."

I sympathised. My thoughts flew back to the gymnasium at school, where I was unfailingly the laughing-stock of the whole class.

"Does that mean they have to go back to school after dinner?" I asked.

They looked puzzled, and then one of them said, "No; they always bring their work home." Light dawned; I suppose it is only in England that the word "Swedish" combined with exercises denotes gymnastics.

But, whether Swedish or not, the Finns do make a cult of physical culture in which gymnastics play a large part. In schools this is manifestly because outdoor games are, for so many months in the year, quite impossible. True, the boys play ice-hockey in the winter, but that is about the beginning and end of their ball games. There were two tennis courts only in Kajaani, and in all Finland I doubt if there are more than two golf-courses. Ski-ing, skating and swimming are the natural recreations of Finnish youth; those and athletics; and all over the country you will find societies devoted to physical culture.

I had not been long in Kajaani when there was a demonstration of gymnastics and dancing in the Town Hall. It had been organised by an Esthonian woman, who introduced the show. When it was all over a small man in a grey suit, whose hair was beginning to show signs of thinning, stepped up on to the stage. He carried a large pot, from which protruded a solitary rose. Once on the stage he spoke for some time, and then presented the rose, pot and all, to the Esthonian. The audience rocked with mirth. I turned to Heljä, who was with me, and asked what it was all about.

"Dr. Savolainen," she explained, "has just stated that the rose is a token of his esteem, but that the pot is only borrowed from the bar, and must be returned."

The show was over. The body of the hall was rapidly cleared of chairs, and Heikki Savolainen and the Esthonian together led off in a country dance. To me the simplicity of the proceedings was eloquent. Heikki Savolainen's wife was one of my pupils, and I had been to their flat. There, to my surprise, for I knew nothing of his achievements, I had found the walls adorned with laurel wreaths and banners bearing the words "Amsterdam," "Los Angeles," "Berlin." In addition, the place was stiff with cups and medals, for Heikki Savolainen was an expert gymnast and had for years been one of the Finnish Olympic team of eight. But he was also the town doctor, whose job it was to cope with the schoolchildren, epidemics, inoculations and the like. How he found time to qualify and afterwards to practise was something of a mystery; but the same might have been said, in his day, of Lönnrot.

The Fourteenth Olympiad must have been a disappointment

for the Finns, who between 1912 and 1936 were second no less than six times, but at least it was gratifying to see that they were first in the Gymnastic Team Contest, and that Heikki Savolainen was again among the team of competitors. In the individual competitions he was third in the Pommelled Horse and sixth in the Parallel Bars, an amazing record for a man who has been competing since 1924. I did not see the events in question, but I did see him once on a news-reel, and if ever the expression "poetry of motion" was apposite, that was the moment. The Finns as a whole take great pride in their athletes, and without doubt Kajaani was proud of its doctor, but lionising in the American sense is quite foreign to them. In many ways it is hard for us to understand the position accorded to athletes, for here athletics have a limited public, but in Finland they are a symbol of nationalism. Athletic prowess, it is felt, puts Finland on the map. The result of this is that sport is acknowledged by all to be a serious business, largely because it is bound up with a deep longing for recognition that is rarely fully appreciated abroad. The judges of the Olympic Sports at St. Moritz were reported in the Finnish newspapers to have had hot grog served to them while distributing the trophies. Knowing how cold it can be, I should never have given this a second thought had not several Finns complained to me about the desecration of so solemn an occasion.

Here, strangely enough, the subject of the Games brings me to the etymology of the word "Finn." The Finns use the word "Suomi," which means a swamp, when referring to their country. In a land abounding in water this is natural enough, and by analogy one leaps to the conclusion that the word "Finn" is a variation of the Anglo-Saxon "Fen." Yet the *Oxford Dictionary* says "Etymology dubious," and while reading I have discovered another school of thought that believes that the "Fenni" referred to by Tacitus derived their name from the word "Penna" or "Wing"—winged because they wore snowshoes. Personally, I like this idea, not because of its scholastic value, of which I am in no position to judge, but because it requires only a small stretch of imagination to believe that they were so named because of their fleetness of foot—fleetness that was later to be personified in Paavo Nurmi, the Flying Finn, the inspiration of countless painters and sculptors, and probably the greatest long-distance runner of all times.

But however dubious the connection between Finns and

wings, there is no doubt that skis and their prototype, snowshoes, are of very remote origin. Prokopios, the Byzantine historian, mentions the *Skrid-Finnen* or "sliders" as early as the fifth or sixth century, and the Norse Sagas certainly prove that they were in general use long before Christianity came to Scandinavia. The earliest known example, however, belongs to the sixteenth century. It was made of leather stretched over a frame that was about three feet long, and pointed at the toe. From these snowshoes the present-day ski has evolved. Those commonly used in Finland are longer, lighter and narrower than their Alpine counterpart. Bindings are very light indeed, a simple toe clip that clamps down upon the sole of the boot, which protrudes on either side of the upper to give it a grip. There are, of course, heavier skis and strong spring bindings for use in the more mountainous country, but they are the exception and not the rule.

* * *

I had one day's ski-ing before the thaw set in. Early on Sunday, April 20th, my dreams were shattered by the ringing of the telephone; it was Eero. "It is a lovely morning," he said. "Come and ski with us. We can lend you skis and Aili will give you breakfast." I hustled into my trousers, and was with them by about half-past seven. Irmeli was there too. We wasted no time over breakfast, but set out almost at once, as when the season is so far advanced the snow becomes very soft when the sun is high. For about three hours we skied through the forest. The sun shone, the snow sparkled, and the country undulated gently. It was a perfect morning, and the last Sunday of the year when ski-ing was possible.

The onset of the thaw was very beautiful. For a brief spell after the ice melted, the great curve of the river above the power station lay like a sheet of pure cobalt between banks of dazzling whiteness. Then all too soon the earth appeared, brown and dead, the streets ran with slush and, during the week or so that followed, the country looked sad beyond belief. Then, almost overnight, the spring green opened and summer came to Finland.

Officially May Day is the first day of summer, and as such is celebrated throughout the country as a national holiday; but the celebrations, unlike their more southerly counterparts, are not rooted in indigenous fertility rites. All direct traces of that nature belong, in Finland, to midsummer, when lighting bonfires, and dancing round poles barely distinguishable from our maypoles, are customary.

In actual fact, the practice of keeping May 1st began late in Finland, where it arrived from Sweden with Roman Catholicism at a time long after a veneer of Christianity had been superimposed on the original pagan ritual. To-day May Day has lost its primary significance and has become first and foremost the students' spring festival, which used, until some thirty years ago, to be held on May 13th, Flora's Day. In Helsinki University the evening of April 30th is the signal for a dance at which the refreshments are traditionally *Sima* and *Tippaleipä*—that is to say, mead and what my dictionary calls *cruller*, and describes as "a cake cut from rolled dough, fried crisp in boiling lard." Sugar shortage prevented me from tasting either the one or the other. At midnight, when the revels are at their height, the undergraduates all put on their student caps to signify the advent of summer. These caps differ little from those worn by students in other parts of Scandinavia, each being made of white velvet with a shiny black peak, and decorated in front with a gold button.

On May morning a procession of students marches through Helsinki to the Kaivopuisto or Brunspark. The procession is in eleven parts, and each part carries its own banners, for the University is divided into eleven student societies. These are organised by districts, and every freshman is automatically affiliated to the district from which he or she comes; the Karelians join the Karelian fraternity, the Ostrabothnians the Ostrabothnian, and so on.

On arrival at the Kaivopuisto there are speeches, one of which is invariably patriotic, while another is always an eulogy of spring. These speeches are followed by singing, and the afternoon and evening are again given over to dancing; the very thought is exhausting.

Students apart, the Finns to-day celebrate very little; at best they congregate to dance and, whatever the weather, put on their summer clothes. Thin frocks and flannel trousers are worn even if snow is falling.

In Kajaani the company gave a large dance at the club, to which I was invited. It was scheduled to start at eight, but, for some reason best known to myself, I did not expect it to begin punctually. I was therefore somewhat disconcerted by hearing a knock at my door before I had put the finishing touches to my summer outfit. Considerate as ever, there stood Yrjö. "We thought you might be feeling shy," he said smiling, "so I have come to fetch you."

Together we joined the party in the big room, which had been elaborately decorated for the occasion. Paper screens adorned with a series of pictures hid the windows and bookshelves. The caption beneath each mural was the same: *Jo riittää* which means "That's enough." Every picture was a variation on this theme: champagne being poured into a glass; a couple kissing in the moonlight. The artist had worked hard and had, so it seemed to me, exhausted all possible variants.

The party began when Niilo Kanto arrived and made a welcoming speech. Then dinner was served. The tables had been arranged in the shape of an "E" and in each place was a little booklet of songs. As the meal progressed it was punctuated by singing, which seemed to begin quite arbitrarily whenever anyone fancied tuning up. All the songs in the book were Finnish except for *My bonnie lies over the ocean*, which all assembled sang with great gusto. All over Finland this tune is very popular and may be heard sung, with equal frequency, both in English and in Finnish.

After dinner they let fly paper streamers in all directions, drink was plentiful, and everyone was very merry and in the mood to appreciate fully a cabaret put on by the younger members of the staff.

When this was over, the room was cleared for dancing, which went on until midnight. Then on the stroke of twelve all those who had ever graduated from school to the University—whether or not they had actually been there—put on their caps and, irrespective of age or sex, continued wearing them throughout May Day. The only variant was provided by the students of the Technical High School, from whose caps dangled long black tassels. As the factory employed a large number of engineers and chemists, there was a goodly sprinkling of these among the company.

Dancing went on until round about three in the morning; then everyone went home. It was a good party, merry but sober, and did not at all bear out the contention which I heard almost daily that Finns drink too much.

I do not know if anything special happened next morning, because I slept late and only staggered up in time for the eleven o'clock meal. After that I walked into the town to see if there was anything doing, but all that I saw was a brass band that had finished for the day and was being driven home in a lorry. Whatever had taken place had taken place early, but I do not think that I missed much as, being International Labour Day, I believe the morning was given over to workers' demonstrations and speeches of which I should not have made head or tail.

By the time I had walked the two kilometres into Kajaani, everything was very quiet and a Sunday-like atmosphere prevailed. The only gay note was struck by the flags that decked the town. The effect of these was charming, because there is nothing garish about the Finnish flag, a slender blue cross on a white background: a river flowing between banks of snow. Every private garden had its slim white flagpole rising proudly above the roof-tops and dwarfing the little wooden house to which it belonged. Those who had no gardens hung flags from their windows, and public buildings flew them from their roof-tops or flanked their entrances with rows of flagpoles. From one end of the Kauppakatu to the other, blue-and-white bunting waved; the hotel flew in addition the national flags of its guests. The whole effect was peculiarly Finnish, and one with which I was to grow very familiar, for the Finns like nothing better than to hang out their flags, which they do on national holidays, official flag days, and on every conceivable pretext.

Not long ago I wrote to Heljä and asked her for a list of national holidays. Her answer began: "All days that are Sundays—even in the middle of the week we have Sundays," which is a not unusual way for a Finn to refer to the Church festivals. When I first arrived I found this most confusing, for although Ascension Day is always a Thursday several people happened to remark to me: "You will have no lessons to-morrow, because it's Sunday!"

Mother's Day, Ascension Day, Snellman's Day and Whitsuntide all fell in May, and on each occasion flags were flown. I am not quite sure when Mother's Day was, but it cannot have synchronised with the day which we know as Mothering Sunday, because that falls in mid-Lent. All that I know is that in theory it is a day of rest for the mother; a day on which she may have a nice long lie in bed. Tradition demands that the children prepare the morning coffee, carry it to her room and there wake her with a song that has been learned in secret and is intended as a surprise. The idea is a charming one and remains so, even though she is probably woken earlier than usual by "noises off" and has later to spend some time in putting her kitchen to rights.

Johan Vilhelm Snellman's Day is kept on his birthday, May 12th. He was born in 1806 and, like Lönnrot, was intimately connected with the Finnish nationalist movement, although he approached it from a very different angle. A Swedish-speaking Finn himself, he believed that no progress was possible for the masses while Swedish remained the language of the administration and all save elementary education. While Headmaster of the Swedish school at Kuopio he edited Finland's first political journal *Saima*, in which he advocated Finnish secondary schools. This publication was promptly suppressed by the Russian Governor-General, and things might have looked very black for Snellman had not Alexander II decided that the time had come to woo the Finnish nationalists. With the Industrial Revolution, Finland was becoming increasingly prosperous, and he feared the effect that this might have on the predatory instincts of the Swedes. But whether from motives of expediency or enlightenment, the result was the same; Alexander's support led, in 1858, to the opening of the first Finnish secondary school in Jyväskylä.

On Snellman's advice, he followed this up by an edict, which he issued in 1863, making Finnish an alternative language in the courts. From this time on the language controversy has raged, the Swedish-Finns fighting an ever-losing battle. In 1886 Finnish was permitted in official correspondence; in 1894 it was allowed in the Senate.

But still the strife persisted and was not even assuaged by the 1919 Constitution. In this Ståhlberg, the first President of the Finnish Republic, laid it down that both were national languages and that the law was to provide for their needs in accordance with "identical principles." A Bill defining "identical principles" became law in 1922. It divided the country into unilingual and bilingual districts, unilingual being those with a less than 10 per cent. minority. This classification, which was subject to revision every ten years, resulted in 454 Finnish districts, 36 Swedish districts, and 64 bilingual ones. Considering the vast Finnish majority, the new legislation was quite amazingly liberal—too liberal by far to satisfy the extremists. Extreme Finnish nationalists complained that the Swedish-

Finns had no right to 20 per cent. of the Government grant made to education, because they were only 10 per cent. of the population. The Government, however, was adamant; they felt that the upkeep of Swedish would be invaluable to international intercourse. There is a lot to be said on both sides, but nothing can eradicate the fact that the maintenance of a dual language is a very expensive business.

There is a great deal too much stress laid on the gulf that is supposed to exist between Finnish- and Swedish-speaking Finns. The reality of this is far from apparent. It is solely a matter of language. Years of intermarriage have minimised any racial differences which may have existed between the Swedish colonists and the local inhabitants. The issue is further clouded by Finns who took Swedish names in the early days, when to have a Swedish name helped preferment. Nor are matters made clearer by the numerous Finns with Swedish names who, at the height of the nationalist movement, took Finnish ones. To-day it is not at all uncommon to find both Swedish and Finnish versions of the same name in use within one family.

J. Hampden Jackson considers that the quarrel is basically between the "haves" and the "have nots," and that the language question has long been a mere peg on which to hang their differences. Be that as it may, the Swedish-speaking minority is steadily declining, and with it should go its attendant grievances. If the issue is truly linguistic, the moderate nationalists have won their point; on the other hand, if it is a question of class warfare, there is little justification for it, as between the wars the right-wing governments were more progressively left than the Communists themselves—their object being to combat the Communist menace by leaving the workers and peasants no legitimate grievances. The result of this was an immense advance in social legislation and a greatly improved standard of living. The post-war deterioration of this standard is nothing short of catastrophic, for, combined with the inevitable propaganda, it has resulted in a revival of Communism, which I am told now claims approximately 25 per cent. of the population. And in this connection it is perhaps interesting to note that the propaganda which reached the Communist headquarters in Kajaani from Moscow included illustrated periodicals printed in English, which not one member of the local Communist Party could read.

* * *

It was Aili Parvainen who introduced me to my first *sauna*. I had been in Kajaani about a month when I met her one morning in the Kauppakatu and she stopped and invited me for the following Saturday. I was delighted, for I had been looking forward to the experience ever since my arrival. The question, "How do you like our *sauna*?" had been on everybody's lips; now soon I should be able to answer it, and I had a strong feeling that I should like it very much.

In Finland the *sauna* is a national institution, and many people claim that it is the one thing which has kept them going through all their troubles. This I feel may well be so, for it certainly has a very comforting and invigorating effect. In general, the Finns do not indulge in a daily bath, but make *sauna*-taking a weekly habit; nevertheless, in summertime the men who work in the fields do quite often take them daily and without any adverse effects.

The ideal *sauna*—the word is used both for the bath and the bath-house—is to be found in the country beside a lake. This is the best possible place, because in warm weather, when you are cooked to a turn, you have only to plunge into the water and swim, while in winter you go out and roll in the snow. At least so I was told, but although during the summer I certainly plunged from a *sauna* into a lake, I never found snow-rolling the subject of much enthusiasm among my friends, except in summertime! But, of course, in many towns both lakes and snow have to be dispensed with, as also, very frequently, does the privately owned *sauna*. People who live in flats generally have one in the basement which is allocated to different flats on different days, while families that live in houses often share their *sauna* with their neighbours. It was to one of joint ownership that I was invited, for at Karolineburg, where the Parviainens lived, several families shared one between them, each family having a specific day for bathing. These semi-private *saunas* are more primitive and therefore more romantic than those in the up-to-date blocks of flats, where electric heating and running water have replaced wood fires and water-butts.

I arrived at Karolineburg about seven in the evening, and Aili and I did not waste much time before setting out for the bath-house complete with towels, soap and a carafe of berry juice, for sweating, she assured me, was a thirsty business. We had not far to go; about 100 yards up a lane through the trees was an unpretentious little wooden house with a cheerfully smoking chimney.

Inside was a small room which led into the bathroom. It was surrounded with benches and hooks, and there we undressed and left our clothes. Opening the door into the *sauna* proper, we were met by a wave of caressing warmth. The room was small and dimly lit. It was lined with wood, and against the walls were broad shelves at various heights. In one corner was a wood furnace on which lay a pile of cracked and blackened stones and beside it were two large water-butts, one filled with hot water, the other with cold. The whole place smelt pleasantly of warm, damp wood.

Taking up a ladle, Aili told me to get up on to a shelf; then, filling the ladle with water, she threw it on to the stones, at which, with a mighty hiss, the steam rose up and engulfed me. Being by nature considerate, she did not throw on much, but even so, to begin with I found it quite hard to breathe and lay there panting with my mouth wide open. Slowly and surely, however, a wonderful feeling of relaxation stole over me, and we were soon increasing the heat and lying back and talking nineteen to the dozen. The warmth which seeped into every pore seemed to loosen the tongue as well as the joints.

When the sweat was running off us in rivulets, Aili announced that it was time for the bath whisks. With some apprehension, I watched her pick up a bundle of birch twigs to which a few of last year's withered leaves still adhered, dip them in water and lay them on the hot stones. Their day was nearly over; in a week or two there would be fresh whisks covered with young green leaves. Their wood would be full of sap and when heated would give off a wonderful aroma. But this was a treat in store, for the spring this year was late in coming and meanwhile Aili was offering solicitously to beat me with something that looked remarkably like a birch rod. Setting my teeth and murmuring to myself, "When in Rome . . ." I accepted her offer. The result was a surprisingly pleasant sensation. When she had finished and I had returned the compliment, with blood racing madly, we got down to the business of washing, for which an assortment of enamel basins, wooden buckets, scrubbing-brushes and soap was provided. First we filled the basins with warm water and scrubbed, then we filled the buckets with cold water for the final douche without which no *sauna* is complete, unless there is a lake close by in which to plunge. It is a moment of mingled anguish and ecstasy.

A rest in the next room, a long drink, and back we went into the steam. You can keep it up just as long as you like, but it is usual to allow about two hours for a bath, after which time you emerge pink and white and very shiny, with your hair hanging in rats' tails.

Dressed once more, Aili took me back to her home, where we drank tea, ate sandwiches and talked. Amongst other things she told me that, contrary to many reports, the Finns do not indulge in mixed bathing except *en famille*; then the babies play with the water on the floor while their parents bask in the steam up above. When I expressed surprise at the children being taken at all, she told me that not only was it always done, but that in the country districts many of the peasant women gave birth to their babies in the *sauna* as a matter of course, because it was such a convenient place. A week or so later this remark of Aili's went down to history in one of my more graphic letters home: "The peasant women frequently have their babies in the *sauna*. In the course of three months I have had three."

But though they do not indulge in mixed bathing, the Finns do in fact entertain freely in the *sauna*, where both stag and hen parties are quite the thing. It was a form of entertainment of which I heartily approved, and one which never failed to amuse me, for it was quite usual for the women to sit round in the nude sweating profusely, yet calling each other by their full titles, thus combining a complete lack of prudery with a sustained dignity that never failed to strike me as incongruous.

Yet, although the *sauna* is to-day an integral part of Finnish life, not even the Finns themselves know how, or when, it originated. All that can be said is that, if Tacitus is to be believed, the early Finns were clearly no *sauna*-taking people; for in his *Germania* Tacitus describes the Fenni—who were then a nomadic tribe living in the Baltic States—as savage, filthy and very poor.

It was during the first century that these people penetrated into Finland by way of the Gulf and the north shore of Lake Laatokka. There in the course of time they settled down and there, it is to be presumed, they took to indulging in steam baths. In fact, in those days, it must have been this custom that chiefly distinguished them from their neighbours; for, by the eighth century, all the evidence goes to show that they were living in single-room cabins that served the dual purpose of habitation and bath-house. High under their roofs they built wooden shelves and through a hole in each roof the smoke and steam escaped.

As time passed, the *sauna* became either a separate room or, more commonly, a separate building; nevertheless, we know that the dual-purpose building was occasionally to be found in the backwoods until quite recent times. Aleksis Kivi, writing in the latter half of the nineteenth century, paints, in his novel *Seven Brothers*, a memorable picture of just such a cabin, and still to-day it is not at all unusual for a man who is building himself a house to construct the *sauna* first and live in it while he is completing his dwelling.

Having thus had occasion to mention Aleksis Kivi, I cannot bring myself to pass on without a word or two about him, because he is the one outstanding figure in Finnish literature for whom I feel a genuine personal affection. Like Lönnrot, he was the son of a tailor, but, unlike Lönnrot, he received no recognition in his lifetime and died in poverty at the early age of thirty-seven. The tragedy this was even we can in part appreciate as, thanks to Alex Matson, we have a very satisfying translation of his masterpiece, *Seven Brothers*. And what a book it is; as I read of their ups and their downs, of their adventures and their absurdities, I find myself constantly torn between laughter and tears. Each brother is essentially human, each is a definite individual; taken together, they are the epitome of Finnish peasantry.

But Kivi's genius does not stop short at characterisation; his work shows a feeling for the countryside that is very nearly comparable with that of Shakespeare. At any rate, the forest in which *Seven Brothers* is set seems to me as purely Finnish in character as the woodland where *A Midsummer Night's Dream* takes place—despite its Athenian setting—is English. Both are saturated by magic and both are imbued with a deep love of nature. But, while to-day the Finnish tradition of magic is probably rather less potent than it was, something of Kivi's great love of the forest is shared by every Finn I ever met. I remember once ski-ing with Toini on a Sunday in early March. The sun was shining and the trees were heavy with snow. On the top of a small hill we stopped and looked out over the forest. "Diana," she said, "I'd love to travel like you; there is so much

I want to see, but you know I could never stay away for long. I should always be homesick for the forest." How silent and how beautiful it was under the snow, so lovely that even I think of it with nostalgia and imagine that I understand how Toini felt.

* * *

May 21st marked the end of a political crisis that had lasted almost ever since my arrival. At the time the Government of Finland was a coalition of Agrarians, Social Democrats and Communist-controlled Democratic Unionists under the premiership of M. Mauno Pekkala. In the Senate were 48 Agrarians, 50 Social Democrats, 49 Democratic Unionists, 29 Conservatives, 9 Progressives and 15 Swedish Party members; it was thus a left-wing Government, but that by no means meant that they were all of one mind.

The crisis in question had been precipitated by differences of opinion on economic policy, but basically it was an expression of the uneasy resentment felt throughout the country at the influence wielded by the Democratic Unionists, which was out of all proportion to their numbers. Nevertheless, ostensibly it was the increase in wages that had been granted to the transport workers that led the Agrarians to withdraw their ministers, and, seeing that the Social Democrats too thought the time was ripe for a change, M. Pekkala, the Prime Minister, was forced to resign.

The task of forming a new government was offered variously to six ministers, but one or other of the major parties foiled all attempts at co-operation. In normal times a General Election would have followed, but Finland's position in foreign affairs made this highly inadvisable, so President Paasikivi was obliged to ask M. Pekkala to withdraw his resignation and remain in office. May 21st, therefore, saw the Cabinet and Prime Minister unchanged and no one any forrarder.

Superficially, throughout these weeks, life in Kajaani had followed an unruffled course, but under the surface people simmered. No one doubted but that Moscow held the whip hand; everywhere one sensed frustration. The Communist element apart, loathing for all that Communism stood for was universal; it transcended all party politics. In desperation, the people shut their eyes to the future and concentrated on the paying of reparations. With ostrich-like deliberation, they tried to believe in the future. Forests must be tended, exports increased; and for what? Their hands were tied, the fatalism that years of subjection had bred in them came to the surface and life went on as usual.

Three days after M. Pekkala resumed the reins of office, came the announcement that Moscow would allow a limited service of five trains a day in each direction to run through Porkkala, the area that the Soviet Union had leased from the Finns in exchange for Hanko. For twenty-five miles the main line from Turku to Helsinki runs through this area, and for some time past trains had been forced into making a considerable detour. But the concession was accompanied by conditions; all windows must be shuttered, Soviet locomotives must be used, and freight must be paid for at a high rate. Rumour had it that if the guards found anybody peeping the whole train-load would be returned to where it started from and all passengers would be forbidden transit. The Finns boiled with rage, most people preferred the long way round and at any rate at the start few Finns would stoop to travel by the direct route. Whether true or not, I did hear tell that the first train that crossed Porkkala carried only four passengers, but if so this state of affairs did not last because, when I travelled by this route the following April, the train was fairly full. Native common sense had asserted itself; after all, they were paying for it: all the same, it is a tedious business and one that is likely to remain a thorn in the flesh.

* * *

By Whitsuntide summer had really arrived, and the young foliage of the silver birch stood out clear and fresh against the sombre green of pine and spruce.

Overnight, or so it seemed to me, the children underwent an astounding metamorphosis. Little boys and little girls, who but the day before had been completely muffled up, suddenly appeared in little more than bathing trunks. Gone were their clothes, and among them went the heavy hand-knitted woollen stockings which I always found faintly comic when attached to suspenders at the knee and combined with shorts. Gone too, as often as not, were their shoes, for many children ran barefoot. How hard their feet must have been, I thought, and how impervious to grit! I, myself, could not walk from the club to Kajaani without acute discomfort caused by the loose, sandy surface of the road.

But few Finns walk if they can help it. In fact, once the thaw was over everyone took to bicycles, and for a nation of inveterate cyclists it was unfortunate that spare parts were in very short supply. In particular, everyone complained of the great tyre shortage. This shortage naturally affected all motor vehicles as well and was, actually, the popular excuse for not using chains when the roads were icebound. But if wear and tear on the rubber was the ostensible reason I doubt if it was the only one, for the Finn is naturally rather irresponsible and inclined to be reckless.

I suppose the first time I noticed this trait in their character was when Heljä and I went together to Sotkamo for Whit week-end. On the Sunday we were invited by a friend of Aili Eho's to go for a trip down the lake in a motor-boat. We accepted with pleasure. To get on board we had to negotiate a long and very rickety wooden jetty, a floating affair that sank beneath the water wherever we put our weight. We reached the boat, however, with no more serious mishap than wet feet, only to find that it would not start. The engine spluttered and hiccupped and the cabin stank of petrol. The aged boatman leant over and tinkered with the motor. From time to time he gave it a crank, and thereby produced a fountain of petrol that spurted in all directions and amidst which he calmly puffed at a lighted cigarette.

"Must he?" I murmured to Heljä. She nodded. "We Finns are like that," she said. "Every so often there is an accident. There is nothing to be done about it."

It was true: as time went on I was to come across instance after instance of a similar kind, all of which appeared to be accepted as a matter of course. I remember, around the following Christmas, someone remarking to me that there had been 900 registered accidents in the Kajaani O.Y. during the year; many, of course, of an insignificant nature, but notwithstanding a horrifying total. Shortly afterwards I went to Helsinki, where I happened to meet the Labour Attaché to the British Embassy. In the course of conversation I told him what I had heard and asked if the paper and cellulose industry was a particularly dangerous one. His answer showed clearly that he was something of an authority on the subject. For some time past he had been busy collecting statistics, and these proved that the industrial accident rate in Finland was shockingly high. Figures for 1946 revealed that, in that year, there had been relatively six times as many fatal accidents in Finnish industry as there had been in British. No one, in his opinion, was especially to blame, nor could the nature of Finland's industries be held responsible; the root cause lay in the national character. It was one thing to provide the Finns with safety devices, but quite another to see that they used them.

There is, however, a much brighter side to the somewhat unimaginative want of prudence that is to be found among the Finns. Lack of concern for the future leads to a great deal of spontaneous kindness that is very refreshing. Many a child, I discovered, was adopted into a happy home and given a good education who would probably never have had either if its foster parents had stopped to ask, "How can we provide for its future?" or "What will happen to it if anything happens to us?" The result of this is that the proportion of adopted children is very high. In one year in Finland I got to know six personally, while in all my life in England I have run across only two.

* * *

The village of Sotkamo lies rather over twenty-five miles east of Kajaani, and is connected with it by the chain of lakes and waterways that stretches all the way from the Baltic Coast to the Russian border. Heljä and I drove there by bus. The bus was crowded, the afternoon hot, and the road dusty and of no great interest. I think roads that run through forest seldom are; they tend to be too straight and there is no distant view. For this reason, Finland should not be visited by road; it should be seen from the water, for its lakes and rivers are not only beautiful, they are the country's natural highways. But to do this is not always easy, as only on the great lakes is there any organised form of transport. So Heljä and I had recourse to the post bus, which reached Sotkamo in about an hour and a half.

On arrival, we ensconced ourselves in the small, wooden inn, ate a substantial meal of potatoes and gravy and then set out for a stroll by the lakeside. There, for the first time since I had been in Finland, I heard the cuckoo—a persistent cuckoo that sang continually throughout the whole evening. And how beautiful the long-drawn-out northern evenings are, when the heat of the day is over and the sun slants through the trees and the breeze dapples the forest with kaleidoscopic patterns. How enchanting it all is and how peaceful; yet, on occasions, how exciting!

I remember once being out on the lake near Sotkamo on a

July evening. It was almost ten o'clock and the sun hung low on the horizon—so low that it seemed to be lighting up the sky from beneath. It had been raining and the great bank of storm clouds that lay ahead had all the strange, subtle contours of those seen from above and, looking at them, I had the illusion that I was flying. And although my air-minded friends assure me prosaically that, however dreamlike in effect, clouds seen from above are never indigo, I still cherish the memory of my illusion. If ever magic was abroad it was that night. It was in the colour of the sky, of the clouds and of the forest, which was of electric intensity; it was in the isolated fragment of a rainbow which shone low above the trees and it was in the path of the sun on the water which had all the silver softness of moonlight.

Together with the neighbouring village of Vuokati, Sotkamo is recognised as the chief beauty spot of the Kainuu district, and to it many people come long distances to ski in early spring.

The village is, by local standards, a large one, and is always referred to as a "church village" for the simple and obvious reason that it has a church, which cannot be said for the majority of Finnish hamlets. Cool, angular and aloof, this church stands beside the lake, but it is neither cold nor forbidding. It is the centre of a large parish; the meeting place where, in an aura of soap and water and Sunday clothes, its widely scattered inhabitants forgather every Sunday.

In bygone days all over Finland the people from the outlying settlements would come to their church village by sleigh in wintertime or by boat during the summer months. The trip by boat took a great deal the longer of the two. The vessels they used were known as "church boats" and were manned by anything up to thirty oars. The idea was to have one for every able-bodied man in the village and room besides for the women and children. Sometimes these villagers had to row immense distances and, in order to be in time for the service, would have to leave on Saturday, carrying with them their Sunday clothes. On arrival they were either taken in by friends or they spent the short, white, northern night sleeping out of doors.

To-day church boats are a thing of the past, and sleighs have largely given place to buses, but the church village remains the church village, and for me at least it still has the power to conjure up the feeling of an age when life was essentially parochial and remote from the realities of the world at large.

In this lies the charm of the Finnish village, for it has little else to offer. Most of them straggle endlessly, houses conform largely to type and wood piles give yards and gardens a very ragged effect. In all this Sotkamo is no exception.

One of the most interesting features of the village is the number of gipsies who live there. They seem to have made the place something of a centre, as a few of them actually own farmhouses in the parish and are reputed to have accumulated considerable wealth; but the majority of them are still nomads. It was a source of constant surprise to me that there should be so many wandering gipsies in Finland, where their lives in winter must be the acme of discomfort. There are said to be two or three thousand in all but they seem far more numerous, for you see them everywhere, from the Gulf of Finland to the north of Lapland. In Kajaani they were continually in evidence hanging about the market-place, the women decked out in frills and flounces and trailing their black velvet skirts through dust and snow in summer and winter alike. Strangely enough, the climate does not seem to have caused any radical change in their way of living—horse-coping, fortune-telling, tinkering and pilfering are still their means of livelihood.

The first gipsies came to Finland from Sweden at the end of the fifteenth century and their dialect still comprises many Swedish words. Ever since their arrival they have been an unfailing source of trial to the patience of successive governments, who have made vain and intermittent efforts to settle them on the land in Eastern Finland. But still no solution to their problem has been reached; they continue to be colourful rogues whose comings and goings remain largely outside the arm of the law. True, some do get roped in for military service and are then given the horses to look after, but those that are caught are few and far between, for most of them manage to keep one step ahead of the authorities. Nevertheless, from time to time their crimes do catch up with them, and when Heljä and I were in Sotkamo the whole village was agog because Hagert, the gipsy king, had just been jailed for having hundreds of forged ration cards in his possession.

The Finnish attitude to the gipsies is one of complete mistrust. When later I went to live with the Freys, Martta always locked my door if I happened to be out and there was a gipsy in Kalle's waiting-room, although it would have taken the most ingenious gipsy to slip in and out of my room under the eyes of the row of peasants that were usually sitting in the hall, awaiting their turn with the doctor. But I was grateful to Martta, she had my interests at heart, and in a strange way I was grateful too to the gipsies simply for being there—for the colour and vitality which emanated from them—at the odd moments when a great longing for the sun and the south would come over me.

Except for one thunderstorm, Whit week-end was sunny, and Heljä and I spent most of the time out of doors, wandering by the lake or through the forest. There is a great sweep of sandy shore beside the lake, of which the Finns think very highly, but I found both shore and forest strangely disappointing at close quarters. Unwashed sand, even though cleansed by winter snow, has not the freshness of sea-scoured beaches, nor the charm of the reeds and sedge that I had expected to find; it is lifeless, and so too was the forest. There were so few birds and I never even saw a squirrel. Perhaps my disappointment was due to the many preconceived ideas I had about it—ideas which its beauty under snow had done nothing to dispel. They sprang from two summers which I once spent at Kedgemakoogie, in the woods of Nova Scotia, in surroundings that photographs of Finland had at once recalled. I had loved those woods and they had played a considerable part in my decision to come to Finland. I shall like it, it is very like Kedge, I had thought; and so it was, but with a difference. At Kedge the forest had been alive with wild life. There had been chipmunks and squirrels, porcupine and skunk, deer and the occasional moose; there had been snapping turtles among the lily-pads, beaver dams across the river; there had even been the offchance of meeting a bear. Much of all this I had expected to find in Finland, but, in fact, the likeness began and ended with the trees and water. Pine, spruce and silver birch they had in common, but here in Finland the trees sprang from sparse sandy soil and shaded, lichen-covered rocks and berry bushes in place of the tangled undergrowth of Nova Scotia. It was all so very tidy; everything was turned to account. Not only the trees but also the red whortleberries and bilberries which grew in profusion were carefully husbanded, for without them there would be little fruit in the winter. The lichen too is important in the life of the country—progressively so as you go north, because it is the reindeer's winter diet. "Poor reindeer!" was my immediate reaction on learning this, for anything more arid and unappetising than the first bank of lichen that I came across would be hard to imagine. But I might have saved my sympathy. Given a little rain, the lichen comes into its own as if by magic. Its dark grey surface turns a yellowish grey-green that is at times so pale that it looks almost white and its brittle texture grows softer and cooler to the naked foot than the silkiest of baby's sponges that has been dipped in ice-cold water. Sometimes in the distance, it looks as if the wood were carpeted with minute flowers; sometimes as if the earth beneath the pines had been sprinkled with star-dust.

On Whit-Monday morning we climbed to the top of the hill at Vuokati, which is the highest point within sight. It took us a bare forty minutes to reach its rocky summit, where a wooden tower had been erected. From the top of this we looked out over an endless expanse of woods and water that stretched in all directions as far as the eye could see. Woods and water, yes, but it was more than that; I had been disappointed hitherto because the Kainuu forest had fallen short of my preconceived notions, but here was something I had never before experienced —a sense of immeasurable distance and an infinite clarity of light. When I think of the Canadian woods it is all close and more intimate; I think of the evening light playing among the trees, of the moonlight falling like blown petals on the lake while the weird discordant cry of the loon echoes across the water; I think too of the flaming red of the maple at the first bite of frost, but here in Finland I think of a clear, silvery distance that seems to go on and on for ever and ever. A distance that is at times a blend of pinks and mauves; at times a symphony of the palest greens and blues. As I gazed the horizon seemed to fade away, it was almost as if it had slipped over the edge of the world and I was looking towards eternity:

> "To mingle with the Universe, and feel
> What I can ne'er express, yet cannot all conceal."[1]

* * *

Heljä and I returned from Vuokati by train, a roundabout journey, but one that best suited our plans. In the carriage we ran into a colleague of Heljä's. The end of the school term was near, and she sat in one corner busily correcting botany papers at high speed and with amazing concentration. I watched her,

[1] *Childe Harold's Pilgrimage,* Canto IV, Verse clxxviii.

fascinated by the assurance with which she marked each answer; not for a moment did she waver or doubt.

"It looks like the end of term," I remarked to Heljä, and so it almost was, for the great day when the "student caps" were to be presented had very nearly arrived.

As usual I was full of curiosity and asked if I might be allowed to attend the ceremony.

"Of course you can," Heljä responded. "You won't understand much, but I'll explain it to you afterwards. It begins at nine and you mustn't be late. Come to the staff-room when you get to school and I'll look after you."

At nine o'clock on the morning of the great day I was there, and Heljä took me down to the main hall, which seemed to be already filled to capacity. It was a huge white-washed room with a platform at one end. Looped ropes dangled from the ceiling and the walls were surrounded by bars, for the hall served primarily as a gymnasium. To-day it had been filled with chairs and decorated with young birch trees. The latter stood in all four corners and encircled the lectern on the platform as well.

The place was thronged with parents and friends. Practically all Kajaani was there, wedged between the schoolchildren who were congregated at the back and the graduating students who occupied the front two rows of chairs. In pre-war days the graduating girls would have been dressed completely in white; now they had been reduced to white blouses. The boys all wore their Sunday best. On a table to the right below the platform were the caps, all previously bought by the students and carefully fitted. Presiding over this array was a dumpy grey-haired little woman who was their form mistress.

Heljä pushed me into an empty chair and disappeared. I found I was sitting next to Kirsti Kivi, who had a very washed and brushed up Pekka on her knee. He looked strangely subdued and gave me a rather over-awed smile. Most of the visitors were clutching bunches of flowers amongst which roses predominated, for tradition demands roses.

The Headmaster advanced to the lectern. He was a minister of the Lutheran Church and wore above his black garments a dog-collar and bands. Birch trees seemed to close in round him; there was one on either side of him and a third, the largest of all, immediately at his back. To me it was irresistibly *opéra-bouffe*.

For over an hour he droned his way through rather a dismal service, and the roses clutched in the hot hands of the donors wilted. Beside me Pekka began to fidget.

At last the service came to an end and the ceremony began. First came the presentation of testimonials to those who were leaving school at the end of their fifth year. Then the great moment arrived, but there was no sense of climax, no apparent jubilation; names were read out in strictly alphabetical order, no prominence being given to exceptional merit. It was the same for all; the name of the graduating candidate having been called, he or she stood up while the Headmaster read aloud the details of his or her individual achievement in each subject group—"*Approbatur*," "*Cum Laude*," "*Laudatur*." This done, the student in question advanced to the platform, bowed or curtsied to the Headmaster, shook hands and received a certificate. From there one after the other they progressed to the table where their form mistress was waiting to put their caps upon their heads. Many of the boys were extremely tall young men and she was very short. The caps got mixed, the result verged on a shambles. Small caps perched upon big heads, and small heads were snuffed out like candles. Yet there was a desperate seriousness about it all, even the moment of capping produced no applause at all. I found the whole ceremony long-drawn-out and monotonous, and I was beginning to feel drowsy when it came suddenly to an end, and the assembled company fell upon the students with printed cards of congratulation and rather forlorn-looking flowers.

Shortly afterwards the party broke up, and the graduating class went first to be photographed and then, in a body, to put their flowers on the graves of the war dead.

From then on it became a family affair, a question of parading the new student before friends and relations, who were invited to coffee in the afternoon. Irrespective of sex, the object of the party circulated among the guests cap on head. I was invited by Anna Ekström, whose elder daughter, Anita, had not only been among the successful, but had easily topped the list, and her parents were glowing with pride. I congratulated Anita and she beamed and curtsied. I did not stay long; it was not the sort of party where people did, for most of the guests had to go the round of several other similar functions.

Thinking of it all as I walked back to the club, I was struck by the staidness of everything. After eight years' grind I would have expected far more gaiety, and I felt sorry for the students. But I need not have done so; that night they had a party all of their own at the club, a rip-roaring affair if the noise they made was any criterion. I know all about that, for I had very little sleep that night. Not only was the sound of their revelry wafted to my room, but about three in the morning a bunch of them burst in on me, their caps still on their heads. They made straight for the window and started cat-calling to friends outside, for, although it was broad daylight, not one of them had as yet noticed me. Smiling to myself, I lay there waiting for the moment when my presence would be discovered. It was a moment worth waiting for. Never have I seen more dumb-founded expressions or a retreat quicker beaten. Not even the great Jasper Maskelyn could have vanished more swiftly.

A few days later I was discussing the ceremony with Toini, Hëlja and Hilkka Pentikäinen. All three are Karelians and all are among my best friends in Finland. Commenting on the proceedings, I asked them why they had to be so solemn and dreary.

"Oh, Diana," they chorused with one voice, "you mustn't judge what happens in Finland by what happens in Kajaani. If you had been in Viipuri when we got our caps you would have seen that everything was quite different. It was wonderful, so gay—in Karelia we were always gay."

There it was again: "In Viipuri—in Karelia."

"But not counting Karelia," I persisted—for if I was not to judge Finland by Kajaani, where was I to look for a yardstick? —"is it so very different here from in other parts of the country?"

"Yes, yes," they reiterated. "Don't you understand this is one of the poorest districts in Finland? Life here is terribly hard. It's made the people dreadfully good and dull. Do you know we even have local laws here that do not apply elsewhere?"

"Such as?" I prompted.

"You can't dance and drink in the same public place; hotels and restaurants may only have a licence for one or the other."

"How does that work out?"

"Drink wins easily; it pays much better."

Whether for better or worse, puritanism, or so it seemed, permeated the social legislation of the district. It was not, therefore, surprising that the school, whose Headmaster was a strict Pietist, should feel its influence. No dancing was allowed within its precincts and all organised theatricals were banned. If the children wished to dance or act they must do so at home, and I noticed that Irmeli's living-room was constantly being cleared of furniture on Saturday evenings so that her daughters, Ritva and Seija, might entertain their school friends. But luckily for Finnish youth as a whole, this veto is a purely local one and in most parts of the country the children enjoy far greater freedom.

Unlike elementary education, secondary education in Finland is not completely State-controlled. There are State schools and private schools in almost equal numbers; the balance being in favour of private schools, for which the fees are rather higher. There is, however, little difference between them, the choice confronting most parents being governed by the locality in which they happen to live. In the country districts most secondary schools are private co-educational establishments; in the towns the sexes are apt to be segregated and the schools to be run by the State. But there is no hard and fast rule about this and Kajaani, for one, had a State school that was also co-educational. Yet, although there are State schools, private schools, boys' schools, girls' schools, mixed schools, Finnish schools, Swedish schools and a few classical schools, the education that the children receive is, in the main, stereotyped. Throughout the country the standard varies very little, the children follow the same basic curriculum and work for identical examinations.

Education in Finland begins at the age of seven, when every child, irrespective of wealth or creed, must go to the elementary school. This education is free and, when I was in Finland, was supposed to last for six years. Since then the school leaving age has been raised a year.

Secondary education starts at the age of ten, eleven or twelve and is at the outset competitive. This is unavoidable because the number of children who apply for the school vacancies far exceeds the available accommodation. In 1947, in Kajaani alone, there were approximately 250 candidates for sixty places—a state of affairs that was common to most towns in the country. For the successful candidates eight years of intensive study follow; that is if they aim at going to one of Finland's three universities. This means that eighteen, nineteen or twenty is the age at which they leave school. Eighteen or nineteen is the most usual, but anything up to twenty-two is not unknown, as failure to make the grade in any one year may mean an additional year's schooling.

But for the unambitious there is no need to worry; five years complete what is known as Middle School, and a fifth year certificate is a passport to the lower grades of the Civil Service, secretarial schools, nursing schools and the like.

Before the war the higher school leaving examination opened all doors to the universities, but this is no longer the case, because the universities are filled to overflowing. Popular faculties, such as medicine, will now only take those who have done exceptionally well in their student exams. Where competition is severe the university year begins with a trial course that lasts about six weeks, after which the students are weeded out and from picked groups several hundred strong about fifty are selected to continue. The remainder may take the initial course twice more, then if they have still not been chosen they must join themselves on to less popular schools.

* * *

One morning about this time I got a letter from my travelling companion, Sylvia, telling me that she was very happily settled in Normarkku and that, far from its being "a mushroom growth of streamline factories," there were no factories there at all. In reality it was a village in which the great Ahlström Combine had built its head offices, and almost all her work was connected with the firm.

She too, it appeared, was principally occupied in teaching, and among her pupils, so she told me, was a young man who always arrived at lessons in top boots, followed by a large shooting dog and carrying a gun. Every now and again he would rise from the table, walk to the window and take a shot at a passing bird. Sylvia found this disconcerting; I rather think I should have done so too, but nothing like that came my way in Kajaani.

* * *

Every since my arrival the club had been meeting regularly every fortnight and the last few meetings had been devoted to reading aloud Laurence Housman's *Victoria Regina* of which the British Council had lent us a dozen copies. Now this had come to an end, and I was faced with the problem of thinking out a new programme for the last meeting of the season. The simplest thing seemed to me to borrow a film strip and projector from the Council, for their offer to lend these was always open. So I wrote off and asked for the loan of one. Unfortunately, the railway delivered it to the men's club in the town, where it sat unnoticed by staff and members alike. Meanwhile, I—or, rather, Toini egged on by me—raised Cain at the railway station. The package was traced a few days later, but too late to be of any use. Not that it mattered, for that great pillar of the society, Elli Hyyrylainen, suddenly produced a Canadian friend, Miss Naomi Jackson, from the Quaker Relief Unit in Lapland. She was ready and willing to come and talk to the meeting about their work. Relief—it was the keynote not only of her talk, but also of my feelings. Truly Elli was an amazing woman. She seemed to have friends all over the English-speaking world, and every so often would produce one of them for the society's delectation as a conjuror produces a rabbit from a hat. She, it was, who had been responsible for Lady Constance's visit, and now here, in the nick of time, was Miss Jackson. And, not content with that, later in the year she introduced an Australian journalist to the society.

Miss Jackson was an immediate success. She was an unassuming and ready talker, and best of all, she made people laugh. It was all very informal, we sat round a table, admittedly rather like a board meeting, and she chatted. She told of the devastation done by the retreating Germans, and of the Friends' efforts to rehabilitate the population. I saw it all later in the summer and nothing that she said was exaggerated.

The money for all this was raised in America almost entirely from among Finnish Americans, of whom there are 300,000 in the United States alone. The expedition had been prepared well in advance, and all personnel had had a year's training before sailing for Europe. During this time they had learnt not only the essentials of their job, but also Finnish, and it was Miss Jackson's incursions into Finnish that appealed most to her audience. They were vastly amused; and one story in particular they liked.

It was the aim of the Quakers to re-open the schools in Lapland and to see that the children who attended were fed there. By this means they were sure of their getting one good meal a day. With this end in view, Miss Jackson set out on a tour of schools. Outside one she stopped her jeep and went inside. The schoolmistress was a staid and worthy spinster.

Miss Jackson did her best to explain her purpose in Finnish, and then asked if she might look at the cooking facilities. These she found were totally inadequate, so, buttonholing the schoolmistress, she declared with emphasis, "What you want is a *kätilö*." The woman looked surprised and not a little puzzled. Miss Jackson repeated herself. "You need a *kätilö*," she said, and with a bold, expressive gesture inscribed a large cauldron in the air. Consternation spread over the woman's face.

"*Ei*, *ei* (no, no)," she said very firmly.

"*Kätilö*," reiterated Miss Jackson obstinately. "*Kätilö*."

There followed a moment of frozen deadlock, then Miss Jackson resorted to her dictionary. "And would you believe it," she laughed, "I'd mixed up *Kattila* and *Kätilö*—cauldron and midwife—and that terrible gesture was just the last straw."

The evening was a great success.

It must have been soon afterwards that one afternoon, when I was giving a lesson at the Freys, Kalle came in, greeted the assembled women, said something to Sirkka, and went out.

"He has gone," said Sirkka, "to do a . . ." the next word completely defeated her. Eventually she got it across to me that he had gone to the maternity home to perform a Cæsarean operation. Casually I remarked that I would be interested to watch one. Without a moment's hesitation, Sirkka rose to her feet.

"Come on," she said. "Let's go."

"Oh no," I gasped. "Your husband will be furious."

"No, no," she insisted. "He won't mind at all." But I was adamant, and greatly surprised when next day, on arriving at his lesson, Kalle immediately asked why I had not come the day before.

I did not know then what I learned later, that Sirkka's suggestion was not as preposterous as it first appeared; that she was in fact a fully trained hospital nurse and that she habitually helped Kalle in the theatre whenever the theatre sister was off duty.

When I returned to Kajaani in the autumn I was given another chance, and this time I took it. I was far from understanding all that happened, but step by step Kalle did his best to explain what he was doing. I was, of course, not helped by being shown a freak case; something simple and straightforward would have been quite difficult enough for me, but none the less I found it enthralling.

* * *

June—the Finns call it *Keskäkuu*, the summer-moon, and the very word seems to go straight to their heads. There was no getting any sense out of them. They were all busy packing up and getting ready to go away, and my afternoon classes, when not abandoned altogether, degenerated into a series of light-hearted outings.

It was Kirsti Kivi who set the ball rolling when she discarded the somewhat telegraphic formula, "Next time to me," with which our lessons usually closed, and substituted, "Next time you must all come to our summer cottage. I will arrange a car." Kirsti seemed to have a way with the firm's cars that was most convenient. Anna, Airi, Sirkka and I accepted gladly.

The Kivis' summer cottage was on the shore of the Oulujärvi, within easy commuting distance of Kajaani, commuting, that is, by bicycle, or, at a pinch, on foot. To be within easy range was actually the aim of nearly everyone, for the average man's holidays were nowhere near as long as those of his children. In pre-war days, of course, boats and cars played their part in getting them to and fro, but now this part was negligible because of the restrictions on cars and petrol. As far as owning cars went, among my acquaintances only Eero Eho, whose legal business took him all over the country, and Aarre Uoti, who was a doctor, had them, and in owning a car Aarre was unique among Kajaani's six doctors. So the people who went further afield depended for transport on the rather inadequate bus service, which often put them down at some little distance from their homes. As a result few people went very far; it was not necessary because Kajaani, as I have already explained, was situated between two easily accessible lakes. Between these two the allegiance of my friends was more or less evenly divided when they migrated to their "villas" for the summer months.

I am always in some difficulty as to what word to use when mentioning these summer hideouts. "Villa" was the one most commonly used by the Finns themselves, but it never seemed to me truly apposite, because it conjured up alternating visions of Mediterranean sunshine and suburban mediocrity. "Cottage" was the most popular alternative, but it too seemed remote from the reality with its associations of thatched cosiness. Most of them were really more like the cabins found in American summer camps, only they were more isolated and showed more individuality. Without doubt this individuality is the root of my trouble, and the reason why I am still at a loss for the right word.

There was nothing, certainly, of the log cabin about the Kivis' place, which was painted cream, flat-roofed and very modern, unless it were the *sauna*, which stood among the silver birches at the lakeside and was built of massive logs and roofed with turf.

Kirsti greeted us smiling. She was dressed in pale green linen and looked absurdly young for her age and very pretty; no one would ever have credited her with three sons, the eldest of whom was already thirteen. I looked around, but there was no sign of the children, not even of Pekka, who I always felt was my particular friend, but later, while we were drinking coffee, he came and talked to us.

After we had shaken hands, the five of us strolled down to the lake and almost at once Kirsti suggested that we should swim. The sun was shining and the lake sparkled. Sirkka, Airi and I allowed ourselves to be persuaded and undressed in the *sauna* at the water's edge. As we emerged the air struck chill so Sirkka and I plunged quickly into the lake. By no possible stretch of the imagination could the water have been called warm, but then it was little more than a month since the last snow had melted. It proved altogether too cold for Airi. She did no more than sit nude on a rock emitting squealing noises as she gingerly felt it first with one toe and then the other.

"Nymph Bathing"—I was suddenly struck by the picture. Poised on a rock against a background of trees, with one foot cautiously testing the water, Airi would have been a gift to any painter of the classical school, for she was beautifully made. Moreover, she was running true to type; like most of her mythical counterparts—at least as depicted on canvas—she was showing little inclination to get more than her feet wet. But, while Airi's courage failed her, I, at any rate, enjoyed my bathe, for I know of no sensation quite so perfect as that of swimming without a suit. It was a sensation which never palled, although the novelty was to wear off as the summer wore on.

When we emerged and were once more dressed, Kirsti had hot coffee and doughnuts waiting for us. It was all exactly right; the coffee was hot, the doughnuts delicious, and Kirsti herself a pleasure to look at. I liked the way she smiled with her head a little on one side, and she had such a pretty speaking voice.

All too soon we had to return to Kajaani. Term was not yet over and I still had some evening classes to give. These evening classes had never been free from strain in the way that the afternoon ones had been, partly, I am convinced, because of the austere surroundings; but there were other contributory causes. In the first place, most of the people who came in the evenings began by being rather less fluent, and were already tired by their day's work. This made them harder to reach, and I had neither books nor experience to help me in establishing contact. Then too there was another factor: it seemed to me that the Finns in their homes felt, in a curious way, responsible for making their lessons a success, whereas once inside the school building I felt that the whole responsibility devolved on me. By hook or by crook, I resolved that before September I would amass quantities of books, which would perhaps make things easier. I had three months' grace, and the thought filled me with heartfelt relief. In this there was nothing personal; it was simply that I was glad to escape from the sense of my own inadequacy. So although I was really happy to say goodbye to my pupils, I was also perfectly sincere when I said that I hoped to see them again.

I recollect making some such remark to a young married woman of about twenty-two or twenty-three. She stands out very clearly in my mind both because I thought her exceedingly attractive and because on the first evening that she came to school, when I asked her her name, she made me laugh by replying "Little Gutter." I found it in the dictionary. Since then she had come regularly both to club meetings and to lessons and, though beyond these occasions I had not come across her, she had always appeared extremely friendly. It was, I thought, perfectly natural that I should hope to see her again and that I should say as much on parting. I was quite unprepared to hear her reply vehemently, "Oh, I hope not." I could hardly believe my ears, and I suppose I must have registered consternation, for she plunged headlong into an explanation.

The root of her trouble turned out to be loneliness, and because she was lonely she hated Kajaani. It was two years now since she and her husband had come north because he had got a job as a surveyor to the Kajaani Town Council, but socially they had made small headway. There were still, she explained, only six families whom they ever visited, and there was no one at all on whom they could drop in without warning.

I must admit this surprised me very much, for at that time I had no true picture of just how clique-ridden Kajaani society was. It had not dawned on me that in so small a town people who mixed happily at club meetings would not mix outside as well. But as time went on the expression, "Oh, but we don't visit with them," became familiar, whether uttered wistfully, snobbishly, or in a matter-of-fact way. There was no gainsaying it, Kajaani society as I knew it revolved in small circles like cog-wheels that met regularly at stated intervals and then parted. There was very little easy camaraderie. It still seems strange to me that this should be so, and that the people who welcomed me so warmly should be so cold to each other.

Later in the summer I ran into "Little Gutter," whose name in Finnish now escapes me, and she told me that her husband succeeded in getting work in the south and that they had packed up and left Kajaani.

One way and another it seemed that I was losing several of my pupils. One lad, for instance, was off to do his military service and would not be back for some time to come, as he was bent on becoming an officer. This meant serving for 330 days instead of the standard 200, both of which periods of service were considerably shorter than they would have been in 1938, when twelve or fifteen months was the rule. The present calling-up age is twenty, but students can always get postponement if they wish it or, alternatively, they may volunteer immediately on leaving school and get it over. But only on the question of age are the regulations flexible, as apart from rejections on medical grounds no exceptions are made. That is unless you count the Åland Islanders, who are immune from military service altogether. They were granted exemption in 1919 on condition that they served for an equal span in one of the many lighthouses of the archipelago. This law, however, has never been implemented and the islanders to date have got off scot-free.

Anja Mustonen was another of my evening pupils who was leaving Kajaani. She was the youthful journalist who had interviewed me on my arrival, and she was now going to Helsinki to study. I had never really got to know her because her appearances at my lessons had been rare. So much so that I suspected she only came for copy, because, having produced a brief column on the subject, she only showed up once more. Her article was shown to me with bursts of merriment by some of my friends.

"What's it all about?" I inquired with natural curiosity.

"She says," they chortled, "that twice a week she sits at your feet and gazes at your eyes, which are the largest in Kajaani"—a statement of very doubtful veracity—"and that you wear the most beautiful nylon stockings"—a statement of even greater mendacity. I remember the ones in question very clearly; they were a present from America, and made of art silk of a startling sunshine hue. Altogether it was too much; my efforts to impress as a teacher were obviously a fiacso—even my stockings were more impressive.

Soon after this article appeared Anja gave up coming to lessons, and the weather being warm I gave up stockings.

* * *

On the last Saturday before the end of term Irmeli and I went with the Ehos on a visit to their summer cabin. Once again my lesson went by the board and we prepared to make a day of it. We had to go about fifteen miles and Eero drove us in his car. The exact distance lives in my mind because at the time there was some question of our having to bicycle as the car was laid up. Irmeli, I remember, had struck, and I myself viewed the prospect with mixed feelings as I thought of the heat and the dust and wondered if I could manage pedal brakes, which is all that Finnish bicycles ever have. In fact, the only catastrophe that I did not visualise was the one that actually overtook us, a brief but very heavy storm which, had we been bicycling, would certainly have soaked us to the skin. But luckily we had the protection of the car, and by the time we arrived the storm had blown over and the countryside was glistening with moisture in the sunshine.

Outside a large wooden farm building we abandoned the car and took to our feet. Our way led through a rye-field, down a woodland path, and on to a clearing by the lake where the Ehos' cabin stood. It was very different from the Kivis'. It was like a square wooden box that someone had painted terra-cotta red and capped with a high-pointed roof. The effect was that of a toy model. It looked exactly as if it had been made to pick up and put down at will. In just such a little house, or so I fancied, the three bears might have lived; that is until, like Goldilocks, we went inside. There, far from finding the table laid for dinner, the house, which had not been opened since the previous summer, inevitably had a shut-up feeling, and we hurried round it, throwing wide the windows.

In the clearing there were several other small buildings besides the house. A shack comprising a woodshed and a spare room was close at hand, and further off among the trees was a children's playroom. This room still housed, among the children's playthings, a dentist's chair, which I must admit seemed a bit incongruous to me, but which apparently had once been useful. Quite a few local farmers and their families had used it, but now with her growing family to house and care for Aili had given up seeing patients in the country.

At the water's edge was what is known as a "smoke *sauna*." This is the oldest kind of *sauna*, but one which many people still prefer. It is different from the others in that it has no chimney and the smoke from the fire escapes directly into the room. What actually happens is this: the fire is lit about two hours before the bath is wanted and all the doors and windows are closed. The room then fills with smoke, through which whoever is feeding the fire must plunge at intervals with armfuls of fresh logs. Later, when room and water are sufficiently hot, the fire is allowed to die down, and for a brief spell the doors and windows are opened to clear the atmosphere. There is a lot to be said for this kind of *sauna* when it is working well. The pervasive tang of wood smoke is very pleasant and the whole place feels peculiarly mellow. But if, as sometimes happens, the smoke does not clear properly, it stings the eyes and catches the throat. Many Finns, however, appear to be largely impervious to smoke. Certainly Eero was, for when, two years later, I was again to visit the Ehos in their summer cottage, I went into the *sauna* while he was tending the fire. I found him squatting beside the stove leisurely piling on wood while smoke poured out into the room. It did not seem to worry him at all, but one look was enough for me—having taken it, I fled spluttering.

But to return to the summer of 1947—basking in the sunshine after a picnic lunch and inhaling the odour of rich damp earth, I decided that life must be very pleasant for the Ehos in summer-time even if their large family did make them rather cramped. Given good weather, it was a lovely spot; remote, yet not too remote, for the people at the farm where we had left the car were very friendly. We had stopped and greeted them on our arrival and they had invited us in on our way back. Someone of their household had a name-day and they were celebrating.

At this farm Aili and Eero kept their one and only sheep. This was a common practice in Finland, where wool was otherwise practically unobtainable. It was quite the done thing to pay a farmer board and lodging for a single ewe, simply in order to have its wool; for wool was badly needed, especially by families who had young children to clothe. But frankly, I was very glad that I never had to wear any of these home-spun garments, because they were usually very rough and, although I am sure that it is better to scratch than shiver, the choice of evils does not appeal to me at all.

The Finns and their animals—I suppose they were not really funny, but they were a source of great amusement to me. The Eberlings kept one cow, the Ehos one sheep, the Freys one pig and Sävy and Yrjö Tähtinen chickens. These last would not have been so surprising if they had not been kept all the winter in the attic. It was one of the first things that Sävy Tähtinen ever told me, and I could hardly believe my ears, for it was early in our acquaintance and at the time her English was still hesitant. But it was none the less true. What she was saying amounted to this: now that the weather was warmer she must go upstairs and fetch her chickens and let them out in the yard. This was the more surprising in that Sävy was very house-proud and did not look at all the type of person to keep a cache of chickens in the attic. She was tall, grey-haired and dignified and, until I got to know her better and appreciate her abundant sense of humour, rather awe-inspiring.

Not very long ago I went with a friend to see *The Wild Duck*, and thought again of Sävy's chickens. Hitherto Ibsen's idea of a menagerie in the attic had always seemed remote from reality to me; now I viewed it with different eyes. If the Finns in the far north kept chickens upstairs, probably the Norwegians would view a menagerie with equanimity. It put a completely new complexion on the matter.

The keeping of livestock among the town-dwellers of Kajaani was, of course, the outcome of wartime shortages, and already it was on the wane. Things were beginning to look up, and by this time the Freys had eaten the last pig that they meant to keep, and the Tähtinens had resolved to part with their chickens before the next winter. But so far as I know, the Ehos had no intention of parting with their one and only ewe, which kept its individual status until the following spring, and then became the proud mother of twins.

About three o'clock we all trooped up to the farm. It was a largish house built of dark wood with white-painted window frames, and grouped about it were the outbuildings. They were of the same dark weathered wood, and together with the farm formed three sides of a courtyard. One whole side of this yard was taken up by an old barn, of a design that was once typical of Finnish farm buildings everywhere. It was a two-storied building, part stone, part wood; that is to say, the lower part was built of crudely dressed stone and used as a byre, while the upper part, which served as a loft, was constructed of wood. This loft had little in common with lofts as we understand them. It was quite unlike the traditionally dim region approached by a ladder through a trap-door in which escaping prisoners are hidden beneath the hay. It was entered boldly by wide wooden doors that were approached from outside by a ramp strong and broad enough to take a hay-cart.

There is something very endearing about Finnish barns, whether large or small, but the small ones in particular have an artless appeal. They are used for storing hay, and are to be found scattered all over the fields, not grouped together about the farm buildings. Often these small barns look very drunk indeed, especially in the far north, for the farther north you go, or so it seemed to me, the more top-heavy they become. But where it occurs top-heaviness is intentional, as barns are often expressly designed to stand upon a small base above which the walls splay outwards and upwards, with the result that the area beneath the roof is considerably greater than that of the floor space. These structures are built of slotted logs and are both simple and strong, yet they tend to look for all the world as if in danger of imminent collapse. This is because they often have a list in one direction or another, for no one seems to bother to make the outward angle of the walls symmetrical. But groggy as the structures look, there is a basis of sound common sense in their design, for it is far drier higher up than it is at floor level, and consequently far better for storage purposes.

Three generations lived in the farmhouse to which the Ehos were now taking me; father, mother, son, daughter-in-law and two small boys. All of them made us most welcome, but it is

Typical Finnish Barn

Smoke sauna

Paltaniemi Church

the daughter-in-law that I remember best because her husband's sister had sent her a royal blue sateen frock from Toronto, and she had put it on for our benefit. It had a very high sheen on it and was short and rather tight; in fact, the poor girl bulged out of it everywhere, and nothing could have looked more grotesque in the depths of the country, yet her obvious delight was moving rather than funny, because it was so unquestionably sincere.

* * *

It was during the drive back to Kajaani that I first noticed I was getting a boil on my neck. This was annoying; I had never had one before, but I was well aware just what a nuisance they could be. I considered the matter ruefully and decided there was nothing to be done about it. Nevertheless, as the day approached when I was due to leave for my holiday I began to wonder whether it would not be advisable to have it lanced, because I knew that I should be alone in Helsinki for at least a week, and that I could not see to foment the back of my neck.

Unable to make up my mind, on my last morning I wandered into town muttering to myself: "Shall I have it opened? Shan't I have it opened?" I had an idea that it would be very painful and I was not feeling at all brave. I think that my courage would have failed me altogether if I had not run into Sirkka. That looked like Fate, so I took the bull by the horns and explained my predicament. She took me straight round to the hospital, where I waited in the hall while she went in search of Kalle. In a few minutes she returned, bringing me a message to the effect that I was to return at twelve o'clock. The die was cast. I thanked Sirkka and walked back to the club thinking to myself that I had just time for a quick lunch.

On arrival I went straight to the dining-room and settled myself in my usual corner. I waited, but nobody took any notice of me at all. After a while I beckoned to the waitress, but she merely shook her head at me. I expostulated—I was in a hurry, I could not wait all day. She, poor girl, quite naturally did not understand a word I was saying, so she went off and returned with the housekeeper. But she too, it seemed, was in league against me, for all she did was to shake her head decisively. It was infuriating, and by now the whole room was watching the pantomime with interest. Suddenly the housekeeper left me and walked over to a table in the far corner where several young men from the factory were sitting. A moment later she returned with Juho Jorma, a young chemist, who was one of my pupils. He was very tall and slight and had an astonishingly deep bass voice. He smiled an amused smile and announced from the depths of his boots: "Dr. Frey telephone, you must not eat."

So that was it! I don't know how I came to be so dense, but it still did not dawn on me that Kalle intended putting me under. In fact, back at the hospital I must have looked very surprised when asked to lie down on the operating table, because Kalle burst out laughing.

"Surely," he said, "you didn't think I'd do it without an anæsthetic? Why even in Finland we aren't as cruel as that!"

When I came round he was standing beside me and apparently still smiling.

"Come into my office," he said, "and have a cigarette."

I felt a little drunk, but did as I was told. When I had finished it he took me home with him to lunch. It was only a few hundred yards, but I was still a bit light-headed and did not steer a very straight course, a fact which, I discovered later, did not escape Kajaani.

By the time lunch was over the effect of the drug had completely worn off and I returned to the club to do my packing. It was not an easy pack to do, for I had planned a very varied holiday. To begin with, my friend Grania was flying from England to join me in Helsinki, and together we planned to go for a tour of the eastern lake district.

With Heljä's help, I had mapped out this tour, but I was still in some doubt as to how it would work out, because the tourist office in Helsinki, to which we had written for reservations, had never let us know what they had succeeded in getting for us. Beyond the barest acknowledgement of our first letter, they had paid no attention at all to our repeated requests for information. It was an exasperating and typically Finnish state of affairs. The chances were that all was in order, but nobody dreamed of putting it in black and white. From Kajaani there was nothing more that I could do bar resigning myself to waiting until I reached Helsinki and then paying them a personal visit. Just what Grania and I would do if all the hotels were full I was at a loss to think.

Grania's visit was to be followed by one from my brother, Michael. Together we planned to go to Lapland and on into

Norway. This involved us in far more complicated organisation than wandering round the lakes, and luckily for me Eero came to the rescue. Hudson Strode, the American journalist, once described him as "the inestimable Eho" and how richly he deserves the name. He knew Lapland well and appreciated to the full all the post-war difficulties we should encounter as a result of the damage done by the retreating Germans. With expert knowledge, he planned everything for us down to the last detail—trains, buses, accommodation. Nothing that was organisable was left to chance. Nor did his help stop short at delving into time-tables and writing letters to Lapland; exactly one week before I left Kajaani, the day on which the sleepers on the night train I was taking to Helsinki were released, he got up at crack of dawn and queued for one for me.

* * *

Having broken the back of my packing, I went out to dinner. I had a long-standing date to dine with the Freys, which, all things considered, was rough luck on them, as they could not have bargained on having me twice in one day, but I, at any rate, enjoyed it very much. It was, for me, a memorable occasion: the first time that I ever sat down to a meal *en famille* in Finland.

Afterwards we all went by taxi to Paltanieme—that is, all but the baby, Petra. It is a village about eleven kilometres away on the shore of the Oulujärvi. There, there is an old church that the Freys were anxious to show me. There, too, was the so-called "Emperor's Stable" in which the Tzar Alexander I had once dined on a visit to Finland in 1819, almost exactly ten years after the Treaty of Hamina had made Finland a Grand Duchy under Russian protection.

Having taken Finland from the Swedes, Alexander set out to treat the country well, and during his reign and those of his immediate successors, Nicholas I, Alexander II and Alexander III, Finland enjoyed a greater degree of independence than the Swedes had ever given her. Remarkable as it seems, four successive Tzars of all the Russias were content to be constitutional Grand Dukes of Finland.

This is an interesting era in Finnish history, for it saw the rise of the Finnish nationalist movement. This in itself seems anomalous, for the country was at peace, prosperous, and to a very large degree independent, but the reasons are not far to seek. The truth is that, in guaranteeing the Finnish Constitution, Alexander I had in fact handed the country over to a small minority of Swedish-speaking aristocrats, a state of affairs that became progressively more and more irksome to the masses.

Nevertheless, there is no doubt that on the whole the Alexanders did well by Finland, whatever their underlying motives may have been. The first gave her what he took to be freedom, the second, with considerable foresight, supported the nationalist movement and the progressive reforms that followed in its wake, while the third continued to pursue a policy that aimed at keeping Finland content. It was left to Nicholas II, with his misguided policy of Russification, to undo all the good work of his forebears and to revive the hatred of Russia that had been latent since the time of the Swedish-Russian wars.

Yet even to-day, in all their bitterness, the Finns revere the memory of Alexander II, whose statue, the only statue of a Russian in the whole country, stands in the Suurtori Square in the very centre of Helsinki, a tribute to all he did for the country.

For better or for worse, the Tzars left their mark, and the Emperor's Stable became one of the historic sites of the Kajaani neighbourhood. It is a small wooden building with a plaque above the door. Inside is a single room containing a few contemporary prints and the table off which Alexander dined. In one corner a ladder leads upwards to an attic, now used to house the boat in which he crossed the lake.

But while the stable is of mild historical interest, the old wooden church is of considerable charm. It was built in 1726 and is one of the oldest of its kind in the country, for the development of wooden ecclesiastical architecture really began in the eighteenth century. It followed a period barren in architecture that had lasted since the Reformation, at which time the building of stone churches, characteristic of the Middle Ages, had virtually ceased.

The church at Paltanieme is a large building with a separate bell-tower, but both are part of the same architectural design. They are painted a rich, creamy yellow, outlined in white and roofed with shingles. I gazed entranced at the twin spires of the church and belfry. They rose in three tiers at the western end and culminated in two small domes of moulded tiles. The evening light glowed warmly on the cedarwood roofing. It threw into relief a pair of stilettos that, hafted in two round balls, together formed the apices of the cupolas. Everything, with the exception of the iron weather-vanes, was fashioned out of cedarwood shingles, even the needle-like stilettos. It was all, or so I felt, directly inspired by the forest itself, for the ball and dagger were each, separately and individually, exaggerated fir-cones; the ball a formalised version of the plump, all but spherical pine cone, the stiletto an elongated replica of the fruit of the spruce.

Down below, above the belfry door, a large white-painted sun encompassed by pointed rays lent the building a faint touch of Oriental romanticism; a touch that was strangely in harmony with the shallow half-moon of grey stone steps that led up to the door.

Cream and white against the azure of the cloudless sky, the austerity of their lines softened by the curving roofs of cedar-wood, the effect of the buildings was very beautiful. They seemed to combine the Quaker-like severity of the north with the grace of the baroque and just a faint tinge of the glamour of the east.

The sacristan opened the church door for us with the largest key I have ever seen; it must have been fully a foot long. Within, the interior of the church far exceeded my expectations. The ceiling and walls had originally been whitewashed, but now they were adorned by paintings that have been recently restored. They are the work of Mikael Toppelius, who lived from 1734 to 1821. There is a simplicity about his work, and gaiety, and looking at it I knew that it was something new in my experience. Here was no atmosphere of dim lights, candles and mystery, but something open, candid and rather childlike in its fundamentalism. Light poured through the plain glass windows and lit the bright colours. At the west end was a great mural depicting Heaven and Hell, a Hell so horrific that part of it had been painted out because it was more than the congregation could stand. What exactly lay hidden beneath the white-wash no one appeared to know, but the part of Hell that survived was apparently reserved for women. The remaining walls were principally adorned with bible pictures in painted frames. They looked like overgrown illustrations from an illuminated manuscript, and as I studied them I felt convinced that the artist was not primarily interested in art and decoration, but that first and foremost he thrilled to his subject, and that what mattered was the story he was telling, and the moral he was pointing. It was not difficult to understand that Mikael had been the grandfather of Zachris Topelius,[1] the magic of whose writing once brought joy to every Finnish child, and whose fairy tales—ever redolent with morals—have spread across the world.

Leaving the church, we climbed the belfry tower. At the level of the two great bells we threw open the heavy wooden shutters that masked the windows and looked out over the countryside. There was an immense sense of space. To the north and to the west stretched the Oulujärvi, calm and gold in the now westering sunlight, its far shore a mere fringe of trees on the horizon, its near shore bordered by immense pines. The trees on the Paltanieme peninsular were the finest I had yet seen, probably because they had been considerably thinned, for the surrounding country has been largely cleared of forest and much of it is farm land. Immediately below us tall pines shaded the tombstones in the churchyard, the warm flush of their stems and the deep green of their needles a perfect foil for the clump of aspens that shivered beneath the window where we stood, their young leaves shot with silver and their upright boles tall, smooth and greenish white.

Here and there the landscape was studded with dwellings. There was one close by the lake at a distance of about two kilometres that I was told was the birthplace of Eino Leino, whose verse is said to be more truly Finnish than that of any other modern poet. It is a small, unpretentious little house whose yellow paint was worn so thin that now only a few faint streaks of colour mar the overall greyness of its weathered wood. It looks out over an arm of the great lake, a secluded creek that seems to overflow with peace and tranquillity. The Finns rate Eino Leino—who died in 1926—very highly and were always deeply concerned, not to say shocked, by an unfortunate tendency of mine to confuse him with Yrjö Leino, the Communist Minister of the Interior, and probably the most hated man in the country.

As we left the church the visitors' book was produced and for the second time—we had already signed in the Emperor's

[1] It is perfectly correct to spell Zachris Topelius with only one "p," and his grandfather Mikael Toppelius with two. The reason is not far to seek: originally the Toppelius family came from Oulu, but Mikael's son moved to Uusikaarlebyy (Swedish Nykarleby) which was a purely Swedish-speaking town. There the second "p" was dropped because of the difficulty most Swedish people have in pronouncing double consonants.

Stable—we were invited to write our names. Harri was properly impressed. He inscribed his name with enormous care in a large round hand and then looked up and said as though weighed down by responsibility: "I'd better write Torsti's name too, hadn't I? You see, he can't write."

From the church we wandered down to the lake shore. Here there must once have been a cemetery, for the sandy cliff that fell away to the beach was full of human bones. More were scattered at the water's edge, for the land is eroding fast. It was a strange place with a haunting quality that seemed to be tempered by the breeze that came off the water. I thought of Ezekiel and of the valley of dry bones that put on flesh. It gave me an eerie feeling and an unreasonable one, for dry was the last thing that these bones were. Sirkka, Kalle and I strolled along the beach, while Harri and Torsti, quite unmoved by the atmosphere of the place, careered along the sand brandishing femurs and tibias until their attention was distracted by some birds that had nested in the cliff face. Promptly they set out to investigate. It must have been nearly ten o'clock, but they were still full of vigour. It was strange; by all the tenets I had been brought up to believe, they should have been in bed and asleep long since; but they were young Finns, and that, I noted as the summer wore on, makes all the difference. Somehow or other, young or old, they do not seem to need sleep in the summer the way we do, but appear to make up for it during the dark winter months.

* * *

Next day I left by train for Helsinki. Juho Jorma was also travelling. No one could have been more helpful. He carried my bags—and they were no light weight—found my sleeper and installed me in it. Being a third-class sleeper it was not the height of comfort, but I could at least lie flat in it. In actual fact there were three tiers of bunks which were so close on top of each other that "lying flat" is precisely all that I could do. As the sleepers were already made up at five o'clock in the evening, I was faced with the choice between going to bed in the late afternoon, standing in the corridor, or walking down the train and sitting in a hot, stuffy and already overcrowded compartment. I was tired, so choosing the first alternative I went to bed and read my book until the last of my companions had joined me.

Part II

Summer Holiday

OLAVINLINNA CASTLE

from *Historia de Gentibus Septentrionalibus* by Olaus Magnus (published in 1555).

See p. 152.

Part II

Summer Holiday

THE sun blazed down on Helsinki across the great Railway Square as the outside porter pushed my luggage to the Carlton Hotel. I followed hard on his heels, but we had not far to go, as the hotel at which we aimed was only a stone's-throw from Eliel Saarinen's much-discussed Railway Station, the building of which was completed in 1919. The Finns are inordinately proud of this building, and not without reason, for not only was it the first architectural achievement of the New Republic, but it is also the most generally admired of all European railway stations. Yet I have to admit that in spite of its pleasing lines, it has never appealed much to me. I have never cared for the reddish granite of which it is built and still less do I like its coal-black roofing and the four grim figures—said to be the genii of light—that flank the main entrance. Each one holds a circular glass lantern and each looks extremely severe, so much so that, when later on I saw them with their shoulders decked in snow, I could only think of the Roundheads in their puritanical white collars. But whether or not you like Helsinki Railway Station you cannot remain oblivious to it. It is, after all, the first place most people see on arrival at the capital. Furthermore, just as in Stockholm every Swede promptly inquires what you think of the Town Hall, so in Helsinki every Finn clamours to know what you think of the Railway Station. Personally, while admitting the actual building to be both spacious and impressive, I cannot help wondering why Saarinen should have designed a terminus in which no platform is roofed or in any way protected from the weather, especially in view of the Finnish winter and the fact that he planned it at a time when Finnish architectural tendencies were all towards functionalism.

In 1923, four years after the completion of the station building, Saarinen went to the United States, where he later became head of the Cranbrook School of Art. His prospects when he left Finland were already rosy. The year before he set out, the *Chicago Daily Tribune* had organised an international competition with the object of obtaining the best possible design for the new building that they planned to erect. Rivalry had been keen and interest in the project widespread. In a field of 260 competitors twenty-three nations were represented, and among these competitors was Saarinen. His entries won him the second prize, a sum of $25,000, and when, together with those of the other prize-winners, his drawings were given wide publicity, they were enthusiastically acclaimed on all sides. Nor was this a passing enthusiasm; it is now universally acknowledged that these drawings of Saarinen's had a profound and revolutionary effect on the subsequent development of skyscraper architecture.

On arrival, the Carlton Hotel struck me as being rather less impressive than its name. It had an unpretentious entrance—a glass door, a desk, a *concierge* and two lifts. The hotel proper began on the sixth floor and occupied the top two landings. It was clean, well-appointed, impersonal and inexpensive. I paid 90 marks a night for my room, which was then the equivalent of about 3*s*. 4*d*., and this in a hotel considered one of the best in Helsinki. Hotel prices were Government-controlled and at the time low rates were general. They are now three or four times as high as they were in 1947.

Somewhat later in the morning I set out for the tourist agency that had been so dilatory about answering the letters that Heljä had written to them for Grania and me. Grania was only coming for two weeks and I wanted to be sure that she would spend them to advantage. At first the assistant to whom I spoke denied all knowledge of our correspondence, but he changed his tune when I produced the brief acknowledgement that Heljä had received to her first letter. Inquiries were set afoot and a file was unearthed containing all the letters that we had sent. It then transpired that our railway reservations had been made, but that not a thing had been done about getting us steamer and hotel accommodation. And now here was the young man blandly remarking that it was far too late to do anything about it, as all the hotels and boats would be full.

What were we to do? It was already June 19th, and on the 26th Grania was due to arrive, and between those two dates was the midsummer holiday. Handicapped as we were by linguistic difficulties and the abnormal post-war dearth of travelling facilities, to start off into the blue was to risk being stranded. Nevertheless, it looked as if this was just what we should have to do, and all because the tourist agency had quietly sat on our letters for a month.

"What," I asked, overwhelmed by a sense of utter helplessness, "is the use of making railway reservations, if they only take us to boats that have no berths and to hotels that have no rooms?"

Eventually it was arranged that the young man should get busy on the telephone in an effort to remedy the situation, and that I should return later in the day to find out what success he had had. This I did, only to be told that he would not know the position until after the midsummer holiday. Never, I felt, had I been in such a maddening country, as for the second time that day I left the tourist office in a state of intense exasperation.

On the first occasion I had gone straight to visit the British Council. I was feeling in need of a sympathetic ear and I had an idea that Stella, my opposite number from the seaboard town of Oulu, was in Helsinki. If so, the Council seemed the most likely place to run her to earth.

This time my luck was in; she was sitting in the office when I arrived, and not unnaturally pricked up her ears when she heard me inquiring for her.

"Who are you?" she grinned. "Another God-forsaken T-sec?" which was the abbreviated and somewhat undignified way that the Council staff had of referring to the so-called teacher-secretaries they were planting all over the country.

Stella was an ex-Wren, quite six feet tall. I liked her; she had a vivid mind, a great sense of humour and immense courage, for, being dogged by ill-health, her life in Oulu was at best uphill. Her health apart, this state of affairs was, I am convinced, due to the size of Oulu. It was four or five times as big as Kajaani, and was thus too large for her well-being to be a matter of individual responsibility and, although she never said so, I think she found her life there pretty lonely. Furthermore, I know that she was exasperated by the prevalent lack of co-operation, because she complained to me on more than one occasion about the lack of team spirit among the Finns and the consequent difficulty she had in getting things done. I saw her point; although I had not half as many enterprising ideas as she had, I knew enough to realise that anything in the way of an innovation requiring concerted effort would be difficult to launch both because the Finns, as a whole, prefer to act independently of each other and because they will never commit themselves if they can possibly avoid it. Experience, however, subsequently taught me that it was a safe bet that things would be done, even though no one actually volunteered to do them, and that I risked nothing more serious by leaving them to chance than the possibility that they might be done twice over. The matter was, therefore, not one of great moment. I had only to reconcile myself to living on faith and to accept, without demur, the fact that most Finns set such excessive store on their personal independence that they are always very reluctant to ask for help and generally very chary of offering it. Yet, proud and self-reliant though they are, they are still Europe's foremost co-operators. As Agnes Rothery says:

"There never was such a country of co-operators! The entire land is peppered with co-operative shops from one end to the other. The entire social fabric is permeated with co-operative societies."

This is, however, not as strange as it seems, because co-operation on a national scale is tantamount to self-help and carries with it no private and personal obligations. Moreover, study of the Co-operative Movement in Finland shows plainly that it has been largely instrumental in the creation of a new class of independent small farmers—men who to-day stand firmly on their own feet where yesterday they did no more than dream of independence.

This was a transition that came about after the First World War, before which, although four-fifths of the population lived in the country and off the land, only a very small percentage of those employed on agricultural work owned any land at all. Security was unknown; tenant's leases could be arbitrarily revoked and employment was uncertain. The peasants were at the mercy of the landowners, and when times were bad their lot was often very hard indeed; so hard, that at the time of the 1918 Civil War, the miserable state in which many were living drove large numbers of them to throw in their lot with the Reds. Small wonder that the first concern of the new Finnish Republic was for land reform.

The first step towards this was taken in 1918, when legislation was introduced making it possible for tenant families to buy up their leaseholds: the second came four years later, when a Bill was brought before the Diet by the Agrarian Prime Minister, Kyöstio Kallio, which set out to provide new holdings for the landless. This Bill compelled landowners, within certain limits, to sell their uncultivated acres and helped the peasants to buy them with State-aided loans. But it is one thing to make land available to the landless and quite another for those without resources to make a living from it, and the fact that the new settlers were able to do so redounds to the credit of the co-operative societies. Ever since the turn of the century, the activities of these societies had been increasing in scope, and by the year in question they had evolved an organisation that might have been expressly designed to meet the needs of the case. It was this organisation that saved the situation. Hard work, the sharing out of farm machinery and breeding stock and the pooling of all marketable produce worked wonders. By 1934 rather over 120,000 new landowners had established themselves and 2,000,000 acres of hitherto uncultivated land had been brought under the plough.

This was a triumph for the new Republic—and for the Co-operative Movement in particular. The *Lex Kallio* had not only accomplished that which it set out to do, but it had virtually immunised a large section of the population against Communism. From every angle it was a tremendous achievement, and it is nothing short of tragedy that it should already have assumed something of the nature of a rehearsal. Finland to-day confronts an essentially similar situation to that which she faced in 1922. Another war has left in its wake another problem of land settlement. 200,000 displaced Karelians have to be settled on the land as well as the evacuees from Porkkala and various other classes of war veterans. Once more the State has been forced to plan new holdings on a vast scale, and once again the well-being of thousands rests largely on the shoulders of the Co-operative Movement.

Whether the Government's new scheme will be as successful as its predecessor it is still too soon to say; I only know that I myself could not avoid a feeling of wholly irrational optimism whenever I found myself in the streets of Helsinki, simply because the familiar initials O.K. were reassuringly blazoned everywhere. *Osuus* being the Finnish for "co-operative" and *kunta* and *kauppa* for "society" and "store," there was indeed no escaping them; for over and above all their other activities, co-operative societies control 40 per cent. of the country's retail trade. It was, therefore, in no way surprising that, when Stella and I inquired where we could get a good cheap lunch, we received the reply: "You'd better try the H.O.K.[1] It's less ruinous than most restaurants and the food's not bad."

Thereupon Stella and I went out to lunch together. We looked in at the H.O.K. in passing and then, because the sun was shining, decided not to stay there. Instead, we went and ate an expensive meal out of doors in the Esplanade Park.

This park is in the very centre of the town, a narrow strip of tree-lined greenery that is sandwiched between the North and South Esplanades. It runs from the Swedish Theatre to the market by the South Harbour and at either end is an open-air restaurant. As time went on we sampled both. One we thought good and expensive, the other poor and only slightly less dear, but the latter had the charm of being close to the waterfront and of having an orchestra. A large part of it was simply a beer-garden, and often in the days that followed, in the intervals between sightseeing, I would rest there in the sunshine drinking weak beer and listening to the music.

After leaving Stella I devoted the afternoon to trying to buy lint. My neck hurt and I knew with a horrible certainty that I had not heard the last of the boil that Kalle had lanced for me before I left Kajaani. Somehow or other, I thought, I should have to manage to foment it, and to do this I must procure the wherewithal—and the wherewithal was lint. Dictionary in hand, I trailed from chemist to chemist, but everywhere I drew a blank. At first I thought that the assistants did not understand me, then that it was a post-war shortage, but, in fact, the plain truth is that the Finns never do use lint. The best I could do was to buy gauze—for my purpose a poor substitute—and I returned to the hotel toying with the idea of substituting a bread poultice and idly wondering whether black bread would do as well as white.

The following evening, having had little success with my fomentation, I went out to dinner in the Esplanade Park. There, in the restaurant, I had the inevitable tussle with the menu, which, though written both in Swedish and in Finnish, remained a closed book to me. Not that this worried me at all; it was a beautiful evening and I was in no hurry. In a leisurely way I ran my eye down the price column, took out my dictionary and set to work to decipher the cheaper items. Soon I was lost to the world. I came back to earth to hear a woman at the

[1] *Helsingin Osuuskauppa*=The Helsinki Co-operative Store.

Helsinki Market

Pihlajavesi, or Rowan Water

Grania at Punkaharju

next table offering, in quite good English, to help me. Thereupon we fell into conversation and, when the time came to leave, she smilingly invited me to return home with her and drink a cup of coffee. I was glad to accept. Her home turned out to be the back of a shop in the Lönnrotinkatu that had been partitioned off to make a small cubicle-like bedroom. The shop, which was in reality two adjacent shops, presented a curious combination. In one china was painted, fired and sold, and in the other typing, stencilling and translating were done to order. Rouva Meders, my new friend, divided her attention between all these activities.

It was long after office hours and we sat in the typing division of the shop. The window gave on to the street but the floor was about three feet below the level of the pavement. There we drank coffee and smoked. Suddenly Rouva Meders caught sight of my plaster which had worked loose. "Your plaster is coming off," she said, and then, as I put up my hand to it, added, "Wait. I fix it for you." A second later she caught sight of my boil, which by now had assumed ugly dimensions. Up went her hands in horror. "Oh!" she gasped. "It will be intoxicated!" I knew exactly what she meant and could not have agreed more heartily. How kind she was; in a minute she had summoned her elder son, Anders, and sent him to the chemist with a list of the things she thought that I needed, and on his return she washed and dressed my boil for me. Nor did her kindness stop there for, when we said good night, her parting injunctions were: "Come back at ten to-morrow morning. You cannot possibly do that for yourself." Thereafter, until Grania arrived, she dressed it for me every day and, when necessary, twice a day, and as she did so she gave me a wealth of good advice. "You must eat yeast," she said, "and *pinattia*. How do you call it, spinach? But you must eat it raw."

So every morning, having first devoured a square inch of baker's yeast, I walked down the Esplanade to the flower and vegetable market and bought a large bag of spinach and generally fell for some wild strawberries as well. Armed with these, I would stroll back through the park, pausing, if I felt so minded, to sit on a seat in the sunshine and eat some, at least, of my spinach. To manage it all at once was more than I could ever do, for spinach in its raw state is extremely tough and unpalatable and, chew as I might, I could make but slow headway with it. Invariably there was still quite a lot left in the bag when I once more reached the hotel, and I was obliged to renew the assault in all my spare moments.

Happily, my perseverance was rewarded. Rouva Meders' treatment worked like magic and my boil, which had been showing hydra-like tendencies, rapidly cleared up with no aftermath at all. This was a great weight off my mind and, in an effort to express my gratitude, I went down once more to the market and did my best to say it with flowers.

As a matter of fact, I welcomed any and every excuse for going down to the market, which during the brief summer season is a blaze of colour. I loved to potter from stall to stall, horrified at the price of everything I saw, and unable to tear myself away. I enjoyed, too, sauntering along the edge of the harbour, where many of the fishwives ply their trade from the boats that are moored stern-on to the quay. The whole place seethes with activity until mid-day by which time the law decrees that the area shall be clear of stalls and booths. Everything disappears like magic. One moment the waterfront is gay with a profusion of flowers and fruit and the next it is a bare open space, and one is left with the feeling that Aladdin's lamp must have been at work.

In 1812 the capital of Finland was moved from Turku to Helsinki, and as most of the present-day town post-dates this event, it is, even by Finnish standards, a new city. Little or nothing remains of the old port, which was in any case of no great importance. Wooden buildings are rarely long-lived and those that existed before the capital was transferred were no exception. Fortunately, the men responsible for the planning of the new city were alive to the danger of fire and the lay-out of Helsinki is spacious and its streets more than usually wide. A happy choice was made when the neoclassicist Engel was appointed city architect and the uninterrupted growth of the capital throughout its first thirty years reflects his genius.

The greatest concentration of Engel's work is in the Suurtori, or Great Market Square, which, to the best of my belief, is never now used as a market. But the present-day market is less than five minutes' walk away and there, too, Engel has left his mark in the shape of the City Hall. This building stands at one end of a row of white houses that overlook the south harbour while at the other, set back a little from the road, is the President's Palace. The houses that go to make up this row are all slightly later in date than the City Hall but, nevertheless, they form one harmonious whole and, cool and dignified, offset to perfection the colour and bustle of the market.

In comparison with the hubbub on the waterfront, the Suurtori Square is a haven of peace and quiet—or would be if there were no trams. To the north rises the Suurkirkko, or great Church of St. Nicholas—to my mind the most distinctive building in Helsinki, in spite of its dead-white finish that comes perilously near to looking like icing sugar. High up on a terrace it can be seen from far out at sea dominating the harbour and the town. Two flights of extremely steep steps lead from the square to this terrace and, as you climb these steps, twin bastions, crowned by pale reflections of the classical temple, jut out to right and left. In conception the whole plan was Engel's, but the great church was not completed until twelve years after his death, by which time his design had been somewhat modified. By classical standards the proportions of the building are magnificently wrong; one glimpse would have made Wren shudder and Phidias turn in his grave, yet this square church with its four-pillared porticos makes up by sheer individualism for any deficiency in orthodoxy. A huge copper dome rises above the centre of the building and below at each of its four corners is a bright blue cupola decorated with golden stars.

On the east side of the square are Engel's University building and library. I never succeeded in penetrating into their precincts because at the time of which I am writing they were closed for the summer vacation. A great deal is closed in Helsinki during the summer months, for the people do not then think in terms of indoor activities. I was almost surprised to find the Art Gallery open. There was no music, no drama, no ballet, and in the smaller country towns even the cinemas were shut because everyone was busy taking advantage of the fine weather and long daylight.

I had only been a few days in Helsinki when Midsummer was celebrated, but I have to admit that I took no part in the festivities. Seeing that it is probably the most popular festival of the year, this was perhaps unenterprising, but I was feeling below par and, having no friends left in the town by Midsummer Eve, I had not the energy to go out in the crowd by myself. From my room in the hotel I heard the sound of exploding fireworks and the scream of rockets, and I knew that round the shores of the gulf great bonfires were burning. All through the evening the crowds had surged out of the city towards the beaches, and merry-making went on all night. It is a very simple matter to get clear of Helsinki, for nowhere are you far from the sea. Wooded islands and sandy beaches are accessible on all sides. They are a paradise for the city children who career about them naked all through the summer, and for the people generally who flock there whenever possible to swim and sun themselves in the scantiest possible attire. In no capital city that I know of are the people who cannot afford a summer holiday better situated.

The attitude of the people to their national holidays is interesting. They are pre-eminently holidays for all and, as such, anything in the nature of an extra train or bus service is the exception rather than the rule, while restaurants, instead of working overtime, for the most part close altogether. I, of course, did not appreciate all this, so scarcely realised my luck when, on ringing for my coffee on Midsummer morning, I got it, though having had it I soon discovered that there was no further service to be had in the hotel that day or, for that matter, anywhere in the town except in the very few open-air restaurants. I do not think that the chambermaids even made the beds, but I cannot be certain on this point. I assume there was a skeleton staff on duty but, if so, they were certainly not in evidence.

Holidays in Finland are thus holidays for all except the poor, long-suffering housewives, who not only have to cater well in advance, but also to cope with their husbands, mind the children and do all the cooking, because most domestic helpers appear to look upon national holidays as theirs by right. I think foreign visitors must often be a little nonplussed by this wholesale downing of tools, especially if not forewarned, as there cannot be many countries where so much store is set on the festivities and so little on turning them to profitable account.

As soon as the Midsummer holiday was over, I returned to the tourist office to find out how our plans were maturing. There the clerk told me that he had managed to procure steamer reservations for Grania and me and that a double room had been booked for us at Punkaharju; but when I asked about Koli I learned that all his efforts to get us accommodation had been unsuccessful.

This was very disappointing, for Koli was reputed to be the most beautiful place in the whole country. The assistant, however, made light of the predicament in which his carelessness had landed us. "Go," he said. "They say they are full up, but it will be all right when you get there." I wished that I could feel as certain. I was not yet wise to Finnish ways and did not fully appreciate the extent to which most Finns will put themselves out on sighting a foreigner.

I shall not dwell on all that I saw in Helsinki, for the subject is altogether outside my scope. Besides, many others have dealt extensively with the city. All that I intend to do is to mention briefly the few remaining things which struck me most forcibly —the statuary, Sirén's Parliament Building and the lilac— before passing on to the arrival of Grania.

Helsinki, as I have already said, is a spacious city, and the people who inhabit it have, like all Scandinavians, a passion for statuary. It is abundant in the parks, in the squares and at street corners. It is good, it is bad, it is indifferent, but first and foremost it is alive, for the Finnish nation is very art-conscious. They are a young people and their attitude to art has all the vigour, the spontaneity and the idealism of youth and not a little of its indiscrimination.

Of the statues in Helsinki, that of Aleksis Kivi is, I think, pre-eminent. The work of Wäino Aaltonen, the foremost Finnish sculptor of the day, it is, to me, at once a worthy tribute to Kivi and a profound expression of Aaltonen's own genius. For this statue is far more than a portrait—which indeed it can scarcely be, as there is to-day but one poor drawing of Kivi in existence—it is the re-creation of the man through his work; the likeness in which he lives on in the hearts of the Finnish people.

Aaltonen, too, is responsible for the five symbolical figures that adorn the great hall of Sirén's Parliament Building, the erection of which was completed in 1931. But, although complete in itself, this building is not yet seen to advantage because it looks straight out over a railway goods yard. This, however, was not Sirén's intention. When he planned this vast, square, faintly Egyptian-looking edifice, the area in front of it was destined to be a park. But the war intervened before the goods yard had been moved and the project has now been indefinitely held up. This is a great pity, as architecturally the Parliament Building is a stupendous creation deserving of better things. The colour of its granite, though pale, is warm, its frontal colonnade, though solid, graceful. It is a public building that any nation could be proud to call its own.

Inside, the great circular chamber is of extreme simplicity; only Aaltonen's five statues risk distracting the attention of the deputies from affairs of state. But this cannot be said of the remainder of the building, which glistens with a myriad reflections. The galleries and passages are of shining marble and everything which goes with them, the glass, the chromium and the wood, is all very highly polished. Light is reflected everywhere. The effect was so like that of a magnificent Hollywood set that, as I walked along the corridors, I should not have been at all surprised to see some pseudo-royal personage come sweeping round the corner; Greta Garbo as Queen Christina of Sweden perhaps, or Elizabeth Bergner as Catherine the Great.

Leaving the Diet, I walked back into the town. I do not think that I have ever walked more in any large city than I did in Helsinki. This was, of course, largely because I was incapable of making intelligent use of the buses and trams; but what a pleasant city it was in which to walk. At Midsummer lilac was blooming everywhere and the air was full of its fragrance. It was the background of the statues in the parks; it was the foreground that framed the blue waters of the harbour. It is still the flower of all flowers that I associate with Helsinki.

* * *

On the evening of July 27th Grania and I took the train from Helsinki to Kuopio, where we arrived at about five the following morning. Sleepily we dumped our cases in the left-luggage office and set out in search of the Atlas Hotel, which our guide-book assured us was the best hotel in the town. There we planned to have breakfast and a wash and brush up. The sun was already high and the heat was intense. It was almost unbelievable that it was barely 5.30 a.m. and less than four degrees from the Arctic Circle.

We found the Atlas Hotel overlooking the Market Square. In the hall a night porter was drowsing in his shirt-sleeves, but he roused himself to tell us that the cloakroom was upstairs and that the prospect of getting breakfast, or even a kettle boiled, before eight o'clock was nil. We were not really surprised for in what provincial hotels do they serve breakfast at 5.30 a.m.? So we accepted defeat, and returned to the station to see if the buffet was open.

It was. A pleasant-looking girl was standing behind a long

counter presiding over fizzy drinks and dry, butterless, tired-looking sandwiches of rye bread and sausage. But here we had not hoped for more; I had long since learned that in 1947 travellers in Finland automatically carried their food with them and we too had providently laid in a supply. Grania had arrived from England well stocked with tea and coffee and we had bought our perishable rations in Helsinki. In the rucksack were bread, butter, tea and Swedish marmalade. I think our coffee must have been buried at the bottom of one of the cases in the left-luggage office, because we did not consider drinking it—it might have been better if we had. Taking the packet of tea to the girl I asked her, as best I could, to make some for us. She took the packet from me and smiled; a few minutes later she came over to our table with the packet of tea I had given her in one hand and a jug of so-called boiling water in the other. Putting them both down in front of us, she indicated politely that we should make the tea for ourselves. We did the best we could, but the tea leaves floated as tea leaves will. Setting our teeth, we drank the warm liquid through them.

We lingered in the buffet for some time after we had finished. We were in no hurry; our boat did not leave till one o'clock and we had plenty of time on our hands. Even so, it was still something short of seven when we set out to explore the town.

Kuopio, the capital of the province of Savo, is the eighth largest town in Finland and about three times the size of Kajaani. It, too, was one of the ten towns founded by Per Brahe in the mid-seventeenth century and, like Kajaani, it suffered almost immediate eclipse and was rapidly reduced to the status of a church village. It was not until over a century after its birth that Gustav III of Sweden granted the town a charter and it is from this era that the importance of the city really dates. In 1775 the Governor of the district settled there, and between 1850 and 1900 the Bishop held his court in the town.

Judged purely as a town, of all those that I visited in Finland, Kuopio is my favourite. It stands beside the waters of the Kallavesi in a basin of low hills, and compared with Kajaani it is very compact indeed. Although essentially modern, part of the old town remains and a few charming cobbled streets stand untouched by the passage of time. They criss-cross each other in straight lines and the simplicity of their outline is absolute. The old wooden dwellings that flank these streets are single storied, rectangular and more or less uniform in pattern. They rise flush and unadorned from the pavement, their colouring preponderantly white, cream or buff and their roofs quite literally pitch black, for they are made of cardboard impregnated with tar. For so northern a clime their slope is very gentle, yet they are remarkably watertight and stand up well to the heavy load of snow that they are called upon to bear in wintertime. Each little house—it may be detached, semi-detached or one of a row—has flat double-framed windows, and each one stands on a grey stone foundation that rises anything from a matter of inches to about three feet above the level of the road, and from these foundations the front door steps jut out with a casual insouciance that is a perpetual menace to absent-minded pedestrians.

Our wanderings soon brought us back to the large market square which is in the very heart of the town, and there, for a while, we pottered. A few stalls floated like islands on its dun-coloured surface, but, as in Kajaani, there was very little on sale. In fact, so empty was it that we had soon exhausted all its possibilities and branched off down the Kauppakatu in the direction of the lake.

This street ran gently downhill past the century-old stone church that had had, in the days before the Bishop moved his court to Oulu, the status of a cathedral. This church was built in 1815 at a time when almost all Finnish ecclesiastical architecture was of wood, and for this reason alone it is of considerable interest. But it is also of considerable charm. I liked the mottled, irregular effect of its stone-work, which was warm and satisfying—the result of a complete lack of uniformity in size, shape and colour of the tawny grey blocks of limestone of which it is built. The masons, in a carefree way, had made up for all lack of symmetry in their material by a lavish use of thick white cement and given a finishing touch to the whole building by white-washing the upper half to the square church tower to match the mortar they had used so freely. Outlined against the blue sky, it was most effective.

Leaving the church, we wandered down to the lake shore and out on to the headland known as Väinöläniemi. There we lay under the trees at the water's edge and watched the sun glinting on its surface and shoals of little fishes darting about in the cool depths beneath.

After a while Grania yawned, stretched and murmured

drowsily: "I suppose we ought to be doing something. You've got the guide-book. What does it say?"

I perused it for a moment in silence. "It seems that we ought to climb Puijo. That's the hill at the back of the town," I volunteered somewhat tentatively when I had finished reading. "There are just one hundred and sixty-three steps up the tower on the top—the book says it's very repaying."

Grania opened a sleepy eye and muttered: "Too hot."

I lapsed once more into silence and lay looking up at the deep blue sky through a weaving tracery of leaves and needles. It was very pleasant where we were and I had no inclination to move, but, in retrospect, I think perhaps that, from Grania's point of view, it was a pity that we did not make the effort, because the view from Puijo is magnificent.

I know, for I returned to Kuopio early in November and then I climbed up through snow to the summit. The cold weather had only just set in, and I think the snow-clad panorama on which I gazed was the coldest I have ever seen. It was the season of all seasons when everything strikes chill. The sky was heavy with snow to come and the landscape an infinity of slate-grey lakes and pools fringed by pale masses of watery ice. White snow, black trees, grey lakes and a leaden sky—nothing could have looked more cruel and desolate. Later in the year, though the thermometer registers a far lower temperature, the feeling is nothing like so cold; the frozen lakes are then a dazzling white, the snow has fallen and during the brief hours of daylight the sun shines in a clear sky.

That afternoon, as I looked down from Puijo, I knew that it was the very antithesis of the June morning when Grania and I had failed to make the effort, and so never saw what must have been a myriad lakes sparkling in an enchanted forest.

"Go on," said Grania. "What else?"

I roused myself to point to a tall red chimney that rose above a cluster of factory buildings on the far side of the lake.

"Over there," I said impressively, "is the largest bobbin mill of its type in the world."

Grania rewarded it with a cursory glance, disposed of it mentally and asked if there was anything more of interest in the book.

"Only that Snellman and Minna Canth lived here."

That was altogether too much for her; she looked blankly at me and inquired who they were.

This was my cue; Snellman's birthday having been celebrated on May 12th, I was able to shoot no end of a line about him, but I had to admit that I, too, had never heard of Minna Canth. However, I made up for it later, and on going into the question discovered that she was not only a champion of feminism, but also Finland's leading woman playwright.

Minna Canth lived from 1844 to 1897 through years that were in Finland, as elsewhere in Europe, years of transition and maladjustment. The Industrial Revolution was in full swing and both industrial and agricultural abuses were general. In Kuopio, Minna Canth took up the cudgels on behalf of reform. A widow with a family of seven to support and no professional training behind her, she became the champion of education for women, but her zeal did not stop there, she fought for the whole of oppressed humanity. To keep her family she opened a wool shop and devoted her days to business and her evenings to writing. Her literary ability was outstanding, her ideals burning and her aim to rouse the people to combat blind obedience to tyranny masquerading as virtue. The drama was her principal medium and she used it with telling force, and her work, which was nothing if not outspoken, soon aroused a clamour of admiration and indignation. But to-day only admiration remains, and in Kuopio, where she lived and worked, there now stands the first statue ever raised in honour of a Finnish woman. Perhaps more pertinently still, the women of Finland have founded in her memory the Social Welfare Minna Canth League and the Minna Canth Literary Society.

Minna Canth did not live to see the new Constitution or to know of the nineteen women who were returned to Parliament in the elections that followed and who occupied almost a tenth of the 200 available seats, because it was not until 1906—nine years after her death at the age of fifty-four—that Finnish women got the vote. Even so they were the first women to be so honoured in Europe, and the first, but for those of Australia and New Zealand, in the world.

Enfranchisement came as a result—one might almost say as a reward—for the stalwart part they played in the passive resistance campaign that brought to an end the first period of Russian tyranny to follow the accession of Nicholas II. The campaign was well timed. It coincided, by no means accidentally, with Russian setbacks in Japan, with the result that the Russians fearing further unrest, placed no obstacles in the way of the new Constitution that the Finns had drawn up. In it the whole adult population over the age of twenty-four was enfranchised, and participation in the government opened to both sexes. In the 1907 elections nineteen women were returned; to-day they hold twenty-four seats and the number in the interim has never greatly varied.

Emancipation, in its fullest sense, came by degrees. The year 1917 saw the doors of local government opened to women and since then about one-third of all seats on municipal councils and committees have been theirs, and their contribution to the common weal, and especially to social welfare, has been enormous.

In 1929 the Marriage Act became law and by it husband and wife became equal partners in everything. In one fell swoop they became equally responsible for their children, their debts, their joint income and all the various aspects of their marriage. In fact, so square a deal is it that in a divorce case a wealthy woman, if judged in the wrong, pays her husband alimony.

In the main the emancipation of women worked smoothly, but without doubt those who have benefited most are the professional classes, for in the professions prejudice against women is negligible and opportunity for advancement correspondingly great. Many become lawyers and architects and many more take up medicine. About 15 per cent. of the country's doctors are now women and about 80 per cent. of the dentists. Of the remaining professions, only the Church and the armed forces remain closed to them; in fact, nothing tangible stands between a woman and the Presidency.

* * *

Over an early lunch Grania and I once more got out the guide-book and studied the map of Finland. We wanted to be quite clear about where we were going. But to be quite clear is not as easy as it sounds, because Finnish maps tend to be very confusing and the maze of waterways they depict very difficult to disentangle at a glance. Furthermore, the map of Finland is apt to be unfamiliar to those who have not visited the country, so I think perhaps, before we embark on our travels, a few geographical remarks may not come amiss.

Before the war Finland, with its population of less than 4,000,000, was the seventh largest country in Europe and covered an area of approximately 148,000 square miles. This area has now been reduced by about 12 per cent., but it is still rather over 40,000 square miles greater than that of England, Scotland and Wales together.

Broadly speaking, the nature of the country can be classified under three main headings: forest land, which comprises 71 per cent. of the total land area, waste land, which accounts for 16·9 per cent., and farm lands and roads, which make up the total. To say that the farm land is in the coastal belt, that the waste land increases as you go north and that the main bulk of the country is forest-clad is an over-simplification of the facts; nevertheless, this is the general outline of the picture. But it must be remembered that the land area itself is only 90·6 per cent. of the country and that the remaining 9·4 per cent. is made up of fresh-water lakes and rivers.

Finland is often referred to as "The Land of a Thousand Lakes." The description is appropriate because it conjures up in the mind's eye an infinity of water, but actually it is a gross understatement. Different authorities compute the number at figures varying from 40,000 to 60,000, but the exact number does not matter: what is significant is the extent of the network of waterways that spreads over the forest area. This is of vital importance because the country's foremost industry is timber, and for this 25,000 miles of natural waterways provide a ready-made means of transport from the interior to the coast.

Of the three main drainage systems that serve the lumber country, the most westerly flows into the Gulf of Bothnia at Pori, while the other two run roughly north to south. The central one reaches the Gulf of Finland at Kotka, and the third and largest—the only one to have no natural outlet in Finland—at Leningrad. To circumvent this early in the industrial era, the Finns cut a thirty-six-mile-long canal[1] by means of which the great mass of water-borne traffic that converged on Lake Saimaa from the north was conveyed to the port of Viipuri. To-day it must all be diverted. What this means to the Finns in terms of transport alone, it would be hard to exaggerate, for the strain that it imposes on all their remaining road, rail, shipping and dockyard facilities is tremendous.

Transport problems are, however, by no means the only economic difficulties to follow the loss of Karelia. Inevitably power problems are another, because the greater part of Finland's hydro-electric power was generated by the Vuoksi—

[1] The Saimaa Canal was opened in 1856.

the unnavigable river down which the waters of Lake Saimaa hurtle through Karelia to Lake Laatokka. In fact, so heavily did the pre-war Finns depend for their electric power on the Vuoksi that, even though the huge plant at Imatra is still in their hands, 30 per cent. of the country's total power was lost with Karelia. The problems arising out of this loss are, however, less immediately urgent than those of transport because, to a large extent this loss of power is balanced by an equal loss in industrial plant. Yet the situation that arises from it is none the less a matter for very real concern. It is clearly not in the national interest that the whole of southern Finland should depend for its hydro-electric power—as depend it does—on the great plant at Imatra; for Imatra,[1] the site of the greatest of all European rapids, lies barely five miles from the new frontier.

But stupendous though the Imatra Rapid is, Grania and I did not plan to include it in our travels. The friends whom I had consulted before leaving Kajaani had all been of one mind: with the limited time at our disposal it was not worth our while to go so far. To do so would mean a good deal of extra travelling and when we got there we should almost certainly be disappointed. Now that the great rapid had been harnessed it was nothing like as fine as it once was. We were too late; too late by almost twenty-six years, for work on the power station had started in 1921. So Grania and I decided to content ourselves with exploring the upper reaches of the Saimaa Lake system.

* * *

Three or four small steamers lined the quayside at Kuopio, but we had no difficulty in picking out the one we wanted because, not only were they all clearly labelled with their destination and time of departure, but they all bore names indicative of the route they were taking. Thus, there being two routes from Kuopio to Savonlinna—one by Heinävesi and the other by Leppävirta—the steamers that coxed and boxed between the two were known, rather prosaically, as the *Heinävesi I* and *II* and the *Leppävirta I* and *II*.

[1] The great rapid at Imatra is formed by a sudden narrowing of the Vuoksi River, which forces its water through a gorge that is half a mile long and in places no more than twenty-two yards wide. The drop within this gorge is sixty feet, not in itself a spectacular fall, yet before the river was harnessed the volume of water that thundered through the canyon must have been tremendously impressive. Lake Saimaa is three times as large as the Lake of Geneva and the Vuoksi is its only outlet.

It was the *Heinävesi II* that was to take us to Savonlinna. She was the exact counterpart of her neighbours, a small double-decker with a low, white painted hull and an extremely shallow draught—an essential feature because there is little depth of water in most Finnish lakes. The general effect was one of top-heaviness; of some curious hybrid that might have been the mongrel offspring of a Canadian lake steamer and a Thames houseboat, for the superstructure was like a flat-roofed house with two stories, each of which was encircled by a covered veranda. The house, however, was divided amidships by a tall, thin funnel round which the passengers on both decks circulated. This funnel finally projected six feet or so into the air above the topmost deck, if deck it can be called, for it served merely as a roof or awning.

Two or three planks had been nailed together to make a gangway and across these we walked on to the lower deck. It was already considerably cluttered up with freight, but there was no sense of imminent departure. Nor did anyone take the least notice of our arrival, so we hoisted our bags up the companion-way to the upper deck and looked around for someone to show us our cabin. Eventually we found the Captain, who seemed to combine the duties of a purser with the task of navigation. He beamed on us, took our tickets and gave us the key of a cabin just aft of the bridge. It was very small and, when we were both inside, the first thing Grania did was to ejaculate with a heartfelt sigh: "Well, thank heavens the door opens outwards!" Inside there was just about as much floor space as there is between the seats of a third-class railway carriage—or would have been if part had not been give up to a rather primitive wash-stand. The remainder of the room was occupied by a settee upholstered in worn crimson plush that by night was transformed into two berths. This was a far from ideal piece of furniture, for when we sat down on it, the window was well above our eye-level and we could not see anything at all. So we stowed our bags and went out on the deck, where, but for the small area around the funnel and an even smaller half-moon at the after end, it was barely wide enough for two people to walk abreast. One tour revealed a few hard wooden benches, some equally hard wooden campstools and—the nearest approach to comfort—three or four wicker armchairs which were already occupied.

For some time we hung over the rail and watched the comings

and goings of passengers and crew until at last the hooter blew, the engines throbbed and the propeller churned up a rabbit's tail of foam. We were off, and as we went about and set our course for Vehmersalmi, the small steamer heeled over like a cyclist on a race-track.

It was a lovely day on the water, the sun was shining and a cool breeze was blowing off the shore. It tempered the heat and filled the air with a sweet smell of pine, and for a while all thoughts of minor discomfort vanished, but retrospectively I have to admit, in the face of all that has been written to the contrary, that Finnish lake steamers are not the height of comfort. I know, of course, that we caught them at a bad time—that the much-vaunted, spotless linen had perforce given way to paper sheets, and that food was expensive and difficult to obtain—but, that the dining saloon should be unbearably hot, the seats on deck inadequate and the view restricted from almost everywhere but the bridge cannot be blamed on the war. Nevertheless, I think that there are compensations to be derived from a certain lack of comfort, because, surely, the more workaday the arrangements, the closer the traveller draws to the people of the country and the greater the sense of adventure he enjoys.

In trying to describe the Finnish lakes, I find myself in a quandary; I simply do not know where to begin. It is probably true to say that to describe one is to describe all, but that only goes to show how misleading truth can be, for their sameness is always with a difference; some indefinable difference of line or colour; some intangible matter of movement or light. This lake may have more islands, that lake be fringed by more leaf green, but there is almost nothing so wholly individual as to be an unmistakable landmark, unless it be some man-made feature, such as a saw-mill or a railway bridge.

Slowly we chugged southwards, now hugging the bank, now ploughing our way into the middle of a great lake and following it until it narrowed and we found ourselves stealing down the reaches of a tree-fringed sound that was calm and wide as a great river. Time and time again the channel would narrow and the forest would hem us in so that there appeared to be no escape; time and time again a hidden bend would reveal another passage, or open out into another lake, sparkling, blue and dotted by a thousand isles. It was impossible to keep any sense of direction, and as we wove our way in and out through the labyrinth it often seemed to us that we must be doubling back on our tracks.

Grania and I spent a lot of our time on the bridge with the Captain, a godlike being who seemed utterly unmindful of the intricacies of navigation, bewildering as they appeared to us. At any rate, he seemed only too pleased to have a little distraction and delighted to have the chance to air his English and point out all the landmarks which we passed.

We stopped frequently; to deliver a parcel, to pick up a passenger, to deposit freight or embark livestock; it was all part of a seemingly leisurely amble which was all in the day's work. As we drew alongside, the small pontoon landing stages groaned and shuddered at our impact. Sometimes a few people were gathered on the quay, but quite often it was deserted and, if needs be, we would abandon a packing case on the pontoon like a calling card on a salver. Often a *sauna* at the water's edge was the only sign of habitation, and disembarking passengers would quite simply vanish up a trail into the woods, firmly clutching their very urban-looking suitcases. More rarely they would transfer from the steamer into a small, high-prowed dinghy and row away to some otherwise inaccessible island.

Every few hours stacks of sawn timber piled close beside a quay indicated that it was time for our steamer to refuel and, as its appetite was as healthy as its food was bulky, taking on fuel was a lengthy business. So there, beside the woodpile, we would wait while two or three men trundled the logs on board in barrows. Meanwhile, small children with wild strawberries for sale on leaves or birch-bark trays would appear at the ship's side and carry on a brisk trade among the passengers.

The bunkers full, we would proceed on our way and once again the intimacy of the islands would alternate with wide stretches of open water—deep blue water outlined in trees that merged with each other in a vast expanse of variegated greenery.

From time to time, as we crossed one of the great lakes, we would pass a small tug with an immense timber raft in tow—a raft that might be as long as 500 yards and that was, in effect, first cousin to the Loch Ness Monster. For these huge rafts are constructed of logs bound into bundles of twenty or thereabouts: giant faggots that, in their turn, are lashed five or six abreast in a long and serpentine column of route.

This is the way most commonly adopted for transporting timber across those of the lakes which are used as highways, because rafts of this kind do not impede the steamer traffic, but on smaller lakes, such as the one east of Kajaani, a much simpler method is used. There the timber is trapped at the river mouth by floating booms constructed of logs chained end on to each other. When full, the ends are closed and the great mass of timber thus encircled has been known to cover an area as large as half a square mile. These immense corrugated rafts are then left to the mercy of the wind and water until such time as a tug arrives to tow them down the lake.

The whole cycle of logging begins with the New Year. In January, February and March the trees are felled and transported to the rivers, as the snow is then frozen hard and the floor of the forest smooth enough for horses to be able to drag the logs to the water, where they remain until the ice breaks up. A cold winter and plenty of snow are thus the first essentials of a good season, but even with them the work is arduous and a considerable strain on the horses that are employed on it. In fact, there was a time not long ago when this strain, coupled with inadequate feeding and shelter, was so bad that a single season might take a toll of half the horses employed; but mercifully this is no longer the case. Conditions both for men and animals in the lumber camps have improved out of all recognition and the majority of the horses can now count themselves veterans of long standing.

But there is more to felling in January, February and March than relative ease of transport, for these are also the months when the growing wood is at its driest and therefore least susceptible to insect pests. Furthermore, the drier the wood the less liable it is to become waterlogged and a dead loss—a fact of some importance because, between the forest and their final destination, the logs may remain in the water as long as three years.

Timber floating begins as soon as the ice melts—that is, any time between the beginning of April and the middle of May. As the logs begin to move, the banks of the streams are patrolled by men whose job it is to keep them moving; to stop them running ashore or piling up against the rocks in mid-stream. This is the part of the lumberman's job to which most of the glamour clings. The upper reaches of the rivers are turbulent and wild. Obstructions grow rapidly and to break them up is often both dangerous and difficult. But where the rivers run wide and smooth, floating booms confine the logs within special channels down which they travel in a steady stream that leaves the fairway free for other craft. At falls and power stations, wooden shoots, deeper, longer, but very similar to those found in many swimming baths, enable the logs to by-pass the obstacles and continue unimpeded on their way.

All this, however, is digressing. The first log rafts that I ever saw were the ones Grania and I passed on our way south, and even then, although we knew little about it, we were struck by the amount of work and patience involved in the process of transport. It was all very well for the *Heinävesi II* to run to schedule, because, where the drop between the lakes was considerable, she had only to enter a narrow canal and pass through a lock just large enough to take her, but the log rafts had to be broken up at every rapid and reassembled at the lower end. To do this each raft has its own crew, who travel with it and who may in one season cover many hundreds of miles.

In the late afternoon we came out on to the Kermajärvi, or Cream Lake, and about seven o'clock we stopped at the church village of Heinävesi. Somewhere in this parish the monks exiled from the Orthodox monastery of Valamo on Lake Laatokka have taken refuge. Just where their new quarters are I do not know, but I understand they have no particular artistic merit. Certainly we saw no monks in the vicinity of the landing stage at Heinävesi, but this is not surprising, as Finnish parishes tend to be very large.

The story of the monks is a sad one, for the island retreat from which they are banished had been theirs since the year 992, and not only are they exiles—the common lot of Karelians —but they appear to be in danger of extinction. To-day there are sixty to seventy monks; in 1938 there were about 200, of whom the older ones were almost all Russian-born, Finnish nationals, for the Finnish Republic had early decreed that all monks must be Finnish citizens and had made naturalisation a prerequisite of joining the brotherhood. Conditions in Russia being what they are, this gradually became tantamount to saying that the monastery must depend for recruits on the Orthodox Finnish community, which numbers 70,000—at least half of whom must be presumed to be female—and in fact their richest source of supply was the orphanage, which they ran for boys of the Orthodox faith, together with forty other youths whom they employed seasonally on the land. Now that the

Orthodox Finns are no longer so heavily concentrated in one area, for the time being recruiting is virtually at a standstill, and the general consensus of opinion is that the order is doomed. But it may be that opinion is unduly pessimistic for at least on one past occasion the monastery has risen phœnix-like from the ashes.

* * *

We left Heinävesi at seven o'clock and in less than an hour had passed Kerma, at the southern end of the lake. Soon after, we were stealing along a narrow canal and entering another small lock. While we waited, penned in, and the water flowed out through the sluice gates, the *Heinävesi I* appeared approaching from the opposite direction. Close inshore she came to a standstill and waited for us to pass. As the gates opened and we drew alongside, the passengers waved to each other and shouted greetings. Then in her turn the *Heinävesi I* moved forward and entered the lock and, when last we saw her, she was slowly rising on the water.

In the cool of the evening we steamed for nearly two hours down channels that seemed to grow more and more intricate. Then at about ten o'clock we tied up for the night at the head of a narrow backwater. As the engines ceased to throb, the mosquitoes started to buzz and, hedged in as we were by trees, Grania and I soon discovered that the cool of the evening was not cool at all. Our small cabin was like an oven and we were plagued by mosquitoes. Luckily, before I had left England, I had been forewarned. Not once but many times, my cheerful friends had assured me that if I was fortunate enough to survive the Finnish winter, I should assuredly be devoured alive by mosquitoes in the summer, so I had armed myself with an American preparation called "Jungle Oil." This oil—which is much favoured by the Swedes—had been strongly recommended to me, so I had laid in a store on my way through Stockholm earlier in the year. We certainly found it most effective. It was anathema to mosquitoes and did not even smell unpleasant. Nevertheless, it had its drawbacks; in the first place it stung painfully whenever, as happened frequently, in an attempt to protect our eyelids, we got it in our eyes; and in the second, its smell was so innocuous that even the mosquitoes failed to notice it until within an inch or so of the anointed area. This meant that they made a nerve-racking practice of power-diving on us like Stukas and then sheering off at a tangent. But the oil did, after all, fulfil its functions and we would not willingly have been without it.

That night Grania and I lay in our bunks in two minds as to whether it was better to have the door and window open or shut. It was unbearably hot and sticky and the mosquitoes buzzed unendingly. Feverishly we tossed and turned and swatted till our paper sheets were in mangled shreds and our tempers equally frayed, until at last, in the small hours of the morning, the ship got under way, the air began to circulate and we fell asleep.

The next thing I knew was that Grania was telling me that it was time I got up, as we should soon be arriving and there was only room for one of us to dress at a time.

"Why," I yawned sleepily, "should I get up first?"

"Because," came the preposterous reply, "you must finish your last bag of spinach before we get there. I'm tired of carrying it about."

A remark to which I naturally retorted: "What's to stop me eating it in bed?"

In the end, of course, we argued so long that we both had to get up at once and, in the ensuing scrimmage, the spinach, too, got dressed—with jungle oil—and was so nauseating that I pitched it overboard.

We came out on deck to find that we were approaching the north shore of Savonlinna—the Castle of Savo—the town which sprang up around the fortress of St. Olaf or, as it is called in Finnish, Olavinlinna. This castle, which is the finest in Finland, was designed as a frontier fortress and built at a time when the Finnish-Russian border ran close by. Thus its site is a strategic one, but had it been chosen on purely artistic grounds, it could not have been more beautiful. It is built on a rocky island in the Kyrönsalmi and from this vantage point commands both the main waterway from north to south and the land route from east to west, for the sound, which connects the Haapavesi in the north with the Pihlajavesi in the south, is the only easily negotiable piece of water in the path of an advancing army.

To-day a great railway bridge spans the sound and, as we passed beneath it, the castle came into sight; a warm mass of reddish brown limestone embedded in the bare rock, its borders fringed by clumps of silvery willows.

But breath-taking as the sight of the castle inevitably is, it came as no surprise, for it is the photographer's dream and, as such, figures on countless picture postcards and looms largely on all travel brochures. It had even graced the 15-mark postage stamp that I had put on my home letters ever since my arrival in Finland, although for some time past I had been expecting a change, as the Finnish Post Office is for ever bringing out new issues.[1]

Yet—however familiar the shape of the castle—it remains a stupendous and eminently satisfying monument and one that surpasses all expectations. Standing in midstream, it is everything that a mediæval picture-book castle should be, and Grania and I gazed at it with rapt pleasure as we steamed by, never taking our eyes from it until the ship rounded a headland and it disappeared from sight. A few moments later we tied up alongside the market place of Savonlinna.

Having said goodbye to our friend the Captain, we made for the Seurahuone Hotel, which, according to our guide-book, was the only alternative Savonlinna had to offer to a hydro or the Y.W.C.A. With memories of Kuopio Station buffet fresh in our minds, we had decided on the hotel. We wanted a good breakfast and we got it, though the dining-room in which we ate was singularly charmless and the whole building merited the adjective "commercial."

A little later, our hunger assuaged, we set out along the waterfront in the direction of the castle.

It was on the way there that Grania suddenly stopped dead in her tracks and ejaculated, "*Gott!*"—for her a surprising incursion into German. Her eyes were riveted on a brand new building and, following her gaze, I saw above it in an ornate, flowing script the words, "Hotelli Gott." It had not figured in our guide-book, but it looked pleasanter than the Seurahuone —which, by the way, was burnt down soon afterwards—so we resolved to eat our next meal there. It was Sunday and, as Grania aptly remarked, with a name like that it was just the place for Sunday lunch.

A straight road that ended in a bridge and a small island brought us to some steps leading down to the water's edge just

[1] Between April, 1947, and April, 1948, the Post Office brought out no fewer than eight different varieties of 10-mark stamp for inland use—and this excluding several special issues that were surcharged and sold for the benefit of certain charities. There never was such a nation of stamp-collectors, and the Inland Revenue profits accordingly.

opposite the castle. Beside these steps hung a big bronze bell and a notice instructing visitors to ring for the boatman. We rang. The boatman, who was sunning himself on the castle steps, bestirred himself in a leisurely way and got slowly into the boat. But as soon as he had cast off, the force of the current galvanised him into strenuous action, and for a few moments he rowed as hard as he could upstream. Then, using his oars to steer with, he drifted downriver towards the opposite bank, where we were waiting; a very necessary manœuvre which he repeated on the return journey, for the water which laps the castle walls runs swift and deep—so swift that it has never been known to freeze.

Once in the castle, a pleasant-looking lad of about sixteen took charge of us and we spent the morning touring the building extensively. No nook or cranny escaped us. We climbed upstairs and downstairs; we walked along battlements; we inspected the great halls, the dungeon and the magazines and all the while our guide dilated graphically, in broken English, on the history, the legends and the architecture.

The first fact to emerge was that the castle had been built in the year 1475, by a Danish knight called Eric Axelman Tott.

"So much for the Hotelli Gott!" I remarked to Grania with a grin. But she was more than equal to the occasion and completely indifferent to small matters of epigraphy.

"Why worry?" was all the response I got. "Tott's really a much more suitable name for licensed premises."

Little would be achieved by describing Olavinlinna in detail, so I do not propose to try. It is a mediæval castle with all a mediæval castle's characteristics, not least of which is that the charm of the exterior transcends everything else. So it is not surprising that the two things that stand out in my memory should be its superbly romantic form and setting and the wonderful view from the top of the three round towers, where, through small medallion-like windows, every circular prospect is an exquisite gem in itself.

Architecturally, the castle represents several historical periods, because it has been subjected through the ages to various alterations, the last of which were made by the Russians in the latter part of the eighteenth century. Yet the castle remains a harmonious whole, perhaps because it has been at all times a frontier fortress, although, when it fell to the Russians in 1743, a literal *volte-face* became necessary. From then on it became a Russian stronghold until 1809, when, with the total annexation of the country by Alexander I, it lost all its strategic importance.

Finland has never boasted more than five important castles; and now, with the loss of Viipuri, only four remain within her territory. Of the original five, Turku, Hameenlinna and Viipuri were Swedish garrison strongholds, and Kajaani and Olavinlinna were frontier bulwarks, but, whatever their purpose, of the four remaining none can hold a candle to Olavinlinna, whose massive walls and courts seem to embody a whole world of romance. Nevertheless, the casual traveller must probe far if he wishes to give any positive form to this world, for the legends and stories attached to Olavinlinna—at least in so far as they are told to the visitor—are in no way remarkable. But perhaps I expected too much, for the castle looks very old for its age—so much so that one is easily deceived into crediting it with a far longer history than it can possibly have had.

Back once more in the town we made straight for the Tott, where, at considerable expense, we satisfied our not inconsiderable appetites. Inside, to our amusement, we found that the hotel was plastered with notices warning visitors not to drink the tap water—presumably the lake water—because of the danger of typhoid. Not that this, in itself, was the cause of our amusement; it was the signature beneath the warning notices that made us smile, for the Board of Health of Savonlinna gloried in the superbly grandiloquent title, "Savonlinnan Terveydenhoitolautakunta."

So the water was still suspect, I reflected, remembering as I did so how, in the course of the morning, our guide had told us that the water round the castle had turned black on the day when the castle pet—a black ram—had fallen in and been drowned. It had been one of the few colourful stories that he had had to tell and we, peering into the depths of the river, had appreciated it to the full. It did not worry us at all that the drowning of the black ram, in 1728, should have occurred almost 200 years after the Swedish Historian, Olaus Magnus, had stated: "At bottom this river is black, especially round about that Castle where all the fishes are black." We had never even heard of Olaus Magnus, and his *History of the Northern Nations* was, in every sense, a closed book to us. It was perusal of the official guide-book that was later to bring this information to light together with another choice morsel from the same source:

"If the Governor of the castle suddenly dies, or if a careless and sleepy guard condemned to death is thrown from the highest point of the wall in conformity with the rules of the Castle, a fairy playing a guitar appears from the midst of the waves, thus foreboding some misfortune, as we have seen above."

* * *

During lunch we debated at some length whether we should stay overnight at Savonlinna. To do so was no part of our original plan, but in the course of the morning we had learned that the Helsinki Ballet was to perform that evening in the main Castle courtyard. Indeed, we could hardly have overlooked the fact, as the stage had already been erected and the place was cluttered up with props. To stay or not to stay? Torn in two we hesitated, then, fearing we might lose our rooms if we failed to turn up when expected, we abandoned the idea. In retrospect, I think we were probably wise because, although I never succeeded in seeing the ballet in Finland, I never heard much that was good of the dancing.

We left for Punkaharju in the early afternoon, heading southwards down the Pihlajavesi—which means, in English, Rowan Water. The small steamer in which we found ourselves was a great improvement on the *Heinävesi II*, because none of the upper deck was devoted to cabins and we enjoyed an unrestricted view over the lake. Like its name, this lake was charming. Wide and open at the start, the farther we went the more densely peppered with islands it became, until the concentration was greater than any we had yet seen. In and out we went, threading our way along channels that were often so narrow that poles had been implanted in the mud to indicate the deep water. And by this I do not mean that an occasional pole marked a mud-bank, but that our channel was picked out by them as if it had been a *slalom* course.

Towards evening we chugged slowly to our destination.

Punkaharju is a ridge of rock, some five miles long and in places no more than six yards wide, which projects southwards from quite a large island. Photographs taken from the air show a sinuous line of tree-clad rock that resembles an uncoiled python of gigantic proportions; a python, moreover, that has just swallowed a big meal, as part of the way along its serpentine course is a large, irregular bulge. This ridge and the nearby islands have been made into a national park because the region is considered one of the most beautiful in the country, and so it is, for unlike many freaks of Nature, this fantastic breakwater is as beautiful as it is curious.

The Hotel Finlandia, where our rooms were booked, was built on the island at the northern end of the ridge and turned out to be the best part of a mile from the landing stage. As no one had thought to warn us of this, we were slightly disconcerted to find on arrival that there were no buildings of any sort to be seen. Nor, by the time we had collected our scattered wits, was there anyone of whom to ask the way, as the few passengers who had disembarked with us had disappeared rapidly into the woods, leaving us standing alone on the dock. No porter from the hotel had come to meet the boat, no arrow even indicated the way we ought to go, so we sat down beside our suitcases to discuss our next move. In the end I went in search of the hotel, while Grania mounted guard over our bags, which were too heavy for us to carry any distance in comfort. But this precaution was scarcely necessary, as the Finns pride themselves, quite justifiably, on their honesty.

The path I selected wound upwards through the trees to a State hotel, but I did not know this at the time. I only knew that after about ten minutes I came to a long flight of concrete steps at the top of which was a building that had all the attributes of a seaside boarding-house; prams, toys and children's litter were scattered wholesale, but of charm there was none. My heart sank. Was this the much-vaunted Finlandia? I went inside and poked my nose into several rooms before finding anyone at all. Oddly enough, though there was every sign of habitation, there was none of inhabitants. At length, in the third or fourth room into which I looked, I found a man. He looked exceedingly surprised to see me, and did not understand much of what I tried to say, but the word "Finlandia" went home and, with much gesticulation, he had soon put me on my way. I had not gone far before I met the Finlandia's porter on his way to the dock with a barrow, so I sat down and waited for Grania, who joined me in a short while, and we strolled on together. Our path led us to a narrow footbridge across an inlet—a delightful backwater strewn with white water-lilies, that appeared to be growing wild, but which, I think, must at one time have been cultivated. As they looked incredibly beautiful, and as water-lilies are among my favourite flowers,

I was quite naturally entranced by them and predisposed to think well of the Finlandia.

The hotel, when at last we found it, stood about fifty yards from the lakeside and enjoyed an unimpeded view of the ridge and the islands across the bay. It was a pleasant place and we spent several very happy days there, basking in the sunshine, rowing on the lake and swimming in the cool, mirror-clear water. It was a simple matter to find secluded spots in which to laze; the sun shone, the water was delicious and the air was saturated with pine. In no time at all we became nudists with all the propensities of lizards: a taste for warm rocks, a tendency to scuttle at strange noises and, if my nose is anything to go by, to shed our skins.

The surrounding trees had all been carefully thinned, which meant that the pines were exceptionally tall and straight and so regularly spaced that they cast a lattice-work of shadow on the floor of the forest. The effect was curiously sophisticated and very beautiful, but though I gazed fascinated at the regular and intricate light patterns, they remained for me always more of a picture than a reality—a sun-drenched landscape that cried out to be perpetuated by an Impressionist, but none the less a landscape that had lost something of its soul, perhaps because it was so tidy and so strangely empty of wild life. Certainly I never caught even a fleeting glimpse of the smallest of wild animals.

As a hotel the Finlandia had points. We had a very pleasant double room, where hot water—always rare in Finland—gushed out of the cold tap as well as the hot. But the place was not really homely, although more so than most Finnish hotels. This is because no Finn thinks of a hotel as of a holiday home; for that he has his cabin in the woods. Hotels are primarily for passing tourists and in consequence they suffer in atmosphere if not in comfort. The Finlandia's sitting-room felt unlived-in, and the dining-room had the impersonal atmosphere that is inseparable from ordering *à la carte* and paying cash. Long as we might for inclusive terms, we could not get them and had to resign ourselves to long-drawn-out meals and carrying money.

A short distance away from the Finlandia was Runeberg's Hill, so called because the view, which it commands along the ridge, is said to have inspired the poet to write the poem which he entitled "The Fifth of July." This poem is one of a collection of narrative poems dealing with incidents in the Russian War of 1808 and 1809, known as *The Songs of Ensign Stål*. Every Finnish child is familiar with these songs, which take the place held here by the works of such poets as Newbolt, Campbell and Kipling.

Unfortunately, any attempt on my part to comment on Runeberg's work must be presumptuous, as the quality of the Swedish in which he wrote is something which I am quite unable to appreciate. Suffice it to say that such English translations as I have read do not inspire me to rate his genius anything like as highly as do his compatriots, to whom he is a poet of the first rank and by whom he is revered, not only for his verse, but also for the profound influence which he had on the nationalist movement, into which he inculcated the idea of Finland as a separate nation—a fatherland—and in so doing gave to the country its national anthem:

> "Our land, our land, our fatherland,
> Sound loud, O name of worth!
> No mount that meets the heaven's band
> No hidden vale, no wave-washed strand,
> Is loved as is our native North,
> Our own forefathers' earth."

This poem, which goes on through eleven verses, was first set to music by Frederic Paucius, and his setting remains, in the face of considerable competition, the most popular. It was sung for the first time in 1848 by the students of Helsinki University at their May Day festival.

* * *

We left Punkaharju very early in the morning *en route* for Koli via Joensuu and Savonlinna. This time we went by train as far as Savonlinna, where we once more arrived in time for breakfast.

Sitting over our coffee in the Tott, we discussed the problem of the moment; how could we reserve sleepers from Joensuu to Helsinki on the night train that left in exactly one week's time? It had to be done at once, if at all, because it was the day on which the sleepers were released, and they were always so much in demand. The obvious solution—to get the hotel porter to telephone to Joensuu to make the reservations for us—was no good at all. We had already tried, and failed signally to make him understand a word we said. Then Grania had a brainwave.

"I know," she announced jubilantly. "The Captain."

"Who?" I responded dumbly.

"The Captain of the *Heinävesi II.* I know she's alongside, because I saw her. I'll go and ask him to help." And off she went, armed with a pencil and paper.

About twenty minutes later she returned triumphant, with all that we wished to convey to the hotel porter neatly written out in Finnish. The rest was easy.

Once again our boat did not leave until early afternoon, so we spent the morning strolling round the town. On our wanderings we came to an ugly modern church, outside which was a statue of a kneeling warrior. It was Wäino Aaltonen's Independence War Memorial, and as a sample of his art I thought it very interesting. I could see in it none of the deep humanity that characterises his Kivi, nor yet any of the undeniable charm of his Marjatta—a mythical figure from the Kalevala who holds high her infant son. Confronted by it, I felt rather as I do when faced by such works as Epstein's Genesis. I neither liked the statue of the warrior nor understood it, but that must be my loss, as Aaltonen's genius is as unquestionable as that of Epstein.

We returned to the hotel at midday to find that the porter had not yet got an answer from Joensuu, and in the end we had to leave without it. Poor porter! How glad he must have been to see the last of us. We had just left the dining-room after lunch, and were standing in the main entrance hall, when Grania's swing-bag knocked our precious glass butter jar, containing quite half our fortnight's ration, out of my hands. The day was hot and the butter in it very soft. The glass smashed into smithereens; butter and splinters flew all over the beautifully polished floor beside his desk and he, kind man that he was, was more sympathetic than put out.

Somewhat dashed by this catastrophe, we sauntered down to the steamer that was to take us to Joensuu—our next port of call on our journey northwards to Koli. As far as we could see, its name, the *Orivesi I*, was the only thing which distinguished it from the *Heinävesi II*, and, what is more, both steamers left Savonlinna together, steamed in line ahead round the castle and continued for the first hour to follow the same course.

Leaning on the rail, Grania and I looked for the last time at Olavinlinna and, as we looked, it seemed as if the afternoon sunshine had cast a spell upon it. The three great towers shimmered in the bright light; the guardian stream flowed swiftly and silently past and the boatman, as though held in an enchanted sleep, still sunned himself upon the Castle steps.

In essence, the trip to Joensuu was very similar to that between Kuopio and Savonlinna, although it was not quite so beautiful. Similar, too, was our time of arrival and, just as Savonlinna had been a stepping-stone on the way to Punkaharju, so Joensuu was one on our way to Koli, which we aimed at reaching the same evening.

To do this we had to choose between going the whole way from Joensuu to Koli by bus or making the journey by train and boat. After some deliberation, we decided to go by rail and return by road and, as the train did not leave until the late afternoon, we had a whole day in Joensuu before us.

Our first object was to get rid of our bags, and the obvious course seemed to be to lodge them at the station. There were no taxis to meet the boat, but we found a horse-drawn barrow with an amiable driver who seemed to be on the look out for people like us. On to this we scrambled with our luggage. It was really no more than a costermonger's cart, and we sat on the floor at the back and dangled our legs over the edge while the pony trotted briskly to the station. It was no great distance, but the driver—amiable as ever—charged us three times the normal taxi fare and we, knowing no better at the time, paid up without demur.

Joensuu is not a very interesting small town. Compared with Kajaani, Kuopio or Savonlinna, it has not much history, being altogether modern and, like so many modern towns, laid out like a chess-board. Such interest as there was centred for me round the Town Hall—because, like Helsinki Railway Station, it is the work of Eliel Saarinen—and Yrjö Liipola's 1918 War Memorial, which stands in Independence Park. This statue is as unlike the kneeling warrior at Savonlinna as it is possible for a statue to be. Conceived and executed on classical lines, the lithe figure it depicts radiates freedom, and as a memorial to those who fell for independence it seemed to me an unqualified success.

* * *

The train that was to take us to Vuonislahti in time to catch the evening boat to Koli left Joensuu in the late afternoon and reached Vuonislahti at about seven o'clock. There quite a number of people got out, all of whom must, I think, have been bound for Koli, or at any rate for destinations on the opposite shore of the lake, for they all promptly turned their backs on the village and made off rapidly in the direction of the water and, presumably, the landing-stage. A hasty glance round revealed that there were no porters, so we picked up our bags and followed them along a narrow track, across an open field and on into the forest beyond. Puffing and panting, we lugged our heavy cases along, but try as we might to keep up, we had soon lost sight of the party. Then, to make matters worse, the boat hooted ominously in the distance. How far away was it? Would it wait for stragglers? Our path wound in and out among the trees seemingly endlessly. I measured the distance afterwards on a map and it was only about three-quarters of a mile, but it was the longest three-quarters I ever walked. And as I walked, I reflected, not for the first time, that journeying in post-war Finland was not a bed of roses. Ever after, when travelling there I have, when possible, limited myself to a rucksack.

Suddenly round a bend we came upon a large launch that was waiting for us. It was already crowded with passengers, but a few people moved up and made room for us to step on board, and barely had we done so than it cast off and headed westward across the Pielisjärvi.

This lake runs rather over sixty miles from north to south and is, at its broadest, only twenty-five miles wide. Along its western shore stretches a low ridge of hills—low, that is, by our standards, for Ukko-Koli, the highest peak in this ridge, is the highest in all south Finland. It rises between 1,100 and 1,200 feet above sea-level, and nestling some hundred feet below its summit is the Upper Koli Inn, to which we were going.

In rather less than an hour we had reached the far shore, where a lorry, filled with schoolroom benches, was waiting to carry us and our luggage up the hill to the inn, or rather to the foot of a steep flight of concrete steps that led upwards from a small plateau to the main entrance.

Everything turned out just as the young man in the tourist office had predicted. Once there, we had no difficulty in getting accommodation and were soon comfortably installed in a fair-sized double room with a beautiful view.

We never discovered whether the hotel was really filled to capacity. It had thirty-one bedrooms—some of which were undoubtedly double ones—but there never seemed as many as thirty-one guests about the place, unless it were in the dining-room, where they could not all be relied on to be residents. It was a pleasant dining-room with large windows overlooking the lake. Each table was decorated with a miniature flag. On the sideboard was a wide selection and in front of Grania and me the Union Jack. I believe all Scandinavian countries indulge in this practice; it creates a bright splash of colour and helps to gloss over the prevalent lack of flowers in wintertime, while in addition it helps the hotel guests to place each other at a glance. Not but that we had plenty of time to stare, for the service was so slow that to get a meal of any sort required the patience of Job.

The waitresses were all dressed in their national costumes: long-sleeved blouses, tightly fitting bodices, aprons and full, striped skirts. The effect was gay and slightly Tyrolean. Colour schemes were many and varied, but the material from which these garments were made was always heavy and warm. The weather being far from cold we felt sorry for the girls; these clothes must have been irksome to wear, especially in and out of a hot kitchen, but they did not appear to mind at all. Though exasperatingly slow at their job, they were a cheerful lot, and I think the probability is that they were all amateurs. They may well have been undergraduates. Before the war it was very usual for language students to spend their summer vacation waiting on foreign tourists, and at different times both Toini and Heljä had been waitresses at Koli; but as none of the girls we came across were in any sense linguists, we were never able to find out much about them.

After we had eaten we climbed several more flights of concrete steps, this time from the inn to the mountain-top, and there on the bare rocky summit above tree-level we looked northwards and southwards along the Pielisjärvi.

I doubt if it is possible to do justice to the view on which we gazed that evening because so much of its beauty was intangible—a thing of atmosphere and above all of serenity. Beneath us lay the lake; its surface calm and unruffled and its shores fringed by an infinity of small bays and inlets, while alongside the low ridge of tree-clad hills reached out into the distance. There were splashes of clear leaf green in the forest; there were stretches of golden sand at the water's edge; there were bare rocky headlands and smooth rounded islands. The lake threw back a thousand mirror-clear reflections and, once again, there was a sense of immeasurable distance. It was a scene of supreme loveliness, for in the light there was that indescribable something that is occasionally found in a boy's treble voice—a transcending, limitless purity.

It was too good to last. The next day the weather broke, the clouds came down and a dense white mist reduced the seemingly boundless visibility to a matter of yards. Then for a while it rained in a steady downpour that transformed the tree-clad world into a place of almost submarine beauty. Everywhere it was damp, dank and dripping, while on the floor of the forest the pallid lichen ran riot, gleaming exultingly in the moisture.

After a day of rain the weather began to clear, although for some time the sky remained overcast and thin wisps of cloud still hung at low level, as if entangled in the pines. It was manifestly weather for walking, so Grania and I set out to explore the numerous footpaths that led along the range, meandered down the hillside or skirted the lake. Our first expedition was along the ridge, where we wandered from peak to peak down a thickly wooded trail that led by sheltered stages from one viewpoint to the next. One minute the forest hemmed us in, the next the trees parted to disclose a widespread view across the lake—a view from which all serenity had vanished, giving place to dramatic lighting effects and a lowering sky.

Then came the day when a marked improvement in the weather led us to roam further afield. For some time past a small, mushroom-like island with a sandy beach and a smooth canopy of pines had been attracting us and we determined to row there. But we never achieved our objective, although we did get as far as hiring a boat. The fact was that it was not a very good boat. No sooner were we well out on the lake than it sprang a leak. As we had nothing with which to bail, we made straight for the nearest land, our intention being to pull up the boat, empty it, plug the hole and proceed on our way. But this was more easily said than done. The approach to the shore turned out to be rocky and shallow and it was quite impossible to beach the boat. Worse still, the boat was extremely heavy and our joint efforts to lift it failed utterly. So in the end we had recourse to laboriously piling stones beneath its stern until the leak was clear of the water. This took such a long time that

Olavinlinna

View from the Bell Tower, Olavinlinna

Koli, between storms

we were forced to abandon all thought of reaching our island and had to content ourselves with lazing away the afternoon in the nearest sheltered cove. This was pleasant enough, the only trouble being that the cove really was sheltered so we never noticed what was happening to the weather until—too late—we started to make for home. As we pulled clear of the headland we were met by a strong wind that had already whipped the surface of the lake into a frenzy of small white horses.

I do not think that we had more than a mile to pull, but I have to admit that Grania did it all. It was not that I did not offer to help, but rather that my offer was flatly rejected. Truth to tell, I believe that Grania rather enjoyed her Grace Darling act. Anyway, the only response I got to my well-meaning if tentative suggestion that I should row a bit was a slightly deprecating "You do want to get there, don't you?" I knew all too well what she meant—my right arm always seems to pull much harder than my left and I habitually row round in circles. So I sat tight at the tiller, with one eye cocked on the far shore and the other on the leak and kept up a flow of maddeningly helpful advice and encouragement.

But although we reached our destination in safety, I had not yet done with that leak, for on returning to Kajaani, I started to tell one of my classes of engineers all about it, and in doing so rashly decided to expatiate on the word "leak." All went well while I dealt with taps, official secrets and hot-water bottles—these latter are almost unheard of in Finland, as also are open windows in wintertime—and in fact it was not until I ill-advisedly added, "And then there's a vegetable, a bulblike affair that looks rather like an elongated onion," that I got into any difficulties. Surrounded by a circle of blank faces, I tried again. "The Welsh dote on them; they're their national emblem." But still I cut no ice at all. Finally, one of them looked up "leak" in the dictionary and remarked, "That's funny; it isn't here." A statement which, to my shame be it said, I not only checked, but endorsed. And there we left the subject and I cannot say that I gave it another thought until the next lesson, when Yrjö arrived with a grin that stretched from ear to ear. "I've found the leek," he announced triumphantly. "We know it quite well, but . . ." Whereupon I devoted fully ten minutes to celebrated English men and women who could not spell.

* * *

It was on Saturday that the peace of the hotel was shattered. Throughout the day truckload after truckload of trippers arrived. They swarmed over the ridge and down to the lakeside, and all sense of privacy vanished. Not that this worried them at all; like many Bank Holiday-makers at home, they seemed positively to enjoy being one of a crowd, for, paradoxically, the Finns, who are by nature unsociable, set great store by human companionship. I used often to watch the people who used the local buses. On getting in, no man ever sat on an empty seat if he could sit beside somebody else, and it often happened that two enormous men would sit side by side on a minute seat when there were plenty of empty ones to be had. But sitting side by side was as far as they went; once ensconced they rarely spoke to each other—a state of affairs that I can only suppose springs from the lonely isolation in which so many of them are forced to live throughout the winter months. After all, while it would be strange if the long, monotonous hours of darkness were to promote lively conversationalists, it is in no sense surprising that companionship should have a scarcity value and be sought, as it were, by instinct.

In any case, as far as sightseeing goes, the Finns appear to favour doing it in a mass, and for one night Koli became a Bedlam. It was lucky that the evening was fine, for it was no part of the trippers' programme to take rooms. The darkness lasted at most for one hour and the nights were still warm; the people simply encamped round the hotel. They were not a noisy crowd as crowds go; nevertheless, when Grania and I eventually dropped off to sleep, it was to the tune of a mouth-organ and the hum of conversation beneath our window.

But if we dropped off to a mouth-organ we awoke to greater things. Through my dreams I heard Grania mutter, "No, it can't be . . . it simply isn't true," and then I heard music. Someone, several people in fact, were playing the Norwegian National Anthem and not playing it in tune. We got up and leaned out of the window. High up on a pinnacle of rock, a brass band was blowing fit to burst its lungs, and all around little groups of campers were sitting up eating their breakfast out of suitcases and consuming quantities of sweet, fizzy drinks.

All through Sunday there was no escaping the crowd. It simply milled around the mountain and went on milling until the lorries returned in the evening and took everyone away;

then, once more, all was peace and tranquillity. We ourselves did not stay much longer, but long enough for me to introduce Grania to the *sauna*. It was not an ideal *sauna*, because it was at the top of the hill and too far from the lake to make swimming from it possible, but it served its purpose, and had one feature that I had not met before—a washerwoman. I am told that these women are common enough in public *saunas*, but this is hearsay: I never went to one to see for myself.

The evening before we left the inn at Koli, the topic of winter sports cropped up. We were standing by the reception desk choosing picture postcards when the girl on duty happened to remark: "You should come to Koli for the ski-ing in winter."

"Rather a lot of trees, aren't there?" I hazarded, fearful that I should be considered to lack *sisu*, the virtue above all others on which the Finns pride themselves, and which is, in fact, a slightly irrational blend of grit and obstinacy.

"Oh yes," she answered cheerfully. "It's very dangerous. We have many accidents. Last year a man broke his leg down by the lake, so the doctor put on his skis and set off down the hill to help him. But he never got there; he broke his own leg on the way."

We left by bus from the bottom of the concrete steps. This was where the bus started its journey, and in this we were lucky, as it meant that we got seats. Once under way we should not have had a hope, as it got rapidly fuller and fuller, and if anyone imagines that by travelling by bus in Finland you can see the country, I can only say that it is a delusion. All I could see was a tarpaulin mackintosh that was strapped to the rucksack of a man who was wedged tightly in front of me. It did not matter that the bus was full; every time we stopped there was a tremendous shove and somebody else got in. I am not exaggerating at all when I say that I have never experienced anything like it, because the Finnish bus companies insist that everyone shall be inside the bus, so that there is none of the hanging out of windows and sitting on mudguards so prevalent in southern climes. I once went in a Greek bus where the majority of the passengers got in and out by the windows, and where many travelled on the roof and the running boards; and I have even been in a Chinese bus with a leaking radiator where, if I remember rightly, a small boy sat astride the bonnet with a watering-can and filled it up as we went along. We proceeded at a snail's pace, and to while away the time a dear old Chinaman who was sitting beside me offered to share his pipe. But in this bus there was no room to smoke and barely room to breathe.

How we made Joensuu was something of a miracle, as round every corner the springs creaked ominously, but reach Joensuu we did, to find another miracle awaiting us at the station—our sleepers. Everything had gone according to plan, but if anyone asks me what the country was like between Koli and Joensuu, I can only reply that I have no firsthand knowledge on the subject.

* * *

Early the next afternoon I drove with Grania to Helsinki Airport and there bade her a hasty goodbye, for she was swept through the barrier with something of a panic rush and I was not allowed inside. Oppressed with a gnawing sense of anti-climax, I returned alone to Helsinki to while away the few days that remained until Michael should arrive.

For me it was not a very good time to be in Helsinki. Almost everyone whom I knew was away and I was thrown very much on my own society. However, I had plenty to keep me occupied. In the first place, I had to see about the police permits without which Michael and I could not go to Lapland. I had applied for these some time before, filling up, when I did so, all the requisite forms, but as yet I had seen no sign of the permits. The time, I felt, was ripe to hurry them along so, hoping that they would be given to me in person, I paid a visit to the Special Police Headquarters. I came away empty-handed, assured, but not reassured, that they would arrive in time, and once again it was borne in on me that you cannot hustle a Finn. Finally, owing to the good offices of a clerk from the Council, they disgorged them at the very last minute—that is, late on the afternoon before we were due to leave.

Then, in addition to the matter of permits, there was the question of Finnish painting about which I was well aware that I knew less than nothing. Impressions had been crowding in upon me and now, if ever, seemed the moment to co-ordinate them. Indeed the time for this was well overdue, for ever since my arrival the art-consciousness of the people had been making itself apparent. In the homes of my friends bare walls were never seen; the invariable tendency was to hang too many rather than too few pictures. Everyone who could afford to buy paintings bought them, and I had the feeling that for an aspiring young artist Finland must be paradise.[1]

Perhaps the most noticeable feature of all was the amount of contemporary portraits that were to be seen. Everyone, or so it seemed, who had money to spare, had themselves and their children painted. It was easy to see that art in Finland was a vital force and worthy of attention. What traditions lay behind it? To what heights did it soar? With time on my hands, I set myself to find out.

The first essential when visiting Finnish art galleries and museums is to discover when they open, as the hours in which the public is admitted tend to be very short. Many do not open until midday and others shut as early as 3 p.m. while, as far as I can remember, the Museum at Kuopio, into which we never managed to penetrate, opened only from 11 a.m. to 1 p.m. As most Finns lunch between these hours, this was something of a challenge—food versus uplift.

To begin with I found these short hours very frustrating. I was continually being foiled by notices that said "Shut," in front of which I would stand aggrieved and incredulous. It seemed unbelievable that such should be the case when the daylight was almost perpetual, but the Athenæum Art Gallery in Helsinki was less obstructionist than most. For six days a week it stayed open from 11 a.m. to 4 p.m.

The cream of Finnish art is to be found in the Athenæum and the paintings are, to say the least of it, revealing. I have read somewhere that the National Museum in Helsinki "teaches the world about Finland rather than Finland about the world." The same might be said of the Athenæum, where Finnish painting and sculpture are abundantly represented, but where the collection of foreign works is negligible. This means that the average Finn has very few means of comparison to go on when judging any work of art, and probably accounts for the prevailing lack of discrimination to be found among many who take a geniune interest in pictures.

[1] "As compensation for all its bad consequences, the war caused a sudden temporary rise in the financial circumstances of artists. During the scarcity there was practically nothing else to buy but books and paintings and sculptures. The years of the crisis saw a heavy boom in the art market. Nearly all pictures were sold, and as a result of this the less gifted amateurs also began to think of themselves as masters. Now, when the normal times—with low prices and few buyers of art—have returned, we are able to see what is left of that multitude of wartime artists." "Post-war Painting and Sculpture in Finland," by Sakarai Saarikivi, *The Studio*, June, 1950.

Apart from the early church murals, Finnish painting grew up under the influence of Sweden and Germany and is not of great moment in its initial stages. In fact, it was not until the end of the last century that it became interesting. At that time—about 1870—the sphere of influence switched to Paris, and to study in Paris became the goal of all Finnish art students. There they came into direct contact with impressionism, the new realism and the doctrine of open-air painting, all of which were revolutionary. To the new realism and to open-air painting they took like ducks to water and, returning to their native land, started painting peasant types and country scenes with avidity. Pure impressionism, however, seems to have appealed to them less which, in a way, is odd, for their country is peculiarly luminous and the people themselves apt to make a fetish of daylight. Pondering on this strange inconsistency, I have sometimes wondered whether the early Finnish traditions of black magic and mystery which colour their literature, have not also influenced their painting, causing them to eschew the more lavish use of light.

The leading painters of this era, and indeed of all time in Finland, were Albert Edelfeld (1854–1905) and Akseli Gallen-Kallela (1865–1931), both of whom were swept into the vortex of nationalism from which, in Finland, there is no escape. Whether the artist be a painter, a sculptor or a musician, all turn at some point in their careers to nationalist themes for their inspiration.

In this line Edelfeld, who was a versatile artist, an idealist and a prolific painter, has left, among other things, a series of black-and-white illustrations of Runeberg's *Ensign Stål*, as well as many large historical canvasses. But it is chiefly as a portraitist that he is renowned, and to the outside world he is best known for his portrait of Pasteur which hangs in the Louvre. His works have a calm, unruffled quality that must, I think, make them easy to live with, but his happiest achievements are his pictures of children. Just inside the Athenæum is a painting of three small boys sailing their boats in a seaside pool. The canvas is drenched in sunlight and the whole composition such a joy to look at that, while I dismissed as too facile for my taste many of Edelfeld's paintings, I returned to this one again and again.

Gallen-Kallela is, however, the dominant figure among Finnish painters. He is also the Finnish painter *par excellence.*

His peasant heads are those of genuine Finnish peasants, dour, stolid and accustomed to battling with the unyielding earth, while his landscapes and black-and-white drawings are not only superb, but they too are Finnish first and last. Nevertheless, to the casual visitor he is pre-eminently the painter of a series of large pictures and murals depicting scenes from the Kalevala. These pictures are essentially illustrations, but illustrations of a very arresting kind. Furthermore, you cannot escape them; they are reproduced in large numbers and are almost as ubiquitous as the legends they illustrate. Personally, I would not, if I could, divorce them from their context, as they have a distinctiveness that makes the Kalevala live for me in a way no translation ever could. Viewed objectively, I know that they are colourful works of a monumental nature, some of which are highly stylised. But the objective approach is exceedingly difficult; the more stylised they are, the better I like them, and the more my critical faculties become enmeshed in the subject-matter.

From the Athenæum I carried away names and impressions of many artists: Pekka Halonen, Helena Schjerfbeck, Eero Järnefelt and Hugo Simberg, to mention only a few. I saw there the work of great portrait painters and, I think, even greater landscape painters, many of whose works speak to me of the country in a way that nothing else can do. A photograph of the Finnish countryside lacks specific character; the trees and the water might be any trees and any water anywhere in the north, but the trees of Pekka Halonen and Gallen-Kallela are Finnish, to the exclusion of all else. Deeply nationalist in spite of themselves, they could be part of no other landscape.

* * *

Michael arrived in due course and we spent one full day together in Helsinki before leaving for the north. There was still a good deal to do and even more to discuss for, though I had done my best to get everything organised, there were some things which we had deliberately left to talk over together. What, for instance, were we going to do after leaving Lapland on or about July 25th? We should have almost a week in hand before Michael's holiday was over and we were due in Stockholm, and the all-important question was: By what route should we travel south and where should we break our journey? Having discussed the matter at some length, we found that we both favoured going via Skibotn and Narvik, but we did not know whether this was feasible because nobody seemed able to tell us whether there was any form of transport between Kilpisjärvi on the Finnish frontier and Skibotn at the head of the Lyngen Fjord. To get from Helsinki to Kilpisjärvi and from Skibotn to Stockholm appeared to be relatively plain sailing; but between Kilpisjärvi and Skibotn there was a gap, a distance of some thirty odd miles that had to be negotiated somehow. Mike, who had been toying with the idea of going this way for some time past, had tried in vain to find out in London how it could be done; it now remained to see if anyone in Helsinki could tell us if it were possible. On inquiry, we were told that our best hope of success lay in consulting the Finnish Tourist Association, so together we set out to pay them a visit. Not that I personally was very hopeful; my past experiences of Finnish travel bureaux had undermined my confidence; but the Finnish Tourist Association was, it appeared, quite different. It specialised in supplying information and running hotels, but it did not undertake to make bookings of any sort.

We found their offices high up, overlooking the station square, and put our problem to them. The girl whom we consulted was most helpful. Having confirmed our suspicions that there was, in fact, no form of organised transport down the valley, she volunteered the information that a Norwegian named Beck made the trip from Skibotn to Kilpisjärvi once every week with a lorry, and added that she thought that if we were willing to fall in with his plans he would give us a lift.

We now had all the information that we needed, as Eero had been at great pains to map out our journey through Lapland and had supplied me with all the necessary data before I left Kajaani. The only question still outstanding—whether we could stay at Pallastunturi—would have to wait until we reached Muonio, where a friend of Eero's would be able to tell us the position. The difficulty was that the hotel—an isolated building in the middle of a national park—had been completely destroyed by the Germans, and nobody in the south knew how far the building of the new one had advanced, or if there was even as much as a *sauna* there in which we could sleep.

Our last remaining problem was that of luggage. Everyone had advised us to take all the food we should need, because no one in Lapland was, at that time, in a position to cater for visitors. I had warned Michael and he had arrived from England laden with tea, coffee and tinned food, but we still had to collect our perishable rations and, of these, bread was our chief difficulty. In the end we decided to chance getting it as we went along; a fortnight's supply would be altogether too bulky for us to carry. After all, we had to strike a nice balance between what we needed and what we could carry comfortably in the way of food, clothes, maps, mosquito oil, etc. Mike's problems, however, were nothing to mine, for he only had to cater for Lapland, whereas I planned to spend three weeks in Sweden after he had gone home and there seemed little in common between the clothes that I needed for trekking through Lapland and the relatively tidy ones that I should want in Stockholm. In the end we filled three small suitcases, a large rucksack and a haversack; the cases were to be abandoned at Muonio, while we went on foot to Pallastunturi, and retrieved when we returned there—as return we must—to pick up the bus to Kilpisjärvi.

* * *

About midday on July 20th Michael and I boarded the train that was to take us to Lapland. Our immediate destination was Aavasaksa on the Torniojoki, about ten miles south of the Arctic Circle and seventy-five miles into Lapland. From there we could go no further by train, as the bridge on the line to the railhead at Kauliranta had been blown up by the retreating Germans and had not yet been repaired.

The journey from Helsinki to Aavasaksa was scheduled to take a fraction over twenty-five hours. The distance being the best part of six hundred miles, this meant an average speed of only twenty-four miles an hour—slow enough in all conscience. The day was hot, the train crowded and the journey uneventful, and although from Oulu northwards the line on the map appears to follow the coast, never once did we catch a glimpse of the sea from the train. At Haapamaki the sleeping cars were attached and not long afterwards Michael and I separated for the night. When next morning we rejoined forces he told me cheerfully that he had shared a compartment with an American journalist who had asked him if he had noticed that six wolves had just been killed at Kilpisjärvi. Of course the story was quite untrue, but, as we were eventually bound for Kilpisjärvi, I inquired with interest how he proposed that we should deal with any we might meet. He considered a moment, laughed and then answered: "I think perhaps we'd better cry wolf and run away," which, seeing how slow we both were on our feet, seemed to me a very dim outlook.

From the head of the Gulf of Bothnia the line to Aavasaksa followed the wide and fertile valley of the Torniojoki, which forms the boundary between Sweden and Finland. This valley is considered one of the most beautiful in Lapland and, in consequence, Eero had carefully planned that we should continue northwards along it by bus after leaving the train. In actual fact the successful fulfilment of all our future plans seemed to depend on our catching the bus which was timed to leave Aavasaksa for Muonio half an hour after we were due to arrive, but right from the start our plans went awry. No seats in the bus were bookable in advance and, being already full up when it arrived at Aavasaksa, it refused to take us—a serious setback in Lapland, where the bus services rarely run more than three times a week and where accommodation is so scarce as to be almost non-existent.

There was now no possible way of reaching Muonio that night. Outside the station we stood in a blaze of sunshine and debated our next move, and as we did so the bus for Rovaniemi pulled in. That clinched matters; Rovaniemi is the principal town in Lapland and our chances of getting on from there were, we surmised, a good deal better than they would be if we stayed where we were, so in we got. At best, we calculated, we should only lose one day.

Broadly speaking, our plan, as worked out by Eero, was that we should go first to Pallastunturi and then to Kilpisjärvi, after which we could either cross directly into Norway or double back on our tracks and enter Sweden by way of Karesuanto. But going to Pallastunturi meant leaving the main road and, in all probability, walking the last sixteen miles of the way, and this could not be done without first spending a night at Muonio. What we were now doing was to advance to Muonio by two sides of a triangle, of which the road up the Tornio Valley from Aavasaksa was the third.

In many ways I regret that we did not see the Tornio Valley, because, over and above its natural beauty, it has points of great interest. For one thing, it is the smuggler's dream, as almost everyone who lives along the river bank owns a boat and on either side Finns and Swedes can move freely inland for a distance of almost ten miles. Consequently, there was, and is, nothing to limit the passage of contraband except the inability of the Finns to pay for large quantities. Swedish crowns are the stumbling block; officially they are not to be had without a very good reason, and the alternative, paying the Swedes in Finnish currency, meant, at the time of which I am writing, paying five times the authorised rate. This sounds exorbitant; nevertheless, smuggling was still a profitable pursuit, and on coffee alone—the Finns being inveterate coffee-drinkers—the profit made by black-marketeers, even at this rate of exchange, was nearly 100 per cent. For a long time it was the main commodity smuggled, probably because it had the most certain market, but it was now getting harder to obtain because the Swedes had found it necessary to ration it for themselves. Even so, a good deal still seemed to seep across the border and the places in Finland where coffee could not be obtained at a price were few and far between. Needless to say, the inhabitants of the border region lived better than those of any other part of the country.

Another interesting point about the Torniojoki concerns the fishing rights. Both in Finland and in Sweden these rights belong to the State, which hires them out to professional fishermen. The proceeds are then pooled and equally divided between the Finns and the Swedes—an example of international collaboration that I am told is without parallel. As for the fishing, I believe it is excellent and that the Torniojoki is considered one of the best salmon rivers in the country, but the best of all is reputed to be the Tenojoki, an almost inaccessible stream on the Finnish-Norwegian border. The salmon fishing season lasts from May 1st to September 11th, but during the war, when food was scarce, all restrictions were lifted.

The salmon, which are plentiful, are caught with flies, trolling spoons or nets, and the largest ever landed is said to have turned the scales at 36 kilos or nearly 80 lb. Yet, to my disappointment, fresh salmon was not eaten nearly so much as the cured variety. Everywhere I was plied with the uncooked salted kind, which I did not care about at all and rarely ate. Kalle always teased me about this, attributing my aversion to the fact that he had once cautioned me that it was apt to give people worms, but, in fact, my dislike—which embraces all raw fish—long antedated his warning.

The bus to Rovaniemi left about half an hour after the one

that we should have taken to Muonio. The afternoon was hot, the flies a constant source of irritation and the road incredibly sandy. Fine particles of sand percolated through every crack and coated everyone and everything with a thin, yellow film and Mike, who insisted upon sitting beside an open window, arrived looking like a statue that had been stored for many years in the undusted vaults of the British Museum. The countryside undulated gently and monotonously and was, on the whole, dull. The trees were smaller than those to be found farther south and homesteads were few and far between. The drive took about five hours and all along the road we passed signs of the appalling devastation that the Germans had wrought.

* * *

The events immediately leading to this devastation are rather less well known than those which preceded them. It is common knowledge how the Russian invasion of Finland in November, 1939, brought about "The Winter War," because at the time it was headline news. The Allies were stagnating on the Maginot Line and the spotlight was on Finland and her heroic struggle. Expressions of sympathy and admiration were heard on all hands, but, to the intense disappointment of the Finns, they were never backed by action; the Western Powers were preoccupied with their own troubles and the Norwegians and Swedes were unco-operative. The much-talked-of expeditionary force never materialised and the Finns were left to fight alone, with the result that still to-day the word "sympathy" brings a wry smile to the face of every one of them. On March 13th, 1940, they capitulated; the Karelian Isthmus was ceded to Russia and a great wave of refugees flowed over the country.

What followed is less widely appreciated, for the focus of interest shifted to other parts of Europe, to the Far East, to North Africa and to Russia itself, and the fate of the Finns faded into the background. Consequently, few people realise that they were at war with the Soviet Union continuously from June 25th, 1941, until September 19th, 1944. The Nazi invasion of Russia had provided them with a golden opportunity to retrieve Karelia. It would have been less than human not to take it. Their intentions, however, were manifestly not aggressive; having reclaimed their own, they penetrated very little further into Russian territory. With Karelia once more in Finnish hands, the people returned to what was left of their homes, but at a cost—thereafter German troops were quartered in Northern Finland and in Lapland.

Then once more the tide turned. In April, 1944, the great Russian offensive got under way and by the beginning of September the Finns were once more forced to sue for peace. This time the Russians not only reclaimed Karelia and exchanged their base at Hanko for the Porkkala Peninsula, but they annexed the Salla District and the area round Petsamo as well and, once again, and in even greater numbers, the country was flooded with refugees. Nor was this all; before any armistice negotiations could take place, it was laid down that all diplomatic relations must be broken off with the Reich and all Germans told to leave the country by September 15th. In all, there were some 200,000 Germans in Finland, and one of the conditions exacted was that the Finns should undertake to disarm all who remained beyond the allotted span and hand them over to the Allied High Command as prisoners of war. This meant that, when on September 4th the cease-fire sounded, the Germans had just twelve days in which to withdraw from Finland.

In the south a few of them retired peacefully, but in the north it was a different story; they quite simply started to dig themselves in and the Finns were obliged to prepare to turn out their former allies—allies with whom, however, it must be said, they had never been in political sympathy. But the Finns were spared the onus of starting hostilities: twenty-four hours before the dead-line date the Germans opened fire.

The main bulk of the German troops being ensconced north of a line drawn from the Oulu River to Kuusamo, it followed that their retreat must be to Norway and that the battleground would be Lapland. The Finnish military authorities, therefore, gave the order for the evacuation of all civilians from Lapland. This was no mean undertaking. It meant the moving of some 110,000 people who were scattered over approximately 60,000 square miles of territory, in which there were only two short railways; one from Tornio to Kauliranta and the other from Kemijärvi to Kemi via Rovaniemi. For such a project the existing rolling stock was quite inadequate and so, too, was the number of motor vehicles available, for the Army's needs were very heavy and left few to spare. Nevertheless, the proclamation went out by radio, by telephone and by runners and, in some cases, took as much as five days to reach the remoter villages. The people, who were caught harvesting, abandoned their homes and took to the roads. Fifty-six thousand were given asylum in Sweden and the remainder converged on Rovaniemi, whence they entrained for the south. Incredible as it sounds, in twelve days Lapland was deserted.

The war against the Germans lasted for eight months and left behind it a trail of destruction which was certainly not limited to military objectives. The Germans scorched the land with a horrible thoroughness and, when on April 27th, 1945, the last of them crossed into Norway by way of Kilpisjärvi, 90 per cent. of all property had been destroyed.

* * *

The first relief mission to reach Lapland was organised by the Quakers. It arrived in the summer of 1945 and based itself on Rovaniemi, the obvious centre of the district from which practically every main road in Lapland radiates. With their arrival things began to hum; the Finnish genius for co-operation asserted itself; U.N.R.R.A. arrived and threw its weight into the struggle and, before long, reconstruction was in full swing. So good was the progress made that, by the time Mike and I reached Rovaniemi, the initial work had been completed, the U.N.R.R.A. Mission had left and the Quakers, prompted by the crying needs of the Karelian refugees, had moved their headquarters further South. Thus, although we were deeply shocked by the sight of the town, we did not see it at its worst, for the bulk of the débris had already been cleared away.

Our bus put us down in the main square, from which we walked to the hotel. It was not difficult to locate, as the place was so full of open spaces that it was a simple matter to pick out any new building. Practically the whole of Rovaniemi having been built of wood, the fire had done its work with ruthless efficiency and beyond the few recently constructed buildings the town was flat.

Clearly there was a tremendous amount of building still to do; and equally clearly a surprising amount had already been done. The new hotel was of concrete and had been planned on a rather grandiose scale, but it was not yet complete, and when we got there we found the management rather loath to take us in. In fact, it was only by dint of considerable persuasion and being too helplessly foreign for words that they agreed to keep us overnight. The rooms assigned to us were on the third, fourth, or even fifth floor—I cannot remember which. I only know that we climbed endlessly up a bare, dusty staircase, for, as yet, there was neither linoleum nor carpet on the floor and, naturally enough, the lift was not working. The passages, too, were in much the same plight, so we were agreeably surprised to find our rooms all but ready for occupation. That is to say, mine would have been completely ready had there been any glass in the window; as it was, it was boarded up and, despite the white nights, I could not see without the electric light. All the same, there were compensations; I had a bathroom adjoining, and into the bath ran piping hot water, so Michael and I at once set about ridding ourselves of the dust with which we were covered, and doing a little laundry into the bargain. It was just as well that we did, for at Rovaniemi we said goodbye to all such things as hot water and plumbing, at least as far as Lapland was concerned.

Clean once more, we went down to the dining-room, which was not only finished but palatial and there, although the diners in it were but a drop in the ocean, we all ate to music.

* * *

Next morning we were about betimes as, come what might, we intended to get on to the bus for Muonio which left at 9 a.m., and after hanging about for some time at the terminus, we succeeded.

Our road ran north up the valley of the Ounasjoki, and a few minutes after leaving Rovaniemi crossed the Polar Circle. The river was wide and very blue and our journey was punctuated by ferries, for the road crossed and recrossed the water at frequent intervals. These ferries took the form of wooden pontoons that were drawn from one side to the other by a man who sat astride the bulwarks and pulled on a fixed cable with a notched instrument that looked like a baseball bat. In his labours he was sometimes helped by the more energetic of his passengers, but even so the process was a slow one—so slow, in fact, that we took nearly eight hours to cover 150 miles.

Scenically, the early part of the drive was not particularly interesting, but from the human angle the whole journey was a shining example of indomitable spirit. The people of Lapland had all returned to their ruined homes and, in the straggling little villages that we passed, almost without exception, every house was brand new. From Aavasaksa to Kilpisjärvi there was nothing to choose between these villages, about whose houses there was a terrible sameness. Every one had been erected at high speed and every one was bright yellow, rectangular and devoid of all decoration. And, as if this in itself were not depressing enough, each one of these new little houses overlooked a square of blackened earth in the midst of which stood a charred brick stove and, rising to the height of two stories, a gaunt chimney stack. Impervious to fire, these mute relics were all that the flames could not burn. No effort had been made to demolish them, nor yet to turn the blackened squares of earth. While there were more important things to be done, these stark relics must stand and the ground remain in mourning; and in the meantime the stoves served very well for boiling the cauldron full of laundry.

The only weathered wooden buildings that we saw were a few hay barns that had managed to survive the destruction, and these, perhaps by contrast with the new houses, appeared far older and more top-heavy than their southern counterparts. Their bases seemed smaller and the outward splay of their walls more pronounced and, looking at them, I felt a sudden overwhelming affection for them, for they alone exuded a sense of normality. Beside them, the rectangular houses and the angular well-heads were so new, so yellow and so sharp-featured that they might have sprung direct from the pages of a geometry primer, and as I looked above the mechanism of each well—the crutch, the slim tree trunk and the pole on which the bucket was suspended—the letters, A, B, C, D seemed to hover in mid-air.

Every so often outside one of these new little houses the bus would stop for a quarter of an hour or so and the passengers would refresh themselves with berry juice, beer or *ersatz* coffee. Sometimes they bought dry-looking sandwiches or, more rarely, hard-boiled eggs, but generally they ate their own provisions.

In the late afternoon we passed through Kittila, a long, thin and straggling village that was the largest on our route. Outside the post office we pulled up and, while we were waiting, Michael drew my attention to a group of gipsies that he took for Lapps. That they were not was disappointing, because it is a fact that we travelled right through Finnish Lapland without ever seeing a Lapp, which is less remarkable than it sounds, as there are but 2,000 all told in the country.

Harri Attila, Pauli Simola, Kauko Tamminen, Eino Juntunen and Juho Jorma

Michael between two students outside the boys' tent at Pallastunturi

Kilpisjärvi

Johanneslund

They are to be found in only four areas: around Enontekiö, Inari, Utsjoki and Sodankylä and, of these, only those who live in the mountains round Enontekiö—in all about 400—are still true nomads who shepherd their reindeer all the year round. The rest have taken to living a more settled existence in villages which, as most of them combine fishing with reindeer breeding, are generally to be found near a lake or a river. They no longer move round after their herds. Instead, as soon as the calving season is over, they turn their reindeer loose to roam free until the great autumn round-up, when the animals are herded into corrals for the winter.

At the time of which I am writing, there were all told some 84,000 head of reindeer in Lapland, but of these only a quarter belonged to the Lapps themselves. This figure represents a serious drop; in 1939 the reindeer had numbered 214,000, and of these the Lapps had owned the majority. The reason for this reduction in numbers is not far to seek. Food shortage during the war had led to the killing off of many and, added to this, the Germans had systematically slaughtered all they found. What is less clear is why the proportion still remaining in Lapp hands should be so very different.

Shortly after leaving Kittila, our road left the valley of the Ounasjoki and curved westwards towards the southern extremity of the ridge of hills that runs southwards from Enontekiö. We were now climbing slowly, if imperceptibly, and very soon we found ourselves among scattered *tunturi*.[1] These *tunturi* are smooth, well-rounded hills that are girdled by trees and bare and windswept above the timber line, but their most distinctive feature is the haphazard way in which they rise up one by one out of the forest rather as islands rise out of the sea. This isolation, however, becomes less and less pronounced as you approach the mountainous border country, until eventually they merge with each other like any other foothills.

Ten miles short of Muonio we passed through the hamlet of Särkijärvi, where a police control stopped the bus and examined everyone's travel permit. Here, had there been anywhere to stay, Mike and I would have left the bus, because it is at this point that the road branches off to Pallastunturi. The very sight of this road was tantalising. It seemed so hard to have to go on to Muonio only to double back on our tracks, especially

[1] The word *tunturi* is a local one and is defined in the dictionary as an "Arctic hill" or "fell."

M

as, by rights, at just about this time we should have been arriving at Pallastunturi, hot and dishevelled after a sixteen-mile trudge. As things were, however, it was far too late in the day to embark on such a walk, even had we known for certain that we could be put up when we got there. So we carried on in the bus to Muonio, determined to seek out and consult with Eero's friend, Nimismies[1] Vuorio, about our future plans.

* * *

Muonio proved to be another long, straggling village. The Post Office was at its southern end, and there, together with the last of its mail, the bus put us down. It now only remained for us to locate the lodging-house Olos where our rooms had been booked. As no one building within sight seemed more likely than another to be it, we went into the Post Office and inquired where it was. Thereupon a pleasant-faced girl left off sorting the mail to point out a ramshackle building on the top of a grassy knoll some 400 yards away. It must have been one of the very few old buildings to survive the war and was certainly a makeshift. The original Olos, like so many other houses, had been razed to the ground. Picking up our bags, we made our way towards it. At sight of us the proprietor, a somewhat scruffy-looking individual, appeared anything but pleased, and proceeded to let off a spate of Finnish that culminated in his producing a greasy dog-eared little notebook to prove—that which we already knew only too well—that we should have been there the night before. It was more than clear that he was not anxious to keep us, but we stood our ground and eventually he showed us into a stuffy little room containing two narrow iron beds, made up with paper sheets, a gimcrack washstand and a very rickety table.

Any hopes we may have entertained of getting a cooked meal in Muonio were rapidly dispelled, but the lodging-house proprietor's wife took pity on us and made some of our own coffee for us, and we dipped into our stores for the rest. No one could have called it a lucky dip; on the way we had bought—with what we had fondly believed to be considerable forethought—some hard-boiled eggs, but now, as I put my hand into the sack, it was all too apparent that they had not been hard-boiled. Jerseys, towels, camp equipment—everything was covered by congealed or congealing egg. Michael fetched some

[1] *Nimismies* is the title given to the administrative chief of a district.

water from the well and we scrubbed our belongings as well as we could, but we failed to salvage much for a meal and were obliged to broach a tin of corned beef.

It was about seven in the evening by the time we had finished and started in search of Nimismies Vuorio. The place name "Muonio" being apparently all the postal address he needed, we had not much to go by; so, with his name written on a slip of paper, we walked down the road showing it, with much gesticulation, to every passer-by, until eventually we ran him to earth in his office at some distance from the main road. It was nearly six weeks since he had received Eero's letter and booked our room for us, and in the interval he had obviously forgotten our existence. However, at the mention of Eero's name, light began to dawn, and by the time he had made a prolonged examination of our passports and permits I think he had us placed.

Our conversation was limited and carried on in very rudimentary German. Nevertheless, it produced results that were entirely satisfactory. To begin with, we learned that a telephone —always a first essential in Finland—had already been installed at Pallastunturi. This made everything much easier, and we forthwith prevailed on Nimismies Vuorio to ring up and find out if we could stay there. We were lucky; the answer was in the affirmative. A party of architectural students from the Technical School in Helsinki were staying there and working on the new hotel that was to replace the one the Germans had destroyed. These students declared themselves delighted to have us, provided that we brought our own food and did not object to sleeping in the *sauna*. This, in itself, was good news, but there was better to follow, for Nimismies Vuorio puckered up his brow and said with an air of deep concentration, "*Morgen es kommt ein Lastbil.*" We were momentarily foxed, then Michael brightly volunteered the information that the Swedes and the Norwegians shortened the word "automobile" to "bil"—the rest, even with our limited German, was easy. By dint of further perseverance, we discovered that the so-called "*Lastbil*" was bringing a couple of students down to Särkijärvi to catch the bus that would be dropping us there shortly after 5 a.m., and that by getting a lift back with it we should reach Pallastunturi at a very early hour—an altogether satisfactory state of affairs, as we should be saved a day's walk and so could get back on to our original schedule.

Transport having been duly organised, our minds turned to bread, or rather lack of it, and once again Nimismies Vuorio proved himself a friend in need. He rang up the baker, explained our predicament and asked him to reopen for us; which he very kindly agreed to do.

Thereupon, with many expressions of gratitude, we said goodbye and set out in search of the baker's shop, which turned out to be a general store. There we bought a lot of hard bread of a biscuit-like texture. At this late hour it was all that we could get but, as it was less bulky and kept better than the ordinary rye bread, we came to the conclusion that it was all for the best—provided, of course, that our teeth would stand up to it. With it we returned triumphantly to the Olos, where we once more sorted out our belongings and, not without considerable argument, decided what to take with us and what to leave behind pending our return.

Outside the Olos a collection of people were sitting round the well-head gossiping and, while I turned in, Michael went and joined them. There he fell in with an old sailor. I remember this well because a little later he banged on the door and claimed a lot of my cigarettes which, being a non-smoker himself, in a truly fraternal way he proposed to exchange with his new friend for a chunk of bacon. Protesting loudly—as a matter of principle—I surrendered them and the deal went through.

* * *

Five o'clock next morning saw us once again in the bus. It had been a very hot night and we were in none too good a frame of mind. A quarter of an hour later the bus put us down at Särkijärvi. The students and the lorry were already there and so, too, were two other girls who wanted a lift to Pallastunturi. No one else being expected, we left almost at once. The lorry was really no more than a chassis which had been stripped of its superstructure to carry logs and, as we bumped along dangling our legs over the edge, we had to keep a firm hold, as the surface of the road left much to be desired. After we had covered about five miles, we stopped by a small lake close to which were a few cottages. Into one of these our driver disappeared. There followed a wait of well over half an hour, during which time I suspect that he had his breakfast. Anyway, whatever he was up to, the other passengers must have known that he would not return for some time, because they straight away abandoned the lorry and plunged into the lake. Nothing would have persuaded me to do such a thing. It was barely six o'clock and, hot though the night had seemed in our airless little room, there was now no warmth in the air.

When eventually we proceeded on our way, the road climbed steadily. Yet, although we were rising all the time, for much of the drive there was no view at all, as the trees hedged us in and only receded at rare intervals to allow us a long-distance view of rolling *tunturi*, undulating forest and small, very deep blue lakes.

These lakes were quite different in character from those that Grania and I had visited. In the south-east there had been as much, or more, water as land and the accent had been on light and space, but here the lakes were widely scattered and of a deep sapphire blue—small oases of brilliant colour amid the prevailing dark green of the forest.

Like the surroundings of both Punkaharju and Koli, the country through which we were passing was a national park and, as such, was much frequented in summertime before the war by tourists. Furthermore, during the spring it had, for some time past, been the most popular ski-ing resort in all Finland and there, in 1938, on the slopes of Pallastunturi, the Finnish Tourist Association had opened a large new hotel. It was this hotel that the Germans had blown sky high and that the students were helping to rebuild. Replace would perhaps be a more accurate word to use as, like everywhere else in Lapland, a fresh building site had been chosen and the new hotel was being built about half a mile lower down the mountainside, in the basin of four hills. It came into sight a few minutes before we arrived and was obviously not nearly finished, but at least we knew that the *sauna* was complete.

The new hotel made no pretensions to rival the old one; it was planned on a much smaller scale and was being constructed of wood instead of concrete, but the view that it enjoyed cannot have been very different. As for the old one, we came to the conclusion that the Germans quartered there must have fired their ammunition store before leaving, as we stumbled over fragments of radiators, basins and other fitments, not to mention chunks of masonry, a surprisingly long way down the hillside. Only the foundations remained to mark the exact spot where the building had stood, and they were a crumbling ruin—just one more scar on the landscape about which nothing had as yet been done.

It still lacked something of seven when we arrived and the camp was not yet awake. It was faintly misty and very cold and we were grateful to our driver for inviting us to share his cardboard tent—an octagonal structure with a stove in the centre and a chimney at the apex of the roof. There, while he coaxed the stove into a blaze, we foraged among our provisions in the rucksack, and very soon the smell of burning pine was mingling deliciously with the aroma of steaming coffee.

Barely had we drunk it than the camp began to stir and a deputation of beaming students came to welcome us. There appeared to be about a dozen in all, mainly girls, but that was not the total for, being the week-end, a few of the boys were away fishing. Their spokesman, a lad called Sakari Siitonen, at once started to show us round the camp and, as he did so, he dilated, with a flow of English that was at moments positively lyrical, on the beauties of the countryside. The gist of what he told us was that a gang of regular labourers was employed on the building of the hotel and that the students were spending their summer vacation in helping them and gaining experience. Everyone concerned was encamped on the spot, where one large hut had been built to accommodate them. On the left as you entered this hut was the students' mess, which was also used by the girls as their sleeping quarters; in the centre was the labourers' dormitory-cum-living-room and on the right was the kitchen. The male undergraduates slept outside in just such another cardboard tent as the one in which we had drunk our coffee.

The students, we noted with pleasure, all seemed delighted to welcome us, and we were no less delighted to be there. It was all so pleasant and, for Finland, so surprisingly informal that in no time at all our self-appointed host was saying, "Call me Sak."

Soon, however, the students went off to work and Mike and I set out to explore the hills. Leaving the camp, we crossed a stream, passed through a patch of scrub birch and scaled the nearest of the four spurs that together make up Pallastunturi. From its summit the view, which should have been extensive, was rather disappointing, for as the day advanced it became hot and hazy and the light was poor. Once on top, we set out to walk from one spur to the next along the ridge, which was bare and sparsely turfed, and as we walked we disturbed a few solitary reindeer. As specimens of their kind they were not very impressive, but they were the first, and also the last, reindeer that Mike and I saw in Finnish Lapland. But though these animals do not loom largely in my recollections of Lapland, I cannot bring myself to leave the subject of reindeer without mentioning a momentous experience that I had in Sweden later in the summer.

It was early one afternoon in mid-August that I set out alone to reach the top of a fell that lay close to the Swedish-Norwegian border. It was not a very high mountain, at most a climb of two hours, but from its summit I hoped to see northwards into the valley beyond. For a short time, I climbed steeply through trees and then came out on to the open fell which rose steadily but gently to a rounded crest. Guided by small cairns, I meandered along, for I was in no hurry. Below in the valley a silver river threaded its way among dense firs, but high above the trees was open moorland, bespattered with colourful swamps and streaked with lush green gullies. The sun was shining and as I walked, there flashed across my mind the words:

> "On the wide level of a mountain's head
> (I knew not where, but 'twas some faery place)."

How apt they seemed, how absolutely right, for in my mind's eye it was against just such a background as this that I had always visualised Coleridge's enchanting poem.[1] Yet, lovely though it all was, I never saw the view that I had set out to enjoy. As I reached the hill-top, a cloud arose from the valley beyond and engulfed me, and the distant fells I had climbed so far to see were shrouded in mist. I turned to retrace my steps, moving as fast as I could, but the cloud moved faster and soon the valley ahead was blotted out also. It was now raining hard and I was drenched to the skin. All thoughts of Coleridge had long since vanished and I was concentrating to the exclusion of all else on getting back, when a shaft of intense sunlight broke through the cloud and, as it did so, a rainbow sprang from the hillside on my left, arched its way across the sky and lost itself in the valley at my feet. Brighter it grew and brighter until it seemed that I had never seen colours of such intensity. Instinctively I stopped where I was to look, and as I did so, a second bow dawned all but as bright as the first and quite as

[1] "Time, Real and Imaginary."

perfect. I do not know how long I gazed enthralled, oblivious to the cold rain beating down upon me; I only know that while I watched, from out of the mist below where the hillside fell away and the trees began, there strode a reindeer; at first a shadowy apparition with an immense spread of antlers and then, as he moved forward, a king of beasts. Once in the open he paused, raised his head, sniffed the air and listened, and then slowly and with awful majesty walked straight into the rainbow's end to be swallowed up in a sea of colour.

Two rainbows and a reindeer—enough to give poor Wordsworth a heart attack—and as I squelched on down into the valley I felt an overwhelming sense of privilege.

But to return to Lapland. It was towards evening that Mike and I got back to the camp, where we looked forward to a hearty meal of bacon. But alas! our hopes were soon dashed; the bacon, for which my cigarettes had been bartered, had not been adequately soaked and was so salt as to be almost uneatable, but fortunately for us the students kindly stepped into the breach and supplemented it with potatoes.

The day's work over, most of them drifted back to the camp. It was Saturday night—that is to say *sauna* night—and the bath house was already being heated. Eagerly they invited us to join them in the *sauna*. They did not have to ask twice; almost before the words were out of their mouths we had accepted. For Mike it was initiation.

When all was in readiness we used the *sauna* in turns; first the labourers, then the girls and last of all the boys. It was a spacious *sauna* as *saunas* go, and my group, which must have been almost ten strong, got in quite easily. Not that it remained ten strong, because no two people take exactly the same amount of steam. Like the ten little niggers, its members simply dropped out one by one when they had had enough, and ran down to cool off in the mountain stream that supplied the camp with water. When my turn came, I found that it was just deep enough to cover me and for a second I lay in the swiftly running burn oblivious to the ice-cold water. But only for a second; the next instant the cold shot through me and I leapt out as fast as I could. A minute later I was rubbing myself down and experiencing that feeling of well-being that only a *sauna* can stimulate.

When everyone had bathed we had a coffee party. How glad we were we had come well supplied, for to these boys and girls, who for some time past had had nothing but water even for breakfast, coffee was a real luxury. Just to see them enjoy it gave us real pleasure, and while we were drinking someone produced home-made doughnuts to go with it. These were quite four times the usual size and somewhat heavy, but they were filled with cloudberries and we all thought them delicious. Everyone was very merry and we sat around talking and laughing until about nine o'clock, when three of the girls suddenly started to cut sandwiches and pack their rucksacks. They were just off for a hike through the night, which, they pointed out, was the pleasantest time for walking. At about ten they said goodbye, assured their friends that they would be back the next evening and disappeared among the hills.

In the end we never slept in the *sauna*. Instead, Michael slept in the boys' octagonal tent in the bed of a lad who was away fishing, and I was given a bunk in the hut with the girls, among whom I already felt completely at home. So familiar, in fact, was the whole set-up that I felt almost as if I had been there before. This, however, is less surprising than it seems, for before the war I had dabbled in archæology and in so doing had run across countless students working on digs—students who had much in common with these young Finns, for they, too, were generally to be found encamped beside their work, roughing it with a will, and keen as mustard on the job in hand.

Early next morning we said goodbye and set out to walk back to Särkijärvi. The day was hot and the walk rather tedious. Our path never left the road, which was shut in and dusty, and I do not recall it with any pleasure. But it may well be that my lack of appreciation was in part due to weariness as, much as I had liked my recent companions—and I had liked them very much indeed—my bunk had been exceedingly hard and my blankets scratchy and for the second night in succession I had not had much sleep. Nor was this all; we were walking against time, for over us hung the fear that if we did not reach Särkijärvi in time to catch the bus, we should have to walk another ten miles to Muonio. And to cap all—as if this fear was not enough—it suddenly occurred to me that it was Sunday, and I fell to wondering whether, in fact, the bus ran at all. I need not have worried; we reached Särkijärvi with half an hour in hand and found, to our intense relief, that there was a Sunday bus.

* * *

We left Muonio next morning by the post bus at the relatively civilised hour of 8 a.m. It was a shoddy, rather uncomfortable vehicle that only ran three times a week. From the outset it was almost full of passengers, amongst whom Mike recognised two Danish boys who had travelled in the same ship with him from Copenhagen to Helsinki. They, too, were bound for Kilpisjärvi, but unlike us they were bent on fishing. They were a pleasant, talkative pair, and to this day I cannot think how we had failed to meet them the night before—or at any rate to hear them—as, according to them, they had arrived in Muonio at about seven in the evening and, finding nowhere to sleep, had encamped on the grass just under our window. Later we found them invaluable interpreters as, without undue difficulty, they could make themselves understood by anyone who spoke Swedish. Nevertheless, absurd as it seems, it is not for this that they live in my mind, but for the abortive war that they waged upon the gadflies that plagued us. Although these flies to do not sting, they are nearly as big as wasps and, if anything, they buzz even louder. From Aavasaksa onwards they had been an almost constant source of irritation and on this particular day they were being even more of a nuisance than usual. There was no disputing the fact that, together with the mosquitoes, they took a good deal of the gilt off the Lapp gingerbread. Even the mosquitoes were easier to cope with, for they could be kept at bay by a lavish use of Jungle Oil—a deterrent that had no effect whatsoever upon the gadflies. So the Danes improvised a lethal weapon that looked something like a catapult and with it they wrought considerable havoc in their ranks. But, though the floor of the bus was thickly strewn with their corpses, it made no appreciable difference to their numbers and after a while the boys lost heart and gave up the unequal struggle.

When we had been going for a couple of hours we passed through Palojoensuu where the road branches off to Enontekio, the centre of the nomadic Lapp district. Perhaps it would be more correct to say that at Palojoensuu our road branched off to Kilpisjärvi as, before the war, the road only ran to Enontekio. It was the Germans who built the road through to the Norwegian frontier post at Helligskogen, and it is, in fact, the only thing of value that they left behind them—their one constructive, if not disinterested, act in a welter of destruction.

From now on, while the road grew steadily more and more

beautiful, the behaviour of our driver grew less and less predictable, until even the local passengers were bewildered by it. It all began in the middle of the morning when, on passing through a village, he stopped outside a store that advertised beer and berry juice and encouraged everyone to get out and refresh themselves. This seemed a very reasonable action and, together with quite half our fellow travellers, we got out and, taking for granted that the bus would wait, went into the store to have a drink. We emerged to find that the bus had vanished. At once there was panic and confusion among the passengers, all of whom promptly leapt to the conclusion that they had been abandoned. What were they to do? Where were they to go? Would they ever see their bags again? They were still standing talking and arguing vociferously by the roadside when a truck-load of soldiers drew up and offered to give everyone a lift, assuring them at the same time that they would soon overtake the bus. So everyone scrambled gratefully on board and careered down the road in a cloud of dust, only to find the bus a mile or so away quietly pulled up beside the Post Office, whence I have no doubt it would have returned eventually to fetch us. Dusty and dishevelled, we all clambered out and waved farewell to the soldiers, who drove off laughing heartily. Then we resettled ourselves in the bus. This sort of thing went on all day, as our driver never once divulged his intentions. Instead, he was continually being lost and refound, eating, refuelling or delivering mail at some distance down the road and sometimes right off the beaten track.

Throughout the whole distance to Kilpisjärvi we followed the valley of the Muoniojoki,[1] a tributary of the Torniojoki, which had branched westwards into Sweden some miles south of Muonio. It was now this river's turn to mark the Swedish-Finnish frontier, and as we followed it to its source in the Kilpisjärvi, first the spruce and then the pine faded out of the picture, and we found ourselves among the open *tunturi*. Here the floor of the valley was marshy and on either side of the road cloudberries were growing in profusion.

Except for a few beside the road to Pallastunturi, I had not seen them growing before, although I had eaten them many times, for the Finns bottle them in large quantities. However,

[1] The upper reaches of the Muoniojoki, that is those north of the Kelottijärvi, are, strictly speaking, known as the Kaokämäeno, *eno* being the Lapp word for a tributary.

I have since been told that they are to be found in the Highlands of Scotland and even in the Border country, where they are known as *nupes* but, even so, I personally had never come across them. The berry is the same shape and size as a blackberry, but the plant is quite different. It grows low on marshy ground and the ripe fruit is bright orange; when overripe it is pale gold, and when not yet mature it varies through countless shades of pink to deep tomato.

At sight of these berries, somewhat to our surprise, our driver suddenly became the soul of consideration. Wherever they grew thickest, he pulled up and suggested to his passengers that they should get out and gather them. Whether this action was dictated by pure kindness of heart, whether the engine needed cooling, for we were climbing steadily, or whether our driver simply wanted a snooze we never found out. But, whichever it was, the result was the same; the passengers spilled out one after another and wandered along by the roadside picking, and the more trusting even strayed farther afield—though why, after all that had happened, they should have been so trusting, baffled us completely. Having no container, Mike and I ambled along eating as we picked and, in so doing, we soon found that gathering cloudberries was far from an ideal occupation for the simple reason that, like the mosquitoes and the midges, they throve on swampy ground. Not that we were badly bitten, for we had taken good care to protect ourselves; it was simply that the game was not worth the candle as, in the hand-to-mouth process of eating, all the berries we picked became tainted with Jungle Oil.

Our driver generally allowed us about twenty minutes before lumbering along in the bus, picking us up as he went. Though he never appeared to be checking his numbers, I do not think that he left anyone behind. He probably relied upon someone in the bus kicking up a shindy if he missed anyone out—a risky business, as the Finns are, of all people, the most aloof and independent and the least likely to interfere on behalf of a stranger.

By early afternoon we were well in the mountains and for the last half-hour or so we skirted the shore of the Kilpisjärvi. There was nothing of the southern lakes about the Kilpisjärvi; nothing even of the small tree-girt lakes around Pallastunturi. Its banks were bare except for an occasional copse of scrub birch, and rocky cliffs and moorland fell steeply down to the lake's edge. How lucky we were that day in our afternoon lights; the blue water and the distant shore were bathed in a silvery pinkness and over all hung a mysterious translucency that it was hard to believe could belong to the realms of reality. It was the kind of landscape that as a child I would conjure up when reading a Japanese fairy tale; a vision of exquisite fragility and beauty that was not quite of this world.

At its further end the lake divided into two short arms, the most southerly of which culminates in the point where Norway, Sweden and Finland all meet. But the German-built road follows the shore farthest from the Swedish frontier and it is beside this road, at the northern end of the lake, that the Finnish Tourist Association have built the hut which they rather grandly call an inn. There is no village in the vicinity. The so-called inn stands alone except for the forest warden's hut, a smattering of cardboard tents, a *sauna* and the Finnish frontier post. The building is painted a rusty red and comprises only three rooms; a large living-room, a small kitchen and a room that is occupied by the women who look after the place. As for the communal sleeping quarters, we found that they were partitions off the living-room and consisted of three cubicles, each designed to take three people in treble-decker bunks, but outside were numerous campers, in genuine canvas tents, who made full use of such facilities as the inn had to offer. Amongst them were fishermen, hikers and cyclists, but by far the greatest number of men, who were sleeping under canvas, belonged to a film company who were making a picture of Lapland called *Maaret*, which is a girl's name. As they all wore national costume, Michael and I were always in two minds as to whether any of them were genuine Lapps or not; retrospectively we decided that they were probably all bogus.

On arrival, we found that bunks had been reserved for us in adjoining cubicles; with Michael were his two Danish friends and with me two Finnish girls, one of whom was an undergraduate and the other the female film star and the only woman in the company. She was short and dark and had immensely wide-set eyes and her Lapp dress suited her admirably. Even when relaxing I never remember her to have changed into any other, although it must have been very heavy and tiresome to wear, for the weather was consistently hot and sunny throughout our stay. The dress in question consisted of a heavy, bright blue woollen tunic which ended in a full skirt, and was embroidered with brightly-coloured wools at the hem, belt, neck and cuffs. It was worn with a gaily-ornamented blue cap of the same material that came very near to being a bonnet, for it had two long earflaps that tied beneath the chin in cold weather. High reindeer boots with turned-up toes gave the finishing touch. These are the traditional footwear of Lapps of both sexes and of many Finns as well, for they have been almost universally adopted by outdoor workers throughout the country, I imagine because of the turned-up toe which keeps the ski-binding in place.

The male costume is very similar, but the tunic is shorter and worn over heavy blue trousers that are invariably tucked into the boots. The head-dress, however, is quite different and takes various forms, the commonest of which is known as "the cap of the four winds." This cap is of a fascinating design and is made up of a deep head-band of colourful embroidery and a square crown that, were it stiffened, would resemble a mortar board. But it is not stiffened; it is made of the same soft blue woollen material as the rest of the outfit and—hence its name —it flaps about with every breeze that blows.

Although Maaret—we never discovered her real name—slept in the bunk immediately beneath mine, our paths rarely crossed because the film unit, of which she was the star, kept quite different hours from everyone else. Consequently, when I got up Maaret was not usually awake and when she turned in I was generally, if not fast asleep, trying hard to be so. This state of affairs was the inevitable result of the company's working hours, which appeared to last from midday to midnight; for, regularly at noon, a lorry, plastered with the words "Suomi Filmi" in huge white letters, would collect the whole company and drive them away to the scene of action, whence they would not return until midnight. This was their time for relaxation. Once back, they would sit around the one and only living-room chatting to each other, smoking and tea drinking until the small hours while the remaining guests were trying to sleep. Thus I found that life, instead of being peaceful and idyllic, was in reality extremely exhausting. When I say that there was a total lack of privacy, it is exactly what I mean. From the top bunk I could both see and hear everything that went on in the living-room and, consequently, the noise was almost ceaseless for, when at last the film party broke up between two or three in the morning, there were barely two hours before the more enthusiastic of the fishermen started getting up and clattering round the hut.

For those who were neither film actors or fishermen, the routine revolved round two meals, one of which was served at about eleven in the morning and the other somewhere between 5 p.m. and 6 p.m. But even these meals were confused and restless because all the campers would gather round one large table armed with their individual rations, so that space was cramped and the table a sea of small pots and bottles. The basic food supplied was porridge and potatoes, but these were almost always supplemented by lake fish, generally in the form of trout soup. There was almost no variety, but what we had was good and we were, after all, lucky to have anything at all, for we had been assured repeatedly that no food of any sort would be provided.

All washing, personal and domestic, was done in a small mountain stream that ran down the hillside a short distance away from the inn. This stream served also as a larder, for in it were immersed everybody's jars and pots of perishable rations. The water was swift-flowing and so bitterly cold that my ablutions were hardly worthy of the name; but at least the butter kept well. All that was really essential was to remember the exact spot where you put your own particular pot, because the common form of glass butter-container was almost invariably the product of the Riihimaki Glass Factory, with the result that they were all exactly alike. Inarticulate as Mike and I inevitably were and quite unable to make our excuses, the whole arrangement was fraught with embarrassing possibilities. What if we were caught filching the wrong butter-pot?

At Kilpisjärvi we just missed seeing the midnight sun, but had we been instead at the most northerly tip of Lapland we should have caught it with five days in hand, for at this point the sun does not set for seventy days. As it was, we were some distance farther south and, a month having elapsed since Midsummer Day, the sun had once more begun to dip below the horizon. Nevertheless, we could still have read a book all night with the greatest of ease.

During the four days which we spent at Kilpisjärvi, Michael and I climbed most of the easily accessible hills and, though none of them was very high, all were well worth climbing. Saana, the one just behind the inn, was if anything the most rewarding. From its summit, some 2,000 feet above the lake and 3,360 feet above sea-level, we looked westwards to a range of snowy mountains and rocky peaks that stretched from the fringes of Sweden far away into Norway. They were sheer and precipitous and one of them looked like a miniature Matterhorn. In the distance they appeared to curve towards the north, where they disappeared behind the immediate foot-hills. Around us, where we stood, rolled tawny brown grassland. It had the colouring of the Yorkshire moors and the same grey, rocky outcrops, and as it undulated south-eastwards into Lapland it enfolded many a small tarn of pure cobalt.

For a long time we sat on the top and gazed into the distance, while in the valley at our feet the lake shimmered—a thin sliver of blue water shot with pale gold and cut almost in two in the centre by a great rocky headland. Seeing it as we did, in almost perpetual sunlight, it was hard to believe that the last winter's snow had not disappeared until June. But it was true enough and, indeed, had it not been for the sunshine, the surrounding moorland would have appeared both barren and desolate—a lonely expanse broken only by a few small lakes, a patch or two of scrub birch or stunted brushwood and an occasional derelict gun emplacement. For this was the frontier zone and the scene of the bitter end of the recent fighting.

To-day, however, there was nothing to mar our peace or desecrate afresh the beauty that surrounded us. Yet, lovely as it was, it was the distant view into Norway that held us in thrall. I have sometimes thought that the Finns and the Swedes must find the beauties of Norway very tantalising, for all their finest scenery lies within full view of the Norwegian mountains, so that the eyes of those who would otherwise be completely content with their surroundings are inevitably turned to the beyond. From the summit of Saana, Norway promised so much that we could hardly wait to be on our way. Yet wait we did, for we depended on Mr. Beck, the lorry driver from Skibotn, of whom we had been told in Helsinki, and he was showing no signs of putting in an appearance. Finally, to set our minds at rest, someone rang him up and extracted a promise that he would arrive in two days' time, and a further assurance that he would drive us back with him. This was just about as late as I dared leave it as, though Mike still had a few days in hand before he had to return to England, I had undertaken to meet a friend in Stockholm on July 30th, and it did not seem fair to keep her waiting, as she only had a limited holiday.

So two days later we packed our belongings and waited for Mr. Beck, who kept us hanging about till evening, by which time we could hardly contain our impatience. It was certainly not our lucky day; when at long last he arrived, his lorry was chock-full of peasants and empty baskets, and he announced blithely that he was going on up the valley to gather berries and would pick us up on his return in four days' time.

There was nothing for it but to walk. So first thing next morning we labelled our bags to Skibotn Post Office and carried them down the road to the Finnish frontier post. There, with the aid of the Danes, we asked the guards to make a point of putting them on to the next Norwegian-bound vehicle that came past. This done, we set out on foot.

* * *

It was about midday when we started to walk the thirty odd miles down the valley to Skibotn, where we hoped to pick up the bus to Narvik that left the following morning at 6 a.m. If by then our luggage had not turned up—a contingency that seemed all too probable—Michael had agreed to wait for it while I went on alone to keep my appointment. In retrospect the whole plan seems to have been blissfully sanguine. Certainly I knew that never in my life had I walked more than twenty miles at a stretch and that that had been more than enough, but I was buoyed up by the thought that the weather had been consistently fine for a long time and that the nights were warm and light. What could be easier, thought I in my ignorance, than to curl up by the roadside and sleep when I felt in need of a rest? After all, we had eighteen hours in hand.

For the first six miles our road ran between low hills that completely obscured any distant view. Then we reached the actual frontier; to the right of the road was a small sign about the size of most notices reading "Trespassers will be prosecuted" and on it was painted the one word "*Norge.*" On the opposite side of the road, facing in the reverse direction, was just such another small board emblazoned with the Finnish lion. That was all—nothing more indicated the line of demarcation.

For the next three miles we followed the shore of a mountain lake that was bordered by lonely moorland. It was a wild, desolate region devoid of all signs of humanity beyond a forsaken looking fisherman's hut and a few burnt-out German

Army vehicles that had been abandoned by the roadside to be overgrown mercifully by deep pink willow-herb.

It was before we reached the end of the lake—it may even have been before we reached the actual frontier—that a bus passed us going in the direction of Kilpisjärvi. It was painted bright red and labelled in large letters "Tromsø." The sight of it was completely unexpected and very heartening, for it did not seem likely that it would go beyond the Finnish frontier post and, if it returned the way it had come—and there appeared to be no alternative route—there was a very good chance of our getting a lift. Nevertheless, we determined to walk on until the bus should overtake us on its return journey.

At the end of the lake we began the long descent that was to take us to the Lyngen Fjord. With every step the country became grander and soon we entered a narrow, rocky gorge, down which the water from the lake foamed tumultuously. From it we emerged into a wide valley that fell away at our feet and stretched as far as the eye could see. On either side the mountain peaks were bare and rocky, but the valley between was green and lush and fed by countless waterfalls and, as we gazed at it, we saw below us a small hut over which the Norwegian flag waved. It was Helligskogen, the Norwegian frontier post and, as we thought, the only habitation between us and the sea, but in this we were wrong, for there turned out to be a fisherman's retreat as well.

By the time we got there—that is, by the time we had trudged about twelve miles—it was raining hard. In fact, ever since the top of the pass, there had been rain in the air and the mountain peaks had been festooned with wisps of cloud; ominous little clouds that had made me think wistfully of my sleep by the roadside and hopefully of the bus marked Tromsø. Already I was very grateful to that bus, for it had taken my thoughts from the gathering storm and allowed me to enjoy the Alpine scenery with an easy mind and one that was free to revel in that strange indefinable atmosphere that hangs over northern Norway. For this region has an atmosphere that is all its own; an atmosphere that is imbued with all the fantasy that surrounds Peer Gynt.

But Norway is a land of contrast and when finally, at about 4.30, we reached the Customs House we were greeted with extreme matter-of-factness. Outside, several vehicles were drawn up, so, while our passports were being examined and we were being issued with ration cards, we inquired hopefully about possible transport. But the guard shook his head; there was nothing going down the valley and, as far as he knew, nothing would be going in the near future. Then we asked after the bus about which, it so happened, he had forgotten. His face brightened. It was, he said, a private excursion and it would be back by five o'clock. The people in the bus were all school-teachers and he had no doubt they would give us a lift.

We sat in the porch on a very hard wooden bench and waited. By now the rain was coming down in sheets. Nevertheless, shortly before the bus was due to arrive we took up a strategic position beside the drop gate that spanned the road; come what may, we did not intend to let it slip through our clutches. It came; the driver pulled up and flung open the door and we were greeted with beaming smiles. Everyone in the bus, it seemed, had been on the look-out for us, for, not only had they noticed us when they passed us on the road, but they had been asked at Kilpisjärvi to give us a lift. It was almost too good to be true—they even had our bags safely stowed away in the back.

* * *

Three days later I took the train from Narvik to Stockholm, leaving Michael to visit the Løfotens and follow in a few days' time. I could not afford the time to go with him, as the friend whom I had promised to meet in Stockholm would, even as things were, have arrived there before me.

In the train I sat opposite to a Dutch boy, a sun-burned lad of about twenty, who was dressed like a Boy Scout and carried only a rucksack. His English was almost perfect and we soon fell into conversation. Not that I really did much of the talking; all that I had to do was to look and listen while he first regaled me with a detailed description of the Battle of Narvik and pointed out the overturned destroyers and then, as we left the fjord and headed inland towards the Swedish frontier, turned to his own recent adventures. It still makes me smile to think of him. He was a student from The Hague on his way to attend a summer course at Uppsala University, and, like all Dutch students, he had only a very small allowance of foreign currency—the bare minimum, in fact, to tide him over the course. Yet he was going to Uppsala by way of Narvik; and Narvik, by no possible stretch of the imagination, could be said to be on the route. Full of curiosity, I voiced my thoughts and was rewarded with the full story.

He had, so he told me, left Holland well before the day appointed for the course to begin, with his rucksack, a return ticket to Uppsala via Malmö and his meagre allowance of crowns. But, awaiting him in Stockholm—and in this he was more fortunate than most—was a small nest-egg that he had managed to accumulate by working for a Swedish concern in The Hague. Thus, on arrival in Malmö, he was in the happy position of having time on his hands and a little money to fall back on and, being an enterprising youth, he decided to see what he could of Scandinavia. I think he used the expression "hitching" when telling me of his journey, but, in fact, he had worked most of his way by sea and was now completing the last lap but one of a journey that had already taken him to Trondheim and Narvik and was about to include a short stop in the mountains of northern Sweden and a visit to the iron-ore mines at Kiruna. As may well be imagined, it was a long story, and I was still listening entranced when the train neared his destination, Abisko, the ski-ing centre on Lake Torneträsk. It was then that he suddenly leaned across the compartment and said with the most engaging smile, "Please tell me: do you think I've got an honest face?" Of course, I fell straight into the trap, and a few minutes later he left the train with all my loose change in his pocket and I found myself with exactly one 50-crown note. The last I saw of him was standing on the platform waving me cheerfully out of sight. But it was not the last I thought of him; I did so ruefully every time the train stopped at a station, because sellers of delectable sweets and delicious-looking ice cream always came down the platform, and not one of them either could or would change my 50-crown note.

A few days afterwards Michael arrived in Stockholm and came straight to the hotel, where, on asking for me at the desk, he found a strange young man who was also inquiring for me. As it happened I and my friend were out sightseeing, so Mike introduced himself and a minute later, rather to his surprise, found himself standing alone in the middle of the hall with a handful of crowns and many messages of thanks. He was still wondering what it was all about when we got back, so I told him the story as far as it went and we learned the rest later when we went for the day to Uppsala. There, by the purest chance, we were lunching in an open-air restaurant when my Dutch friend passed by. Seeing us, he promptly abandoned his companions, joined us and entertained us with the last instalment of his adventures—which is how I happened to know that he went to Kiruna. I was delighted; never, I felt, had fifteen crowns been stretched farther or used to better advantage.

* * *

On the afternoon of August 16th, I left Stockholm once again for Turku, this time on board the S.S. *Wellamo*, a very much larger ship than the one in which Sylvia and I had travelled through the ice the previous April. In warm sunshine and with clear visibility, how very different it was steaming down the Saltsjön towards the open sea, and how changed my feelings were. For the last four days I had been alone in Stockholm; and returning to Finland felt almost like going home, and I found myself looking forward eagerly to seeing my friends in Kajaani once more. But first, as I still had a fortnight's holiday to run, I was going to stay at Johanneslund, near Kiikala, Irmeli Virkkunen's family home, where she and her two children were spending the summer with her mother. It was in the depths of the country about midway between Helsinki and Turku and roughly fifty miles from both.

It was very pleasant lying back comfortably in a deck-chair enjoying the sunshine and reviewing from a distance the uncomfortable morning that I had just spent trudging round Stockholm in my new rubber overboots. I had not had much time to enjoy the sunshine during the last few days because I had had to devote them to shopping; that is to say, to collecting anxiously all the things that I thought I should need during the winter that were not available in Finland, and of these the aforesaid boots were by far the most important item. Throughout the winter they were to prove a godsend, but they had not got off to a flying start as only a few hours before I was due to leave the hotel porter had assured me that I would not be allowed to take them out of the country unless they had been worn. This was an unexpected blow, for I knew that I could not do without them. There was nothing for it—the boots must be worn even, though the weather was fine and bright and had been for as long as I could remember. So I put them on and, clad in a flimsy cotton frock, set out in a blaze of sunshine in search of a puddle, of a little mud, of anything, in fact, that would make my shining new boots look as if I had worn them. My search was a dismal failure; never were streets cleaner than Stockholm's or feet hotter than mine, as I wandered here, there and everywhere on my fruitless quest, feigning an indifference I was far from feeling to the unspoken comments in the eyes of the passers-by. In the end I gave it up as a bad job and somewhat apprehensively went down to the dock with my boots still blatantly new, but they were not even queried, nor for that matter were any of the other essentials I had recently acquired.

Though pleasantly sunny, this crossing was nothing like as impressive as the previous one, nor did it take anything like so long. With no ice to slow us up, we docked in Turku early in the morning and there, by arrangement, I was met by a friend of Irmeli's, who, of course, did not know me from Adam. Not that that worried him; rather to my surprise, for I am nondescript enough, he had picked me out from among the crowd on deck, raised his hat and said, "Good morning, Miss Ashcroft?" before even the gangway was in place. Nor was this all; from every point of view he turned out to be an admirable 'meeter of boats,' for, no sooner had I stepped ashore than, with a lordly "Mark those bags," he had whisked me through the Customs in no time at all.

From the dock we drove straight to his home, where we at once settled down to breakfast in a room whose walls were more heavily laden with pictures than any I had yet seen. Barely, however, had we started our meal than Irmeli herself arrived with her brother, her two daughters, Ritva and Seija, and her young nephew, Arto. Arto was a contemporary of Ritva's, a lad of fifteen, with a round, beaming face and a blue-and-white knitted cap perched on the back of his head. As a cap it was one of many, as Finnish boys, though frequently stripped to the waist in hot weather, seem to have a peculiar aversion to going about bare-headed and a special affection for their round woollen caps. They take to them almost as soon as they can walk and go on wearing them until they are thirty or thereabouts. Arto was no exception; he was wedded to his cap and, though of course he took it off indoors, I never think of him without it. As headgear, these little caps were a source of unfailing amusement to me; perhaps because of their utter uselessness—they protect neither the eyes nor the back of the neck, and are discarded just when the bald patches that need covering tend to appear—or, perhaps, simply because they look so very ingenuous. But there is one thing to be said in their favour; on the one and only occasion that I attended the Olympic Games, just such another little blue-and-white cap as Arto's enabled me to pick out the Finnish competitor in the Marathon Race without a moment's hesitation. He not only started off wearing one, but he finished the twenty-six-mile course with it still on his head.

Like me, the children had never really seen Turku, so after breakfast we all went out to see the sights of the town.

Turku, the old capital of Finland, has to-day a population of 105,000, roughly a quarter that of Helsinki. But, though a much smaller city, it is a much older one, for it dates from the early thirteenth century and owes its existence to the arrival of Christianity. From the time of Thomas—incidentally an Englishman—who in 1220 became the first governing Bishop of the mediæval Church in Finland, until 1812 when the Russians transferred the capital to Helsinki, Turku was the capital of the country. Thus, throughout the era of Swedish rule, it was the seat of the Government and the Church and the natural centre of all learning. Moreover, it was also a commercial centre, for it carried on a thriving trade with the cities of the Hanseatic League. To-day little remains of this once flourishing town, as it was almost completely destroyed by fire in 1827. But even before this time the Government offices had been transferred to Helsinki. A year after the great fire, the University followed them. Nevertheless, Turku still maintains much of its early tradition; it remains the seat of Finland's only archbishop, the site of one of the country's three Courts of Appeal and the home of the Swedish University that was founded in 1918 and the new Finnish University of Turku that followed in 1922.

As a city I have to admit that I found Turku disappointing. This was unreasonable, for although the glimpse I had had on arrival had been confined to the hotel, the railway station and the docks, I knew perfectly well that most of the old town had been swept away in the great fire of 1827, and that it was inevitable that the city would be a new one. Yet its tradition of antiquity is such that I had persistently thought of it as old, and assumed, without any grounds whatsoever, that it would be picturesque. But, in point of fact, the Cathedral and the Castle, both of which originated in the thirteenth century, are the only buildings of moment to have survived the fire, and consequently we went straight to visit them.

The Cathedral is a massive building of limestone and brick, austere in outline and curiously pock-marked in effect, for it has undergone so many vicissitudes in the course of its history, has been altered and restored so frequently, that its exterior now boasts a most unusual amount of apertures that have at one time or another been bricked up and replaced by others. Of the building, Onni Okkonen, Professor of the History of Art at Helsinki University, writes: "Of the stone buildings of mediæval Finland only the Cathedral of Turku attains the high plane Continental architectural style." Not being an expert, I can only accept his statement, but I cannot help feeling that his level of comparison is not a very high one and that most Europeans need not go far to see much finer examples of ecclesiastical architecture; that, in fact, the Cathedral of Turku deserves attention chiefly as an example of the mediæval architecture of the north and that, even when viewed as such, full appreciation must depend on a wealth of local historical knowledge.

Like the Cathedral, the Castle no longer belongs exclusively to the thirteenth century, as part of the present-day building is a seventeenth-century addition. The original Castle is, however, complete in itself; a massive fortress, devoid of all ornament, that is strongly suggestive of a prison. Owing to recent war damage, we never managed to penetrate its precincts. Instead, we paid an exhaustive visit to the adjoining museum, about which, I must confess, I remember very little beyond that it was full of furniture and pictures that, like the interior of the Cathedral, depended for much of their interest on a knowledge of local history that I did not possess. From a distance, "dull" is the adjective that suggests itself to me whenever I think of Turku, and I have sometimes wondered whether it is altogether fanciful to imagine that the city reflects the character of its inhabitants or vice versa, for the people of Turku are reputed to be stiff, unfriendly and lacking in graciousness, and are said to form a closed society that it is very hard to penetrate.

I cannot claim that my limited experience bears out this generalisation, for my acquaintance with the people was so slight as to be negligible. But whatever the truth may be, however staid and unforthcoming the inhabitants, however uninteresting the town, Turku has broken out in recent times and allowed Erik Bryggman to build a new cemetery chapel that is without exception the most fantastic piece of church architecture that I have ever seen. As I remember it, three sides of the building were of unrelieved concrete, the fourth of plate glass; while the interior was distinguished by a mass of highly polished surfaces and a calculated lack of symmetry that was far from restful to the eye. To my mind the whole place lacked atmosphere and, after a while, I reached the conclusion that the only beautiful effect to be achieved was that of the great mass of flowering plants that were banked beside the long window. This being so, it seems to me to raise the question: Ought not a building to stand or fall on its own merits rather than on those of its floral decoration?

* * *

Towards evening, we left for Johanneslund, driving through highly cultivated country that is renowned for its farms. Even so, it is far less extensively cultivated than it appears at first sight, because the farmlands very naturally cling to the roadside, and seeing them one tends to forget how much forest there still is in the background. It was only much later, when I had a chance to fly over part of south-west Finland, that I realised that almost three-quarters of the country is actually still forest-clad.

On arrival, we were greeted by Irmeli's widowed mother, Rouva Silvan. She was an old lady of immense personality who, in her determination to be understood, brought her Swedish-English dictionary to every meal. Hers had always been a Swedish-speaking household, but now things were changing and, more than once during meals, I was struck by the ease with which Irmeli switched from one language to another—the perfect common denominator, who spoke Swedish to her mother and brother, Finnish to her children and English to me. The old lady and her son, needless to say, understood Finnish perfectly and the children Swedish, only rather less well; I was the odd man out.

Rouva Silvan had come to Johanneslund on her marriage and had lived there ever since, for her husband had run a small glass factory that was just out of sight of the house. This factory, which had now been taken over by her son, was a thriving, homely concern that, as far as I could make out, specialised in producing green glass beer bottles and, as a side line, some remarkably heavy glass balls that were to be found crowning the gate posts at the bottom of the drive and decorating the garden in the most unexpected places. But the thing I liked best about the factory was the way in which the children used to bake potatoes in the furnaces after working hours.

The house itself was a large, low, white wooden building that was typical of many a Finnish country home. It was entered through a glass porch and, broadly speaking, consisted of two parallel rows of rooms. In the centre was a small hall, but there were no passages, so that almost every room had three doors, one in each inside wall. Thus every room was in a sense a passage and, as all doors were habitually thrown wide open, there was no real privacy.

Here through the long winter months—with every comfort except indoor sanitation—Rouva Silvan lived alone with her son and a maid who had been with her for many years: an invaluable woman who knew her job inside out, but who—paradoxically, for she was Seija's devoted slave—grumbled ceaselessly as, with each successive summer, Irmeli and the children arrived to stay. Matters came to a head while I was there and she gave, or was given, notice. There was nothing unusual about this; it was almost a matter of routine. What was unusual was that when we went, so did she. But she did not stay away long; six months later she was back and I have an idea she is there for life.

Dearth of domestic help is one of Finland's problems. As a topic of conversation it is as done to death there as here, but with the introduction of the new Domestic Servants' Charter in Finland the position is beginning to ease. By the new regulations, no maid may be asked to work for more than ten hours a day, and these hours must be between 6 a.m. and 7 p.m.; anything else must be paid for at overtime rates. Further, all maids are entitled to one free half-day a week, alternate Sundays and every other national holiday. In addition, they get a fortnight's paid holiday in the year, rising to three weeks when they have been five years in the same situation. Their minimum wage has been fixed by law at 4,000 marks—roughly £6 10*s*.—a month all found and, in addition to this, most employers pay their taxes for them. This paying of taxes is, of course, a hangover from the days when help was extremely scarce and was, in origin, tantamount to bribery, but it has produced a system whereby to-day few, if any, girls will work for an employer who does not do so.

Life at Johanneslund was one long blissful orgy of sun-bathing and swimming in the lake nearby—an occupation that was punctuated by excellent meals, frequent *saunas* and one bout of feverish activity, when Irmeli declared that it was time to pick all the apples in the garden. Not that they were either very many or very good, for Finnish apples are nothing like as good as ours.

After about a week of this gloriously peaceful and lazy existence, I went for a few days to Helsinki, largely in order to buy books for the next term, as I had no intention of being caught inadequately supplied a second time. The selection was good and I managed to lay in quite a satisfactory assortment and, in between shopping, to consume vast quantities of crayfish, which were then in high season. These crayfish are looked upon as a great delicacy, but, to be truthful, I consider them more trouble than they are worth, and it has crossed my mind more than once to wonder how much of their vaunted attraction is inherent in themselves, how much in their decorative value, which is that of a Dutch still life, and how much in the almost unlimited *schnapps* that is their invariable adjunct.

From Helsinki I returned to Johanneslund, where the few remaining days of the holidays are primarily associated in my mind with Seija's frenzied last-minute efforts to do her holiday task; for Seija, Irmeli's twelve-year-old daughter, had now, in the space of three days, to finish collecting 120 wild flowers, press them, mount them and label them with their Latin names. Poor Seija, she had not collected nearly enough flowers, and she most certainly did not know their Latin names. However, things were not as black as they looked, for the simple reason that there is no originality at all about Finnish holiday tasks, which, for years past, have repeated themselves with clockwork regularity and can always be calculated well in advance. Seija was only doing now what Irmeli had done before her—except that she was getting away with 120 flowers, whereas, in her day, Irmeli had had to collect 200—and Irmeli, with considerable forethought, had hoarded her collection against just this contingency. By which thoughtful act the major difficulty, that of looking up all the Latin names, was happily by-passed. Down came Irmeli's folder from the attic; a combined operation produced an adequate number of flowers, and while Seija, with many sighs and groans, copied out the labels, Irmeli, armed with the iron, pressed and mounted the fresh flowers. Much the same, I am convinced, takes place annually in every household where there is a Second Form child. Yet perhaps something is achieved as, on an average, the Finns know far more about their country's flora than we do about ours, and almost all of them show something akin to ostentatious familiarity with their Latin names, especially when one considers how very few of them have even a nodding acquaintance with the classics.

A last *sauna*, a last swim, and we all left for Helsinki together in time to catch the night train to Kajaani. Irmeli and the two children shared one third-class sleeping compartment and I was next-door. There was only one other girl in with me and we both turned in early. I had the lowest of the three berths and she the one immediately above me. The top berth was unoccupied. About two hours later, when we were both fast asleep, the train stopped and an enormously stout middle-aged woman got in. She took one look at the empty berth and announced clearly and with conviction, "I cannot possibly get up there," or words unmistakably to that effect. One glance and I knew she was right. Shamelessly and without compunction, I closed a sleepy eye and left her compatriot to cope. After all, I did not speak Finnish.

Part III

Northern Winter

THE RUNNING REINDEER

from *Historia de Gentibus Septentrionalibus* by Olaus Magnus (published in 1555).

Part III

Northern Winter

ON arrival next morning at Kajaani I was met by Sirkka Frey and her two small boys and from them I learned that there was a temporary hitch in my plans. Instead of going straight to the Freys as I had expected to do, I was to spend a week at the Maakunta. This was unavoidable because Kalle being away from home, his *locum* was installed in their only spare room—the one I was destined to occupy.

At the time the Maakunta was the best hotel in the town—though not a very good best. I knew it well, for I had already stayed there during Niilo Kanto's birthday celebrations. It was in the Kauppakatu and occupied all except the ground floor of a large concrete block that was quite a modern building, although old in comparison with most of the concrete buildings in the town. As time went on it grew more and more familiar to me; for not only was it a general meeting place, but Heljä and I lunched there together daily. This was a mutually happy arrangement, as Heljä lived alone and always lunched out and, my teaching hours being irreconcilable with Kalle's consulting hours, I also went out to lunch every day except at week-ends. As we were neither of us particularly flush, we always ate the set meal. This had the dual advantage of being both cheap and ready; an advantage that was unfortunately counterbalanced by the extreme monotony of the menu which, when translated by Heljä, invariably read: "Some sort of meat," "Some sort of fish," "Some sort of porridge"—a rendering which reflects not on Heljä's English, which was excellent, but on the excessively nondescript character of the dishes.

Things, however, began to look up some weeks later when a new hotel, the Seurahuone, opened a little farther down the street. To it we transferred our custom as, although a shade dearer, it was considerably more than a shade pleasanter. True, there was no central table of *hors d'œuvres* such as the one in which the Maakunta, Scandinavian-wise, indulged; but this was no great loss for the *hors d'œuvres* in question had always been of the most uninteresting. Nevertheless, dreary as they were, they were not altogether devoid of novelty. Now and again an element of surprise would creep in, and I clearly remember a day on which a dish piled high with revolting-looking yellowish grey marbles appeared.

"What in the world are those?" I asked Heljä, my eyes popping out of my head.

There was a moment's pause while she considered the matter and then replied, half apologetically, "Tunny fish roe, I think. Don't take them; I don't think you'll like them." A feeling with which I readily concurred.

Such novelties apart, my recollections of the Maakunta are largely centred round the one and only setback that I suffered there. The bedroom keys were all attached to wooden balls of more than golf-ball size, on which the room numbers were engraved. This, no doubt, was to stop visitors from walking off with them by mistake and, as a precaution, I for one found it all too effective. Once deterred from putting my key in my bag or my pocket, I never could remember it, and as a result I managed to lock myself out my own room almost every day. Nine times out of ten this did not matter, but the tenth time it did. Returning from school in the evening, I found that the floor maid had gone off duty taking with her the pass key. It was the only one; the girl lived out and, to make matters even worse, no one in the building knew where. That there was no other room available was simply the last straw. It was one of those occasions when, I feel sure, I scored by being a foreigner. Instead of throwing me out, there was general concern over my predicament and a good deal of animated and somewhat frivolous discussion that centred round the locksmith and the fire brigade. At the end of this I retired quietly to the house-keeper's private sitting-room, where there was a divan which she had made up for me. And there she entertained me with tea, sandwiches and German conversation as halting as my own, until it was time to go to bed.

It was in the Maakunta that I first came up against the question of drink, although, of course, I had often heard it discussed, for the Finns are all too conscious of drunkenness as a national weakness, and are for ever drawing attention to it by bewailing the fact. But for this constant lamentation I doubt if I should ever have given the matter a thought; that is, before spending this week at the Maakunta, because it was only then that it became in any way noticeable. Then I did find that when I returned of an evening I was apt to have to step over recumbent figures asleep on the doorstep and to shake off all too garrulous individuals in the lift. But this was not altogether surprising, for the Maakunta was one of the only three places in Kajaani licensed to sell spirits for consumption on the premises.[1]

I still find it difficult to sum up the situation. Certainly nothing that I came across compared with Stella's description of the heavy drinking that went on in Oulu; but then Oulu, being a port, is probably not representative of the country as a whole. All that I can say is that, while I am prepared to believe that Kajaani is for Finland an unusually sober town, I am not prepared to believe that the situation is as black as it is painted. In a recent article by Alexander Werth, I came across this statement:

"During a recent visit to Helsinki a Finnish friend told me: 'What a pity you've arrived late. Yesterday we had a *really* good wedding: seventeen people were knifed!' "[2]

Assertions like this are deceptive because they imply that the exception is the rule. Hard drinking may be prevalent, but it is not as hard as all that.

The sale of alcohol in Finland is restricted and is all in the hands of a Government monopoly, the O. Y. Alkoholiliike A.B., whose stores are only to be found in towns and urban districts. Consumption for the many is, therefore, regulated partly by the need to travel quite long distances to get drink, partly by its high price and partly by a system of so-called rationing that has been in existence since the war. By this system cards are issued to all over twenty-one years of age, which entitle the bearer to buy two litres of strong alcohol every day and five to six litres of wine—but wine, being all imported, is prohibitively expensive. On the surface, this allotment would appear more than ample, and so it is, despite the fact that in practice no one can draw their full quota every day, as the system is not really one of rationing, but of control; and whereas in theory everyone is entitled to draw their daily ration, in practice the authorities watch lynx-eyed, and if they consider that anyone is drawing too freely they remove his or her card altogether. To-day, some 14,000 persons are disqualified from buying.

[1] For the purposes of licensing and price control, hotels, restaurants and boarding-houses are divided into six categories. The highest grade are fully licensed and forced to sell at maximum prices while the lowest sell only beer at minimum rates.

[2] *The Manchester Guardian Weekly*, July 13th, 1950.

For the private individual the whole arrangement is tiresome in the extreme, as only the privileged few are granted a licence to buy what they want and store. For the rest, giving a party means fetching supplies daily for some time in advance or going to the trouble of obtaining a special permit from the police for the occasion. But I fancy that the difficulties put in the way of the consumer look greater on paper than they are in practice, because they never seemed to put a stop to entertaining any more than the great prohibition experiment, while it lasted, put a stop to drinking.

I suppose the fact that prohibition was tried out in Finland between the wars is one of those nebulous facts about the country that are more or less generally known. In origin, it was another manifestation of the will to reform that in the late nineteenth century gave rise to the co-operative movement and led ultimately to the *Lex Kallio.* Like the cry for land reform, the movement towards temperance was rooted in the appalling living conditions into which the Industrial Revolution had plunged the masses—conditions that had driven many people to drink; and drink, for the poor, meant strong spirit distilled from wood.

The first prohibition Bill passed the Diet in 1906, but for economic reasons—how was the inevitable loss of revenue to be made up?—it never passed the Senate. But the temperance advocates were not to be silenced and in 1909 a similar Bill came before the Diet. This time is was pigeon-holed because the Tzar refused to sign it, and pigeon-holed it remained until the birth of the Finnish Republic. In 1919, one year before the United States embarked on a similar experiment, it became law. But from the outset it was a failure; the country as a whole was not behind the Government, and without its co-operation the long, indented coastline could not be controlled. Things went from bad to worse, following much the same pattern as they were doing in the United States; notwithstanding, the Act remained in force until 1932, when the issue was decided by a plebiscite, the result of which was a 70 per cent vote in favour of repeal.

The new laws created a state monopoly in the form of a joint stock company which controlled the manufacture, import and sale of liquor, and which greatly augmented the national revenue. The company prospered and illicit traffic fell away to such an extent that whereas in 1933 contraband amounting to 651,560 litres was seized, in 1945 only 250 litres were impounded. The annual profits of this company, after reserves have been set aside and dividends paid, are allocated to the communes who devote 30 to 40 per cent to old age and disability insurance and the remainder to social welfare with the accent on temperance.

*　　*　　*

Early September saw the end of cotton frocks and the reappearance of woollen clothes, for autumn came quickly to Kajaani, and with it the people settled down once more to the serious business of living. Holidays were over, the children were back at school and the nights were drawing in. From one end of the Kauppakatu to the other the road was a shambles, as the pipes beneath it had to be relaid before the snow came, and the time was all too short for the work in hand. Not that the workmen themselves appeared in the least hurried; to watch them no one would have dreamed that the job was urgent. It was the local inhabitants who did the worrying, although the state of affairs was an all but chronic one and they should have been used to it. After all, everyone freely admitted that Kajaani without excavations in progress would not be Kajaani, and certainly when, almost two years later, I returned on a visit the first sight that met my eyes was that of the inevitable barricades.

It took me about a week to arrange my classes and when I had done so, I found that I had very nearly the same number of pupils as I had had the previous summer. On paper the gains all but compensated for the losses, and in practice they more than did so, as some of those who had given up learning English had at best put in such scanty appearances at my lessons as to be scarcely missed. Teaching, moreover, was not as hard to resume as I had anticipated; the summer holidays provided an almost endless topic of conversation and, over and above this, I was now more or less adequately supplied with books.

As for the general conversation, the ratification of the Peace Treaty and the prevalence of strikes were the topics of the moment. The upshot of the former was that normal diplomatic relations were restored and the British and Soviet Control Commissions were withdrawn from Helsinki and this, if it did nothing more, at least relieved the Finns from the onus of supporting them financially. But, while the Control Commissions were withdrawn by October, the series of Communist-inspired strikes continued throughout the country on and off until Christmas. It was the age-old question of wages and inflation, and every time the workers came out the Pekkala administration compromised. I do not remember exactly which industries were affected, but the other day I came across an old letter of mine in which I stated laconically, "The railways and the sausage-makers are out." If there was a marked decrease in the available sausages—a form of food as popular in Finland as I understand it is in Germany—I cannot recall it, but I do remember the railwaymen's strike because they made a habit of stopping work systematically on Sundays only, and the first time that they did this, several of my pupils, who had gone to Helsinki for the week-end relying on catching the night train back, failed to turn up for their lessons on Monday.

As soon as Kalle returned and his *locum* had left, I took up my abode in the Seminaarinkatu with the Freys. There I had a small room opening off the entrance hall that was used by the patients as a waiting-room. In my room was a large green-tiled stove, typical of many, whose performance I found nothing short of miraculous. Ten small logs would keep it going for twenty-four hours. As the weather grew colder Martta, the cook-general, took to lighting it for me first thing every morning, and it was wonderfully easy to get going. Martta was a pearl of great price; a talkative individual who worked extremely hard and was devoted to the family. Some time in the past, Kalle had operated on her for goitre and, when she got better, had discovered that she was in need of a job. This was providential, for Sirkka wanted help, so it was suggested to Martta that she should fill the bill. To this she readily agreed, but, to the astonishment of all concerned, with the unusual stipulation that she did not have to take a holiday or go out on her days off. What she wanted above all things was a home; and a home she found on which she expended such unbounded energy that on more than one occasion I found her on her knees scrubbing the waiting room floor at ten o'clock in the evening. But she was not only an efficient housemaid and an excellent cook, she was also very good with the children. Thus Sirrka had only one anxiety; near Kuopio there lived a farmer who had his eye on Martta. But luckily for all concerned—except the farmer—Martta persisted, in the face of Sirkka's conscientious, if somewhat half-hearted, encouragement, in treating him as a joke.

Martta, however, was not the only string Sirkka had to her bow, for there was Kaisu, a sentimental, kindly old soul, who came daily to lend a hand, sterilise Kalle's instruments and spoil all three children, and Petra in particular.

I was very happy with the Freys for there was a wonderful feeling of content about the house. I think this was largely due to the fact that Sirkka and Kalle were exceptional parents. They played with their children, they talked to them and they encouraged them, but they neither fussed, worried, nor spoiled them. In consequence, they were altogether adorable and, as families of small children go, no trouble at all. I think it speaks volumes that, in the seven months which I lived with them, I only once saw Harri in tears, and Harri did not have his seventh birthday until after I had been four months in the house. Naturally, this could not be said of Torsti and Petra, who when I arrived were both under four, but squalls blew over very quickly and whining was never heard.

The Frey ménage was all the more remarkable because the general impression left with me was that most Finnish parents confine their activities almost exclusively to the physical well-being of their children, at any rate until they are of school age; a circumstance that is largely, but not entirely, due to domestic shortage. The children are thus left very much to themselves, with the result that when, at seven years old, they start school, they are by our standards mentally very backward. By which I do not mean simply that the majority of them cannot read, but that they are surprisingly lacking in imaginative enterprise. At any rate, it always seemed to me that, in their pre-school days, they made remarkably little use of their opportunities for wandering off and getting into trouble; which is perhaps an argument in favour of letting their youthful minds lie fallow.

No one, however, could accuse the little Freys of being backward. Harri, though small for his age, had started school early and more than managed to hold his own in a class of children two years his senior. Of the Frey children I thought him the most sensitive and, watching him, I used often to think that he would have made a fortune on the films, for he had an extraordinarily mobile and expressive little face and could look a poor little waif to perfection, than which nothing could have been more misleading. I can see him now sitting at the table, his legs dangling and his chin cupped in his left hand, doing sums with a look of desperate earnestness, and I can see him, too, his face alight with mischief, hatching some plot quite blatantly under my nose because, of course, I could not understand.

Torsti was very different both in disposition and physique. He was plump, sturdily built and possessed of enchanting dimples. He was a terrific chatterbox and never tired of telling me long, long stories—in Finnish, of course—with a touching faith that sooner or later the penny would drop. And as he talked, he always made full use of his hands; so much so that, on one occasion when he was well away, Kalle remarked to me with a grin: "How is it, do you think, that I have a little Jew for a son?"

Torsti's English was a joy. There was not much of it, but there were certain words that he liked the sound of enormously and often at meals he would sit back and remark, quite out of the blue and as if the whole world depended on it, "Yes," "Blueberry," "Hurry up," "Aeroplane" or "Boat"; but "Yes" and "Blueberry" were the sounds he liked best of all. He and Petra were often in and out of my room, for both of them liked company, even inarticulate company and, in addition, Petra took an enormous interest in the contents of my top drawer, and I often surprised her standing on tip-toe peeping into it. I can see her, too, sitting in her high chair waiting to be fed, with her mouth wide open like a baby bird, and I can hear her romping with the boys and making more noise than both of them together. But the most indelible picture that I have of Petra is of her waking one evening and escaping from her cot and, looking incredibly pink and white and cuddlesome in her nightie, toddling into the sitting-room, where there were guests. There was no question of putting her back to bed; she stayed and was made much of for quite twenty minutes before being tucked up again, and when the moment came she dropped off without a murmur.

I loved them all, and now there is a fourth, Maâret, my goddaughter. I remember one evening when we were talking about the advent of the new baby that I asked if the other children would be pleased. It was Kalle who answered. "I'm sure they will," he said, "but Harri may take a little while to get used to the idea. I remember taking him to the maternity home to see Petra when she was a day old. He was only five at the time and he stood just inside the door of the room and wouldn't budge. So I said 'Harri, don't you want to look at your sister?' But nothing would persuade him to move; he only shook his head and replied firmly, 'No, I can't. I haven't been introduced.' "

In the spring before I left, I had a birthday; a memorable occasion for two reasons. The night before I went to a party, a small friendly affair where there was dancing to the gramophone. Somehow or other—just how is a mystery—word must have gone round that my birthday was approaching, because on the stroke of midnight all the men of the party suddenly bore down upon me, picked me up, threw me up to the ceiling, caught me and proceeded to toss me up and down until they were exhausted. This appears to be a good old Finnish custom among university students who wish to feature one of their comrades, and should be taken, I was assured, as a great compliment. But however it should be taken, I can only say that I personally was taken so completely by surprise as to be bereft of all other feelings.

Early next morning, just as I was going up and down for the hundredth time, my dreams were shattered by a commotion outside my door and a lot of whispering. Then it opened and in came a procession—first Petra, then Torsti, carrying a book high in front of him as if he were a page and the book a crown on a cushion, and last Harri with a vase of pink tulips that were so tall that they spread out like an umbrella over his head. Beaming from ear to ear, they lined up beside the bed, took a deep breath, looked at each other and said—almost with one voice—"Happy birthday!"

* * *

The club season started well, for at the opening meeting we had a visit from Georgie Henschel, who was touring the country for the British Council and who came to lecture about the B.B.C. Yrjö and I met her at the station and installed her, somewhat prematurely, for it was not yet officially open, in the Seurahuone. To this day I cannot think why we did this or why they consented to take her in, for they were certainly not ready for guests.

Before the meeting there was a dinner party, to which about fourteen people turned up. This, for Kajaani, was a very good showing; nevertheless—possibly because of this—it was a very sticky affair. I learned a good deal at that dinner, but chiefly that, if an English-speaking party was to be got going, it must be kept small and helped by alcohol, at any rate in the initial stages. Unfortunately, dinners were expensive even without drinks, and because of this they were always rather a problem, for it meant that attendance was limited not only to the interested, but also to the well-to-do. As a result, the entertainment of English visitors was always in danger of being regarded as the prerogative of a clique—a state of affairs that all agreed should be avoided. The question was then—and I am afraid still is—"How?"

After dinner we all repaired to the factory club, where things warmed up considerably. Georgie was an admirable visitor; an entertaining speaker herself, she was also a sympathetic listener who took a deep interest in all that she saw and heard—a quality that rapidly endeared her to one and all. She left behind her an indelible impression and has remained a good friend to the people of Kajaani ever since. When, later, the question of play-acting was mooted, it was to Georgie that I wrote and it was she who, with firsthand knowledge of the English Club members and a shrewd idea of their capabilities, chose out a selection of suitable one-act plays and sent them to me.

* * *

The next landmark that stands out in my memory is the trip that Irmeli and I went with Aili and Eero in their car to Kuhmo, a church village that is situated east of Kajaani and close to the Finnish-Russian border. The distance from Kajaani to Kuhmo was about sixty miles and on the way there we hoped to see the autumn colouring at its best, but luck was against us. Shortly before the appointed day a gale swept over the country and stripped most of the trees bare. Yet, even so, the beauty of the autumn lingered on as, here and there, a birch still lit the forest like a tongue of golden flame or a rowan glowed red as a Canadian maple.

Beyond Sotkamo the countryside grew increasingly sparsely populated. On either side of the road the great wall of the forest was broken only by a few small lakes. For the rest, the trees stretched interminably and screened the distant view, which, on the rare occasions when it did appear, was one of low hills vaguely outlined against the sky. The landscape was completely indeterminate; except for flashes of transitory colour, it was devoid of all salient features, and for this very reason in 1939 it had shown itself to be the nation's best defence. A mile or two to the south-east of Kuhmo lay Rasti, a visible proof of the strategic value of the terrain, for here one great drama of the Winter War was played and, luckily for the Russian soldiers concerned, was not played out.

This being recent history, as we approached Kuhmo it was natural enough that our conversation should turn to the great *Rastimotti*. The word *motti* is used by the Finns for a pile of sawn timber held in place by upright stakes, but during the war it came to signify by association a tactical manœuvre whereby large numbers of the enemy were encircled and held at bay by patrols of eight to twelve Finns, armed with automatics, operating under cover of the forest.

It was the Russians who made these tactics possible. They played straight into the hands of the Finns by ignoring the nature of the countryside and invading at intervals the whole way along the frontier from the Gulf of Finland northwards to Petsamo, and this when they should have realised that only in the extreme south was Finland really open to attack. To the Russians the operations in the north were catastrophic; on the Suomussalmi front alone they left 36,000 dead for the cost of 150 Finnish lives.

The story behind this slaughter of the many by the few seems all but incredible. The Russians crossed the border and advanced down the main road in a long column, only to be cut off from their supplies by a handful of men operating in the forest. Yet although this took place at the very outset of hostilities, the end of January found the Russians staging a repeat performance some eighty miles to the south in the vicinity of Kuhmo. Willy-nilly, it seemed that they were bent upon advancing down every available road that led from the frontier into Finland, and that with only the Leningrad-Murmansk railway to bring up their supplies. The Russian soldiers pushed forward with guns, tanks and propaganda, with all the paraphernalia that had served their armies so well on the plains of Poland. But here, in Finland, they were ill-equipped for the cold and, furthermore, they were entirely unused to the vast, silent forest that hemmed them in, for they came, most of them, from the Ukraine and the central Russian steppes. The Finns, who were born, bred and at home in the forest, had them at their mercy. They simply let them advance unmolested, except by snipers, down the roads which they knew full well were often too narrow for large vehicles to pass without one or other of them getting bogged in the soft snow beside the road. Once under way, no mechanised column could turn back; their boats were burned and fear of the invisible was ever present, for the Finns saw to it that the advancing troops were kept in a state of constant apprehension and that those who left the road were never seen again.

Briefly, the Finnish tactics, both at Suomussalmi and at Rasti, consisted in cutting the enemy off from their supplies and in destroying their staff headquarters and food kitchens. Cold and hunger did the rest, for there was no ammunition to spare. To the Finns it was simply a question of choosing suitable sites from which to cover the road with small artillery and there erecting strong-points both in front and in the rear of the advancing army. Small ski patrols, at one with the forest, were then enough to harass the invader's flanks. It was merely a matter of waiting until the spearhead of the column had reached the advance gun emplacements, halting it and then cutting it off in the rear.

Range of vision apart, the governing factor in choosing these positions was mobility on the enemy's flanks, for they had to be deceived into thinking the Finnish patrols far larger and more numerous than they actually were. For this the lay-out of the winter roads—as opposed to the permanent roads used by the Russians—had to be taken into consideration. These winter roads are the roads which disappear each year with the spring thaw—the roads that do not appear on any map, the roads from the lumber camps to the water's edge down which the newly-felled logs are dragged and on whose icy surface small compact groups of skiers can manœuvre at high speed. Thus the problem confronting the Finnish General Staff was how best to utilise the winter roads that were already in existence and to build when necessary new ones parallel with the main road down which the Russians were streaming.

Of the 16,000 Russians who crossed the border to the Kuhmo area, 7,000 to 10,000 were saved from destruction when the peace was signed. Most of these men had dug themselves in along a five-mile stretch of road on either side of which for a distance of half a mile they had cut down every tree. This enclosure comprised the main *Rastimotti*, but to the rear three smaller groups of men were encircled, one of which was composed almost entirely of Orientals.

However you look at it, the Winter War was a ghastly tragedy. The ultimate outcome was never in question. Finland was mutilated and in her vain struggle against aggression lost, chiefly in the Karelian Isthmus, the cream of her youth. Meanwhile, the Russian High Command achieved its objective —at a cost. Thousands of intrinsically harmless Russian peasants were sacrificed apparently to no purpose, or if to a purpose, to one so callous that the whole mind boggles at the thought.

* * *

Long before the end of October all the leaf green in the forest had disappeared and by the middle of the month the first snow had fallen. But it was only a foretaste of things to come, as the last fortnight in October was relatively warm and the early snow very soon turned to slush.

About this time we had two visitors: the Parliamentary Secretary to the Labour Party, Alderman Carol Johnson, and an Australian journalist called Redrup, who was studying European agriculture at first hand, and who was one of those friends of Elli's whom she was given to conjuring out of her hat at a moment's notice—that hat which, as Lady Constance said, "sat where nobody else's hat sat."

But while the society as a whole welcomed all English-speaking visitors with open arms, to me they were doubly welcome. I not only enjoyed talking to them, but I was delighted to be spared the onus of thinking out programmes for the meetings they attended. We did the honours; they supplied the entertainment—or uplift, as the case might be. Thus, at no trouble to myself, the club enjoyed two very pleasant evenings during which it is to be hoped that its members imbibed an insight into *British Social Services* and *Life in the Bush*. But somehow or other, I suspect that all that they really remember is the spirited and spontaneous rendering that Mr. Redrup gave them of "Waltzing Matilda." I cannot say whose idea it was that he should sing it, but I do know that it was a special request and that we were all sitting round drinking tea at the time. Formal as the atmosphere was, he was not the least disconcerted. He rose to his feet and sang it the whole way through with unaffected gusto, and very soon the whole party had picked up the refrain and were joining in the chorus.

Visitors from outside were, however, not very frequent, and in the main the weeks which passed have all merged with one another in my mind. Day followed day in a regular routine that varied only with the changing topics of conversation. As October wore on, Princess Elizabeth's forthcoming wedding held the floor. I was amazed at the amount of interest it aroused and quite bowled over by the degree of knowledge the republican Finns displayed. When it came to the crowned heads of Europe, they had all their genealogies at their finger-tips, and there was no gossip, true or untrue, that they did not know about them. Often in my surprise I queried the source of their information. The answer I got was always the same: "We got it from Sweden."

Wherever I went, interest in the wedding predominated and the daily papers were scanned for details of the preparations that were being made, while I myself was constantly plied with questions that I was seldom able to answer. About this time I was sitting one afternoon with Sirkka, Airi, Anna and Kirsti—in theory, they were having a lesson; in practice, we were having a gossip—when Anna remarked to me in rather a puzzled way, "Isn't it rather a strange present that Queen Mary has given to Princess Elizabeth?"

"What is it?" I asked, not being very up-to-date.

"A jewelled brassière."

Visions of Fatima floated before my eyes. It certainly did seem a bit out of character.

"Are you sure?" I queried. "I don't think you can be right."

"I read about it in the newspaper and I looked the word up in the dictionary."

I took the matter up and foraged through *The Weekly Times* and all the available picture papers until I discovered the answer. It was a stomacher, an object that I had some trouble in describing, because I was very hazy myself as to what it was.

Towards the end of the month a rival topic of conversation cropped up. The fifteen-year-old son of a prominent man in the town failed to return home one evening and was found next morning in the lock-up. He had set out the evening before to go to the cinema, but instead had found an empty taxi parked in the market place and driven off in it for a joy-ride. In good film style, the police gave chase and he, panicking, fetched up against a telegraph pole a mile or so out of the town. Thereupon, he abandoned the wrecked vehicle and climbed up on to the roof of a nearby house—every Finnish house has a ladder leading to the roof in case of fire and to facilitate the clearing of snow. From there the police fetched him down and, when he refused to give his name, locked him up. How it came about that in a small place like Kajaani the police did not know who he was, nor how, confronted with a badly rattled fifteen-year-old, they failed to find out, I have never understood, but such was certainly the case, and as a result his parents passed a very anxious night.

As may well be imagined, Kajaani talked and went on talking until the court case was over; but had the boy been a year younger it is possible that the general interest would have died down sooner. There would certainly have been less publicity as, in Finland, those under the age of fifteen do not come under the jurisdiction of the courts. In the normal way they are dealt with by a board of school teachers and parents, and only in exceptionally bad cases does the local welfare board have to be convened to cope with the situation.

Between the ages of fifteen and eighteen, however, young law-breakers come into a different category. They are arraigned before the ordinary courts. But, in dealing with them, the judicial and welfare authorities work hand in glove with each other and the system allows of great elasticity. In this particular case the boy was let off with fine and a reprimand, the only charge made being that of driving without a licence. This meant that he was allowed to return to school, where, to this day, he is known by his companions as "Chauffeur," but his unfortunate father had to pay through the nose for his escapade. The court awarded the taxi-driver heavy damages and also, because his taxi was his means of livelihood, maintenance during the time that it was being repaired. In this way the driver made a good deal of easy money, as the motor mechanics promptly came out on strike and considerably prolonged the period for which maintenance had to be paid.

Basically, the Finnish legal system is a heritage from Sweden and contains no such procedure as trial by jury. Most offences come before the rural or municipal courts, above which there are three courts of appeal,[1] various highly specialised courts and

[1] The functions of these three courts are identical. One is at Turku, one at Vaasa and one at Kuopio. The last-mentioned has only been at Kuopio since the war; before that it sat at Viipuri.

finally, over all, the Supreme Court. Treason trials and those of high-ranking officials all begin in the courts of appeal, but the rural and municipal courts take care of the rest, at least in the initial stages.

For legal purposes, the country is divided into roughly fifty circuits that are in their turn subdivided into assize areas, in each of which courts must be held twice in the year.

I once went to a rural court, which was sitting at Hyrynsalmi, a church village some thirty miles to the north of Kajaani and about halfway to Suomussalmi. Eero, who was staying in the village while defending several clients, arranged for me to go on the last day of the session so that we could return by car together. Consequently, I travelled alone to Hyrynsalmi, but before I left Aili gave me minute instructions as to where to find the court, which was sitting in a bakery. Then, to make assurance doubly sure, as she put me in the post-bus she had a word with the driver, who undertook to see me to the very door. But things did not go according to plan; the spring thaw had sent in, and on reaching Kontiomäki, a railway junction roughly one-third of the way there, we learned that the road to Hyrynsalmi was no longer safe for heavy traffic as thereafter it continually crossed and re-crossed the river on the ice. However, the driver did the best he could; he found someone to explain the situation to me and saw to it that I joined the train with the other stranded passengers.

It was not long after the train had started that a completely strange man came and sat down opposite to me, saying as he did so, "I know who you are, I know what you are doing, and I've seen the room you live in. Please may I talk to you?" I was not a little disconcerted, but it soon transpired that he worked for the Red Cross, that the Red Cross owned the Freys' house and that he had recently been to visit them on business connected with the lease. There was no gainsaying him; he talked incessantly all the way to Hyrynsalmi, where our ways parted.

The church village of Hyrynsalmi is as spread out and scattered as most others in Finland and is a long distance from the railway station. I must have walked a good mile through the forest before reaching the village proper, and even then my difficulties were not over, for the bakery showed no outward —or for that matter inward—sign of being a bakery and I tried several wrong doors before running Eero to earth.

The court was already sitting, but a new case was just about

Harri, Kaisu, Petra, Martta and Torsti

Yrjö Liipola's 1918 War Memorial, Joensuu

It was early one morning during the last week in October that Ritva Virkkunen was rushed into hospital with acute peritonitis. There Kalle operated and when, later in the day, he told me what had happened I have rarely seen anybody look more dejected. In an isolated small town like Kajaani everything takes on such a very personal aspect. At the time, though of course he would not commit himself, I do not think he expected her to live and it was, in fact, a full month before she was out of danger.

As a result November was coloured by an anxiety which, in varying degrees, we all shared, and during this period my attention was drawn to several significant facts. One was that Kajaani had no ambulance, a deficiency that has since been rectified, but which at the time was viewed with astonishing complacency. The Virkkunens lived not more than five minutes' walk from the hospital and Ritva had been taken there in a taxi, but what of the whole large district of Kainuu that was served by the same hospital? The only answer I ever got was, "You do not understand; we are so poor," which in reality I understood very well. It was the priorities the local authorities gave to their expenditure that I so often found incomprehensible.

Living on the fringes of the medical world in Finland was very interesting. The personal relationship between doctor and patient was so very different from any to which I have been used. I think it was the lack of personal touch that surprised me most, although, there being so few doctors to go round, it was really only to be expected. G.P.s rarely visited privately in a professional capacity; everyone who possibly could went to see them, and clearly they were far too busy to make daily rounds from house to house. Nevertheless, I was surprised when Kalle told me that it was unusual for him to be called out at night more than twice in a month.

Another factor that made extensive private visiting out of the question was the dearth of cars. Only one of Kajaani's six doctors owned one and in this there was nothing uncommon. Yet even had they the means of getting about easily, I am convinced that most Finnish doctors would continue to maintain that it was better for their patients to come to them; that practical considerations, such as having everything to hand, were far more important than the study of their patients' environment.

A medical man of any kind who panders to his patients is a very rare phenomenon. The tendency is for them all to behave like dictators, and the public as a whole respond with docility. I remember Kalle, who at heart is very far from being a dictator, explaining to me how he inoculated all and sundry against tuberculosis. "I don't ask them if they want to be done," he said. "I do them. It's for their own good." A wise measure, for tuberculosis is the scourge of the country.

But overwork is only one of many reasons why the family doctor, as we understand him, does not exist in Finland. Another reason is their attitude to fees. The theory is that medical men do not charge doctors and their families, nurses or pharmacists. In this there is nothing very original, but what, in fact, seems to happen is that exemption is extended to all their personal friends. This has serious repercussions, because the Finns, being aggressively independent, cannot bear to be indebted to anybody. They therefore tend to say to themselves, "I can't possibly trouble Doctor X again; he didn't charge me last time. This time I shall ring up Doctor Y." And ring they do on the slightest pretext, and a really rather frightening amount of prescribing is done over the telephone.

But there is more to this tendency to call in first one doctor and then another than mere unwillingness to be beholden to anyone. It is in the Finnish nature to love anything or anyone new and any doctor or dentist who sets up in practice can be sure, at least to begin with, that he or she will have plenty of patients, for the public as a whole will be unable to resist the temptation to try them at least once, just to see what they are like.

There is, however, another factor which may mitigate against a long-term, personal relationship between the G.P. and his patient, and this is that the rising young men frequently do not stay long enough in one place. Private practices are often of necessity set up on a short-term basis, because State hospitals generally appoint their juniors for a period of three years and pay them so badly that they are forced to run one concurrently with their hospital work in order to make both ends meet. At the end of three years, as a matter of course, these men move on and set up elsewhere.

The surprising fact to emerge from all this is that medicine ends up by being one of the most lucrative professions in the country, despite the fact that State salaries are so poor that Kalle, in his capacity of Assistant Surgeon at Kajaani Hospital, received only about one-third of what the foreman in charge of the workmen digging up the Kauppakatu was paid.

But if the salaries paid out by the State are small, so too are the demands made on the patients, a flat rate of 160 to 165 marks, or approximately 3*s*. 8*d*., being the inclusive charge for each day spent in hospital. This charge is compulsory and must be paid by all but the destitute, whose expenses are met by the commune in which they are domiciled—a ruling that leads to not a few disputes among local authorities.

As for Finnish hospital buildings, they vary from the primitive and inadequate to the super-modern and magnificently equipped and, indeed, the new children's hospital in Helsinki is without parallel anywhere in the world. But even here there is one great need. There is only one professional anæsthetist in the whole of the country. Instead, anæsthetics are given by the nursing staff, whose normal training is prolonged by six months to teach them the job. The result is the predominant use of ether and the fact that the finer shades of analgesia inevitably have to go by the board.

* * *

With November came the first real snow of the winter. It fell, I remember, on a Friday night for, it being half-term, I had arranged to spend a long week-end in Kuopio, and the morning that I left Kajaani I awoke to a white world.

My counterpart in Kuopio, Hope Castren, had invited me. She was a Scot, the widow of a Finn, and she lived there with her eight-year-old son in the home of one of the leading local families. I thoroughly enjoyed my visit, for kindness was showered upon me and I lived in the lap of luxury. But perhaps the greatest luxury of all was having someone to talk to who understood half sentences and shades of meaning.

Kuopio under snow looked most attractive. I thought then, as I have continued to think ever since, that Finland is far more beautiful in winter than in summer; the dust disappears and the drab little gardens and untidy wood-piles are transformed. At once the smallest light shining among the trees is a fairy tale come true. Lighted windows abound and curtains are rarely made to draw. The fact that only a narrow strip of material frames most windows has little or nothing to do with post-war shortages; closing up is simply not a national custom. It was a long time before I got used to sitting in brightly lighted rooms looking out into the darkness, and I still think that the effect of them is naked and cheerless. Nor is this effect lessened by the Finnish passion for covering their floors with shining linoleum and—curiously enough—using their rugs as mural decoration.[1] But if the indoor effect is cold, the light which is thrown from within on to the snow outside is warm and welcoming.

In more ways than one the long hours of darkness had their compensations. They were nothing like so dark as I had pictured them and there was none of the Stygian gloom my mind had conjured up. Instead, the snow reflected not only the moonlight and the glow from the windows and street lamps, but also the brilliance of the Northern Lights, which would often stream across the night sky. There was no method in their madness, no fixed shape or form. They might shine out like searchlights or drift across the night sky like opaque sea monsters. They were sometimes white and sometimes tinged with mauve or pink, but the first that I remember seeing was a great silver arc that spanned the entire firmament.

Northern Lights are an integral part of the winter and the background for a wealth of legend and fantasy. Robert Crottet has recently produced a book called "The Enchanted Forest" that contains a collection of legends told to him by the Koltta Lapps[2] from the Petsamo region. In it I came across the following passage:

"About the Northern Lights. When the leaves of the trees begin to turn yellow in the autumn, it is because they're going to die. And the souls of human beings do the same thing. They become brighter as death draws nearer. But instead of falling as the leaves do, they fly away right up into the sky. As long as they are on the earth and hidden by the body, one could not see them clearly, but in the sky there is nothing that hides them.

"When the shadows of winter lie on the earth the souls of the dead come too and show themselves to the living, so that they may have patience and courage enough to wait for the return of the spring and the sun. From one end of the sky to the other the souls dance in the Northern lights and give us much better light than the moon and the stars."

* * *

[1] The Finnish craft of weaving loose-piled variegated rugs for use as mural decoration is one that originated in mediæval times.

[2] The Koltta Lapps have now been evacuated to the shores of Lake Inari.

Shortly after I returned to Kajaani I received a large parcel from Hope. Full of curiosity, I cut the string and out fell a heap of letters. With them was a note beseeching me to deal with them as best I could. It seemed that Hope, in an excess of zeal, had had a brainwave. She had put an advertisement into a Scottish newspaper asking for pen friends for her pupils, and the response had been such that she was now knee deep in answers. The result of this was that she had had another bright idea—namely, that I should deal with some of them. Being kindly disposed towards her, I waded through the letters she had sent me and chose out the possibles—about thirty in all—and relegated the remainder to the waste-paper basket. The pathetic truth was that these ardent letter-writers were in the main so illiterate that my pupils would never have made head or tail of their effusions. Nor was it simply a question of literacy; a bond of mutual interest is, after all, the first prerequisite of a "pen pal," so, having jettisoned the useless, I set about allocating the remainder.

A week or so later, having disposed of some twenty letters, I found myself still with a dozen in hand. It was then that I encountered Elli in the Kauppakatu. "Let me have some," she said. "I can find people to write." I did not need a second bidding; I handed over the lot. At the next club meeting I inquired if she had managed to get rid of them. Unexpected as she always was, I was still taken aback by her reply. "It wasn't necessary," she said. "I answered them all myself."

* * *

At the beginning of November Gretel Eberling returned to Kajaani. She had not been back since her departure for Exeter in June as, on completion of her course there, she had gone straight on to Sweden to get some first-hand experience of the latest Swedish dental practices.

Kajaani was all agog to welcome her back and to find out what the latest fashions were, for Gretel had long since established herself as the glass of fashion in the town. Hence the excitement, for, as she was earning Swedish crowns, everybody was certain she would bring back a lot of new clothes. Consequently, it was unfortunate for all concerned that the Swedish income tax authorities should have made sudden last-minute claims on her earnings. But with or without new creations—and there were some—everyone was delighted to have her back, as Gretel was a live wire and life was never dull when she was around.

Not that Kajaani lacked entertainment; considering its remote position on the map, I thought it did rather well. There were, for instance, two cinema houses each showing two pictures a week. These pictures had a distinctly cosmopolitan flavour as, besides the Finnish and Swedish films shown, there were English, American, French and German. They varied from the very old to the most up-to-date, but, barring the home produce, it was the French pictures that tended to be the most recent and the German ones the most archaic.

Over and above the films there was a concert almost every month, given either by a visiting artist or by a local choir, and last but not least there was the People's Theatre, which produced on an average nine plays every year between September and May.

Nearly every Finnish town, however small, has its own theatre, and in this Kajaani was no exception. Moreover, the organisation prevailing there was one common to most of the smaller towns. Neither professional nor purely amateur, the theatre boasted a paid staff of three—a producer, a costumier and a stage decorator. The cast were all amateurs, spare-time enthusiasts who devoted their leisure to rehearsing and playing, and who were from time to time supported by a visiting professional.

Naturally enough, for linguistic reasons, I benefited very little from the theatre; in fact, I only went there once with Toini and that was out of sheer curiosity. It was a Sunday afternoon, when they were giving an operetta which I felt might be within my grasp. As was only to be expected the standard was not very high, but the hall was full and the audience, many of whom had come in from the outlying country districts, was most appreciative.

Even in the big cities the organisation behind the Finnish theatre is very different from ours. Scattered over the country there are some forty purely professional establishments. About half of these employ actors and actresses who are engaged by the year and the other half are hybrids, where a permanent nucleus of professional players is supported by visiting artists. A producer who hires a theatre and collects his own cast for the purpose of putting on a single play is practically unknown.

But, in Finland, it is the amateur theatre that is the most

interesting, because it is ubiquitous and vital and thrives on the most seemingly unlikely soil. All the time I was in Finland I only saw two theatrical performances, one amateur in Kajaani, the other professional in the Swedish theatre in Helsinki, and the amateur by amateur standards seemed to me to outshine the professional by professional ones. To be truthful, however, I found both performances uninspired, but whether, in their respective classes, they were representative of the nation's talent I have no idea.

No official visitors came to the club in November so once again I found myself faced with the problem of providing the meetings with entertainment. On one occasion Gretel stepped into the breach with a description of her travels, and on another Stella. I had sent an S.O.S. to Stella in the form of a pressing invitation to come and help me out, for Oulu, by Finnish standards, was not very far away,[1] and furthermore I knew that she was supremely interested in the drama league and that the subject was likely to go down well. A talk from her seemed therefore to be an excellent idea, but I had also an ulterior motive. I cherished a hope—vain, as it turned out—that she could sing, for Christmas was approaching and I was diligently and unsuccessfully trying to teach club members to sing English carols. The first snag that I encountered was that most Finnish voices are pitched farther down the scale than ours so that every tune had to be transposed into a lower key. The second was my own ineptitude, for the spirit of the music was so foreign to most of my pupils that they did not assimilate it at all easily and were constantly asking me to show them how it went—in other words, to sing—and all that I could do was to croak like a melancholy frog. This really was hard, for the Finns love to burst into song, and I could not help feeling that the job of a teacher secretary who could play and sing, even a little, would be money for jam. But no amount of wishing could ever give me a tuneful voice—even in my early schooldays I was thrown out of the singing class and given extra dictation instead, with results scarcely more successful—so I pinned my hopes on Stella. But, alas! they were soon to be dashed; Stella, with the best will in the world, was no better at it than I was.

* * *

[1] The distance from Oulu to Kajaani is 120 miles—a train journey of five and a quarter hours.

It must have snowed on and off all through November, for the snow-plough was kept busy keeping the streets clear, but the curious thing about it is that I really cannot remember it actually snowing, or at any rate only on very rare occasions, so I can only suppose that the snow must generally have fallen in the early hours of the morning. Certainly the picture that I had conjured up in London of struggling head first through a permanent blizzard was far from the truth. Short as the daylight was, in Kajaani it was nearly always sunny. Nevertheless, the snow fell and was swept to the sides of the streets where, between the pavements and the road, it was piled in long mounds that rose to a height of anything from two to four feet. It was only in the main thoroughfares that these heaps were systematically carted away, and by the time this happened in the Kauppakatu—which was long before they had assumed the mountainous proportions they reached elsewhere—picks were needed as well as shovels and the great frozen lumps of snow were striated with multicoloured dirt.

The roads in winter presented a series of hazards for the uninitiated. These risks were not great, but for the newcomer they were almost continual. Before Christmas they came from below, after Christmas from above, for with the spring thaw the eaves began to drip and the snow to fall or be shovelled from the roofs on to the unwary. All winter long the pavements tended to be very slippery and, what was far worse, to teem with wooden chairs on metal runners six to eight feet long.[1] These contraptions are very light and are used by the general public for a variety of purposes. They may serve to carry their luggage or their shopping baskets; they may strap their children to them in lieu of a pram, or they may even use them to give their wives or grandmothers a lift, but the activating principle is always the same. Hold on to the back of the chair and scoot down the road until you come to a hill and then, ignoring all cross-roads and other possible pitfalls, glide to the bottom. So far so good, as there was not much heavy traffic in Kajaani, but on reaching the Kauppakatu, which is long and flat, the trouble began. The chairs were manœuvred on to the pavement to facilitate shop-gazing, and in pushing them along, their owners were apt to tack or go about without the slightest warning as if completely oblivious of the six feet of metal that were sticking out behind them. There is no doubt about it,

[1] The Finnish word for these chairs is *potkukelkka*. There is no translation.

common courtesy and consideration for others are sadly lacking in the streets of Finnish towns, where the very old and the very young get shockingly jostled.

I mention this because "We Finns have no manners" is almost as common a lament as "We Finns drink too much," and one for which I personally think there is a good deal more reason. Because of this, my first instinct was to skate round the subject altogether, but, on second thoughts, I have changed my mind, as by omission I shall risk being accused of insincerity, and the Finns, I am well aware, deserve better of me than that. I remember well how, soon after my arrival, I was lent Constance Malleson's book *In the North*, and how, seeing me reading it, Kalle asked me what I thought of it. I was not yet very sure of my ground, so I countered his question with another: "How did you like it?"

"Very much," he answered. "All that she says about the Winter War is correct, and it's nice that anyone should like us so much. But, you know, we Finns do not always wear our Sunday clothes."

I laughed; I understood so well what he meant. Constance Malleson's enthusiasm for the Finns and everything Finnish is such that the picture she paints is scarcely human.

"You'd better look out," I retorted. "Who knows, perhaps one day I'll write a book about you and then you'll be in your dungarees all right." In the face of which, I can scarcely pretend that the manners of the man in the street are endearing when in public places they most certainly are not. They are both actively and passively bad; in the streets it is the weaker that always go to the wall and nowhere is the spirit of helpfulness in evidence. In fact, the number of Finns who would simply stand by and stare when they might have lent a hand never ceased to amaze me.

Treatment of the foreigner is a thing apart, an altogether different matter. Those who speak a foreign language can usually find plenty of people ready and willing to carry their bags, secure them seats in trains or buses and be generally helpful, for visitors from abroad are always treated with the greatest politeness. Furthermore, should there be an exception to this rule, the offender is liable to get into hot water, as being rude to a foreigner is a legal offence and one which may land the perpetrator in trouble with the police. It is not, so I am told, by any means unheard of for a tram conductor to stop his vehicle and, in a high-handed way, give a drunk in charge simply because he considers him to have been offensive to a foreign passenger. But this is pure hearsay; I never witnessed any such scene, though I saw much that made me realise the lack of common courtesy between Finn and Finn.

Perhaps the climate is responsible and the jostling and pushing the natural outcome of its rigours, for in outlying districts survival is still often only of the fittest. And in the same way the prevailing lack of helpfulness may perhaps be attributed to thoughtlessness engendered by the soporific effect of the long hours of darkness. I think it was a Finn—it was certainly someone who had been in the country—who once said to me, "I can always spot a foreigner when travelling by train in Finland because their eyes are alive all the time. A Finn's only light up when you speak to him." Of course, this is as exaggerated as all sweeping generalisations, but I quote it because in a way it seems to bear out my theory. But let me make it abundantly clear: in the homes that I visited, the behaviour of the Finns must often have put ours to shame, as it left nothing to be desired, unless it were a rather greater ease of manner.

* * *

The great excitement of November was the Civil Service Strike, which took place during the last week of the month and lasted for three days. Trouble had been brewing for some time among Government employees because they were grossly underpaid in comparison with all other workers, persistent strikes in almost every other sphere having led to higher wages and a universal rise in the cost of living. But protest as the Civil Servants might, their protests fell upon deaf ears. The Communist-controlled administration was apparently indifferent to their plight and their strike, which was without precedent, aimed at bringing home to the Government that they were, in fact, essential and deserving of notice. Their actual demands centred around two points: that their salaries should be increased and tied to the cost of living index and that so-called temporary civil servants should, on completion of a specified time in Government service, be entitled to the same rates of pension as the permanent staff.

The strike paralysed the country and cut it off from the outside world completely. Post, telegraph and telephone services all came to a standstill, railways ceased to function and,

Customs and immigration officers being implicated, all sea and air services were suspended.

Altogether some 70,000 civil servants were involved, the term "civil servant" being used to embrace all Government employees. Thus a very large part of the responsible world was on strike and, alone among state employees, the doctors and nurses in the state hospitals continued to function as usual. State schools shut down and university teaching fell into abeyance.

In Kajaani, as elsewhere, the inhabitants were marooned. Only the children, who started on a period of indefinite holidays, were delighted. Heljä, who was on strike, was in a frenzy; torn between her sense of justice and fear of the bad effect the teachers' example would have on the schoolchildren.

On the second day things started happening. The Communist Prime Minister ordered the police to occupy the postal, telegraph and telephone buildings, and by so doing effectively isolated all strikers from each other. Then he broadcast to the nation. There was deep anger at his broadcast, which was singularly abusive and paid but scant attention to the root causes of the strike. In it he first threatened to call up all the men on strike into the armed forces—in which he was within his constitutional rights—and then proceeded to put out a false report that the strikers in the capital had gone back to work and that all those in the provinces who did not promptly follow suit would lose their jobs.

Consternation was general because no one knew what to believe. It seemed impossible that so wholesale a threat could ever be implemented. In Kajaani—as indeed all over the country—the burning question was: what was happening elsewhere? If the strikers in Helsinki were indeed back at work, it was obviously courting disaster to hold out, but, being unconvinced, they held.

As it turned out, those in Helsinki were not back at work, although things were moving. On the second day of the strike —that of the Prime Minister's broadcast—a deputation, headed by M. Järnefelt, the head of the Civil Service, had visited President Paasikivi. High-level discussions had taken place, and the day following M. Järnefelt himself broadcast the order to return to work.

Individual reactions were interesting and showed that in many cases the habitual Finnish phlegm was no more than a veneer. Everywhere one heard talk of reprisals. There would be a drastic purge of the Government offices; all the best people would lose their jobs and the Communists would take full advantage of the situation to further their designs. But nothing of the sort happened. Wage increases were granted and, if not so large as had been demanded, they were at least tied to the cost of living index and the temporary old-stagers got their pensions.

Meanwhile, I too was feeling the effect of the strike. The Finns always celebrate Advent, which they refer to as "Little Christmas," and the club was giving a party. The date had been fixed for November 28th, which, as it turned out, was the last day of the strike. That it should have coincided with the strike was unfortunate, for the whole party pivoted round the Press Attaché from Helsinki, who was to be the guest of honour and who, it was hoped, would supply at least half the evening's entertainment. He was known to be in Kuopio, and there was just a chance that he might be able to come by car, but there was no way at all of getting into touch with him and finding out. Nor was this my only headache, for at the last club meeting the members had been at their least co-operative. In the absence of Yrjö, Gretel had asked for volunteers to provide refreshments for the party. Her plea had been met first with an exasperating silence and then with a few half-hearted undertakings which I was still too green to appreciate at their proper worth. Consequently, when I was not worrying about possible alternative entertainment, I was wondering whether or not there would be anything to eat and drink. I need not have bothered, although our guest failed us; there was enough food to have fed an army and the party went with a great swing.

* * *

On December 4th municipal and communal elections were held throughout the country and in Kajaani, as elsewhere, everyone went to the polls.

These elections are held every third year, generally in November, and all Finns over twenty-one years of age are entitled to vote. The strength of the Municipal Councils varies throughout the country from fifteen to fifty-nine members. In Kajaani there were twenty-nine and, of the members going out of office, fifteen had belonged to left-wing parties and fourteen to right.

The election was fought on national rather than on local

issues and, considering the political tension in the country, everything went off very quietly. I myself would hardly have noticed that the election was in progress had not a solitary car with a loudspeaker been cruising round the town and the Kauppakatu been enlivened by waves of broadcast propaganda interspersed with the melodies of Schubert and Strauss.

The results of the election, which came out next day, showed a slight swing to the right. The numbers were reversed, fifteen right-wing candidates being successful and fourteen left. The nation-wide results followed much the same pattern and the right-wing parties, together with the Social Democrats, profited in all by 10 to 15 per cent of the seats lost by the Communists and Democratic Unionists.

Like the life of the municipal councils, that of the Diet lasts for three years unless dissolved. The present system of government by a single chamber goes back to 1906, when the Diet of Four Estates was abolished, but it was not until the Russian yoke had been cast off that it achieved supreme governing power. Now parliamentary elections are held every third year on July 1st. The total number of deputies balloted for is 200, and for electoral purposes the country is divided into fifteen areas, each of which elects members in proportion to the number of its inhabitants, the smallest number returned by any one area being eight and the largest thirty-one.

The presidential elections are a thing apart and take place every sixth year, the President being elected by a college of electors who are themselves balloted for in January of the appropriate year. The power invested in the President of Finland is very great. He has supreme executive power, the right to summon or dissolve Parliament, the right of veto, the command of the armed forces, the appointment of all high officials and the right to decide on foreign policy except when it is a matter of war or peace, in which case he must have the approval of the Diet. He has not, however, the power to amend the law without the consent of the Diet; nor can he embark on a foreign policy that involves special legislation or public expenditure without the Diet's approval.

In November, 1945, the misuse of the President's right to decide on foreign policy was the excuse given for the impeachment of ex-President Ryti, who was in office from December, 1940, to August, 1944. Together with seven other members of the War Cabinet and the wartime Minister in Berlin, he was arraigned for war guilt before a special tribunal. It was held that they—the members of the Foreign Affairs Committee—had neglected to consult the Diet and sometimes even omitted to inform the other Cabinet Ministers of the steps they were taking. That, at least, was the peg on which the charges were hung, but so poor a peg was it that under the existing law there was no case against them, and retroactive legislation had to be introduced in order that the clauses of the armistice relating to the trial and punishment of those responsible for the war might be executed.

As President, Ryti came off worst. In February, 1946, he was sentenced to ten years' imprisonment[1] for the crime, if indeed it can be considered a crime, of having backed the wrong horse. Certainly, at the time when he led Finland to throw in her lot with that of Germany, his policy was endorsed by the majority of his fellow countrymen, who do not now hold it against him. The whole sad business was a political necessity which, it was plain to see, went severely against the grain of the people. For had not Ryti's astounding financial ability put Finland on her feet between the wars; and was not this ability, even now, at his country's disposal? At any rate it was generally assumed that the Governor of the Bank of Finland sought his advice on all financial matters of moment; the basis of this assumption being that the Governor's official car was constantly to be seen waiting patiently outside the prison where Ryti was confined.

Shortly after Ryti's trial, his successor, General Mannerheim, was forced by ill health to resign the presidency, and Juho Paasikivi took over, and has held office ever since. He is a man of great personal integrity and one who enjoys the confidence of the people, who fully appreciate the limitations imposed on him from outside and the courageous policy with which he continues undaunted. And if this policy was courageous in 1947, it has been even more courageous since. Take, for example, his handling of the 1948 pre-election crisis: fearing a Communist *coup* on the Czech model, he calmly alerted the Army and the police—as distinct from the State Police—over the head of and without any reference to, the Communist Minister of the Interior, Yrjö Leino. This done, he proceeded to dismiss Minister Leino from office on the grounds—real enough, but somewhat out-of-date—that he had exceeded his

[1] Ryti was the last of the so-called Finnish war criminals to be released, and he came out of prison on May 20th, 1949.

authority in the handing over of certain individuals to the Soviet Union. Nor did his courage stop there; having thus cleared the decks of the Ministry of the Interior, he instigated an inquiry into the very questionable activities of the State Police—an inquiry that led to their dissolution in the following December.

But in writing all this I am preceding myself. The year in question should not be 1948, but 1947, and the time, two years before President Paasikivi, at the age of seventy-eight, was re-elected by a grateful nation for another six years in office.

* * *

On December 11th we held the last club meeting before Christmas, and this time the Press Attaché, who had been prevented by the strike from coming to our "Little Christmas" party, turned up, and we had a pleasant informal evening, after which the society closed down until mid-January and everybody devoted themselves to Christmas preparations. Now more than ever I noticed the paucity of goods in the shops, where books still seemed to be the only things worth buying; books, that is, and Christmas cards, and paper wrappings which were charming, and looking at these gaily coloured wrappings I frequently found myself wishing wistfully that there was more to wrap up in them. All the same, with or without goods, there was a pervasive sense of festivity and bustle which was not a little enhanced by the gipsy horse fair that took place about this time. During several days the town teemed with gipsies, and people from the countryside poured in, either making the fair an excuse to do their shopping or their shopping an excuse to attend the fair. In any case the result was the same and sleigh bells rang out merrily as farmers drove their steaming little chestnut horses hell for leather through the town with the usual gay disregard for pedestrians.

At this time, too, the traditional 'copper kettles' to be found in all Finnish towns at Christmas-time appeared hanging from their tripods in the market place and at street corners. These vessels are, in reality, cauldron-shaped pots and they are put there by the Salvation Army, so that the people may put their season's alms for the poor into them.

About a week before Christmas two minor calamities occurred: Harri and Torsti went down with measles and a filling fell out of one of my teeth. As a result, the little boys were put to bed and I contacted Gretel and embarked forthwith on a series of visits that lasted on and off until Easter.

Gretel had her consulting-rooms in the town on the ground floor of one of the Kajaani Company's blocks of flats. They were small but exceedingly up-to-date, and her apparatus, which included an X-ray plant, was a shining symphony of chromium and powder-blue paint.

As a dentist I have yet to meet Gretel's equal. Never before had I been so painlessly or so thoroughly treated. She took infinite trouble and all the while she worked she kept up a running commentary, explaining step by step exactly what she was doing and why, and stopping every now and again to illustrate her point with a human skull that she kept handy. The jaws of this gruesome object were laced with red and black threads to indicate the nerves and blood vessels and, to prove any further points, a framed series of abnormal teeth hung on the wall.

My teeth turned out to be badly in need of attention and, in all, I must have had about twelve major stoppings done. I also had a dead tooth replaced—a lengthy proceeding, but one that was well worth while. When at last my new tooth was ready it was perfection in porcelain, and Gretel, as she critically surveyed her handiwork, uttered this solemn warning, "Beware of caramels and crayfish." Later, when the time came for me to return to England she gave me a spare tooth as a parting present and a safeguard against possible disasters.

Eighteen months have elapsed since then and I have not yet needed to use it. It remains securely lodged in the family safe among the heirlooms. As for its twin, I still look with admiration at it in the mirror and brag about it on occasions. On the last of these I was lunching with a friend and her small daughter when the conversation turned to dentists. "Talking of teeth," I remarked across the lunch table, "Do you know that one of my front teeth isn't my own?" This was altogether too much for the small girl on my right. She pricked up her ears and said with bated breath, "Oh, Diana, whose is it?"

* * *

As Christmas approached the temperature fell and by Christmas Eve the thermometer registered 30° C. below zero. These bitter, frosty days were as beautiful as they were cold, so, putting on several layers of clothes, I set out with my camera

Kalle, Maaret and Harri on the beach at Kalajoki

The author at Oulu

to take some photographs. I had to make the most of the daylight, for it now lasted a bare two hours.

By eleven o'clock I was down by the river watching the sunrise. Ice clung to the banks, but out in the main stream the swift-moving water flowed freely and, because it was warmer than the air, it steamed like a boiling cauldron. The light from the rising sun caught the vapour, which flushed with a rosy glow, and all along the river banks the trees glinted and glittered as though made of pure glass. I shall never forget the frosted trees of Finland; weighed down by ice crystals that were often over an inch long, the birches wept. The effect was magical beyond belief—lovely beyond words. Every twig, and indeed every plant that showed above the snow, was crystalline and sometimes so powdered with rime that the effect against the sky was that of dazzling white blossom. All through the frosty weather the forest was a fairy place, but on this particular morning, with the warm blush of the sunrise suffusing the gently swirling mist, it was more than usually enchanting. Yet the cold was such that I could not dally and as a photographic expedition it was largely a failure. I only managed to take a few pictures because manipulating the camera meant removing my gloves, and the resulting cold was almost more than I could bear. On the bridge I stopped to look at the castle. Its massive walls were capped with snow—thick white snow that smoothed away the angles and filled my head with greedy thoughts of pre-war Fullers cakes. Black water swirled past lapping its walls and as I watched the glow of the sunrise on the mist began to fade. I took one more photograph and then gave up, for the pain in my hands was agonising. Climbing the hill to the town at full speed, I plunged into the Maakunta's cloakroom and there hugged the radiator until my icy fingers ceased to hurt.

Late that afternoon Sirkka, Kalle and I trooped over to the hospital, where one of the male choirs was giving a carol concert. The singers were massed on the main staircase between the first and second floors and, all along the corridors, the doors of the wards were thrown wide open. In these corridors the staff and their families were congregated. The choir sang beautifully and I listened with pleasure, although Finnish carols are so solemn that not for a moment do they make me think of Christmas.

We walked home when it was over, taking with us the hospital

Father Christmas. To Finnish children, Father Christmas is known as the *Joulupukki*—literally the "Christmas goat"—and he lives on the top of a *tunturi* in northernmost Lapland. There —because, of course, no one man could cope with so many parcels—he is helped in his preparations by the *Tontut*, a pack of small urchins in red caps and grey jerkins. Children dressed up as *Tontut* are always much in evidence at Christmas parties, but on Christmas Eve the *Joulupukki*, covered from head to foot in furs, comes alone in a *pulkka*—the small boat-like sleigh that is used by the Lapps and drawn by a single reindeer. He always makes his visits in person; for him there is no slipping unseen down the chimney in the middle of the night.

Back in the nursery, the little boys were waiting, all keyed up with anticipation. A tall Christmas tree stood in the window, and on a low table by each child's bed a candle was burning. Harri was already sceptical about Father Christmas, but he was none the less excited for that, while as for Torsti, he was a firm believer. He sat up in bed, tense with expectation, his dimpled face still mottled by measles spots and his eyes shining like stars. When at long last the *Joulupukki* did arrive with his great birch-bark basket full of gaily coloured parcels, he was absolutely speechless—a pretty rare state of affairs for Torsti. As for Petra, at sight of the *Joulupukki* she burst into tears and hid her head, which was not at all surprising, for the mask he was wearing was more than enough to scare any two-year-old.

His visit did not last long, for he had a pressing date at the hospital, but he stayed long enough to distribute his presents and to crack a joke with each child, excepting Petra, who would not look at him. His departure was followed by a regular riot of excitement as the parcels were unpacked and the attractive paper wrappings, in which the Finns excel, were cast aside. Their contents were nothing to write home about. Good toys, like so many other things, were difficult to get, but the children, who had nothing with which to compare them, were supremely happy. Someone had procured three fine rubber balls, which were soon flying from bed to bed with a total disregard for the burning candles on the tree and the bedside tables, not to mention the discarded paper wrappings that were strewn all over the floor just asking to catch fire. While, adding to the confusion, there was Petra who, now that the *Joulupukki* had gone, had quite recovered from her fear and was dancing madly about in her excitement.

The uproar lasted until dinner-time, when everyone in the household sat down together, as Christmas is an essentially homely affair. We were ten: Sirkka, Kalle, Sirkka's mother, who was staying over Christmas, Harri and Torsti rolled up in rugs and arrayed in Red Indian feathered head-dresses, Petra in the high chair, Martta, Kaisu, her husband, Jussi, and I. Jussi was a dear old man who was unfortunately suffering from the results of a stroke. He hardly spoke at all, but sat throughout the meal smiling quietly to himself and when it was over retired happily to the nursery with the children.

We ate by candlelight. On the sideboard beneath the portraits of Kalle's great-grandparents, four candles burned in silver candlesticks. Normally these pictures lacked vitality but now in the soft light they lived as never before. The table, too, was lit by candles whose mellow radiance dimmed all contours and threw new features into relief. Yet withal there was none of the warm intimacy generally associated with candlelight. It was banished by the lack of curtains. It was as if the night were in the room with us and, in a strange way, as if the room were outside in the night, for in the dark depths of the windows, every pin-point of light was reflected.

There was no holly and no mistletoe; instead there were evergreens, paper hangings and, as at Easter, the inevitable straw decorations. There were straw angels, straw animals and the peculiar pendant straw boxes known as *himmeli*. But of all the Finnish Christmas decorations it is the candles that strike the dominant note. They are everywhere, indoors and out, for on Christmas night they burn outside in the churchyards and the cemeteries. As soon as it is dark, the people come and light them on their family graves and soon the whole churchyard is alive with twinkling points of flame. The candles used are thick and solid and, when necessary, they are protected from the weather by glass shields. They burn till morning when, in the country villages at 6 a.m. and in the towns at 7, the people flock to church through the darkness.

Finnish Christmas food, even at its best, does not compare favourably with ours. The traditional fare is boiled ham and peas, rice porridge and plum tartlets, and over and above this, there is the Christmas fish. This last is known as *livekala*, and is described in the dictionary as "Cod steeped in lye." It is the fish so often seen in photographs of northern Norway, hanging out on racks to dry. From Norway it is imported into Finland, where it is bought by the Finnish housewife well before Christmas because it has to be soaked in ash water for two weeks before it is eaten. In actual fact, I never yet met a Finn who really enjoyed eating it. Its annual appearance is a pure matter of tradition.

As on all festive occasions, this Christmas Eve dinner began with *hors d'œuvres*. The ham followed. With it we ate tinned peas, turnips, mashed potatoes and a delectable sweet sauce. The ham was put on the table and, for the one and only time while I was in Finland, I saw a joint carved in the dining-room. The Christmas fish being reserved for Christmas Day, the rice porridge followed, thanks entirely to an American food parcel, for rice was not then obtainable by any other means. To me it was just like a milk pudding without any skin on the top. Floating about in it was one lucky almond which fell to Jussi. As so often happens when the mince-pie stage is reached, no one had much room left for the plum tartlets—which, for want of plums, were made of apple—and we all rose from the table happily replete.

The meal over, the little boys were put back to bed and we cleared away the dishes and washed up. Order restored, Kalle got down the family Bible and, sitting at his desk, read the Christmas story aloud to the assembled household. This Bible is a very treasured possession, as it dates back to the year 1642 and is one of the first complete edition ever to be printed in the Finnish language. Of the 1,200 copies that composed this edition, only 200 to 300 exist to-day, and their language, which is that of the original translation, is archaic. This is not the text in general use. The modern Finnish Bible is up-to-date in language and has none of the outstanding literary merit associated with ours. But, of course, the finer points of translation were as wasted on me as they were on Petra, who suddenly shattered the solemnity of the occasion by hurling first her new ball and then herself into the midst of the listening circle.

When the reading was over and the Bible had been returned to its place of safety, the children were tucked up for the night. This took some little time, for by now they were a bit over-excited and Harri suddenly evinced a whole-hearted desire to take his sharp new skates to bed with him.

With the children settled, peace reigned once more and the grown-ups opened their presents. When everything had been unpacked and admired—a proceeding that was quite a lengthy one—we all drank coffee and madeira, after which we decided unanimously that the time had come to call it a day.

Christmas Day was very quiet. There was only one service in the church, and that was at 7 a.m. Not realising this, I went expecting to find one at 10 a.m. but the place was deserted. Obviously I should have inquired in advance and not taken Heljä's definition "A Sunday in the middle of the week" so literally.

For lunch we had the Christmas fish and, long before we had it, we smelt it. It arrived on the table covered in a blanket of delicious sauce which I cannot but feel is its chief justification for existence, as the fish itself has nothing to recommend it. It was of a leathery, opaque consistency and looked horrid; but I have to admit that, eaten with the sauce, it did not taste as bad as it looked—or smelt. Unfortunately, Sirkka had got rather a lot and, as nobody cared for it much, it haunted the dinner table for several days to come.

I spent Christmas afternoon quietly with the Ehos, and in the evening Hilkka and Toivo Pentikäinen gave a small party. It was the first of a series of evening parties that lasted all the week. They were all great fun. We put on evening dress and set out to enjoy ourselves. The houses where we gathered were different, but the company did not vary much. On Boxing night Gretel produced a turkey and plum pudding. They were as good as any that I have tasted, but the plum pudding was a highly unorthodox shape, as Kajaani did not run to pudding basins. And, talking of orthodoxy, I found that it still required all my attention to drink at the right moment, to drink the right amount and not to upset the routine by having a full glass when it should have been empty, or an empty one when it should have been full. It was just one of those things, I reflected ruefully, that one must be born to.

Just before the New Year, I left for Helsinki. I had been given a generous holiday which lasted until January 12th, and there were several things that I wanted to do in the capital. When I told the Freys that I was going, Kalle said at once that I must stay with his cousin Madge, and as promptly fixed it all up for me over the telephone. I felt that this was hard on Madge, but Kalle was adamant: "Madge will be delighted," he assured me, "and it will be much cheaper for you. Besides, Madge's flat is very central."

At this point, I cannot resist repeating a story told to me quite recently by a friend. She had, it appeared, just received a letter from a certain very celebrated Finn, in which he began by saying that he was coming to London for a conference and ended by asking if she could manage to engage a room for him in a hotel—a hotel, mark you, that he expressly stated must be "central oh so and convenient very!"

In some ways it was a pity that I went to Helsinki just when I did, as by so doing I missed seeing the film of *Maaret*, which came to Kajaani during my absence. This was disappointing, as, after our visit to Kilpisjärvi, both Mike and I felt a very personal interest in it and I would have liked to be able to write home and tell him all about it. As it was, I could only pass on the general opinion that beyond having a certain scenic value, it was not up to much. But the Finns—possibly with reason—are always the first to decry their own film productions.

The showing of *Maaret*, however, was not the only event of interest that I missed; there was a wedding and the christening of the Eho's new baby, born in Christmas week. As these were the only functions of their kind to occur in my circle during the year, I would naturally have liked to see both. As ceremonies I know that I should have found them interesting, for in the Finnish approach to all such things there is frequently an intriguing blend of the romantic and the practical. Nor is the practicalness of the Finn in any sense a veneer; it has existed, side by side with their romanticism, since the beginning of time. To-day the urge to give flowers on all occasions of importance is nation-wide; so too is the highly practical system by which they may be replaced by cards. Whether the occasion demands good wishes, congratulations or condolences is completely immaterial. Anyone who so wishes may go to any bank, where, in aid of certain specific charities, a card appropriate to his needs may be bought. All that the donor has to do is to choose which charity he intends to support and the extent of the subscription he wishes to give. He then despatches the card in lieu of flowers. By this very simple means the charities benefit enormously and the people themselves save a good deal of money, for throughout most of the year in Finland the cost of flowers is exorbitant.

* * *

Madge gave me a warm welcome, and very soon I felt completely at home in her flat, and indeed Madge's flat was far more homely than most, for it gloried in an altogether un-Finnish disorder. But then Madge was only a Finn on her father's side. Her mother had been half English and half German and her childhood had been spent under the Tzarist régime in St. Petersburg. She spoke English, Swedish, German, French and Russian with equal ease and Finnish only slightly less fluently, but at bottom she held tenaciously to her English strain and preferred to talk English whenever possible.

Madge's flat was tiny, being little more than a bed-sitter which we had perforce to share. This made me feel extremely indebted to her, for, after all, I was a complete stranger and her room was already well filled with knick-knacks, photographs and a Christmas tree. But it would have taken more than a small matter of space to worry Madge, who was kindness and hospitality itself.

I arrived on the morning of New Year's Eve, and in the evening we set out together to the Suurtori Square to see the New Year in. As a festival the New Year means a great deal to the Finns and in this, as in many other respects, they resemble the Scots. People who never go to church the whole year round will turn out on New Year's Eve, and in Helsinki all who can flock to the great Church of St. Nicholas. Consequently, long before we arrived, it was packed with people who, having overflowed from the pews, were standing shoulder to shoulder in the aisles.

Having failed to wedge ourselves into the church, Madge and I waited outside. The terrace where we stood was thronged and so was the area at the foot of the steps, where a magnificent Christmas tree, brilliantly lit with white lights, towered above the statue of Alexander II. We had a long time to wait and all the while our feet grew colder and colder, so that when at last things started to happen, I was so torn between interest and discomfort that I cannot remember very clearly what took place, and certainly I cannot swear to the sequence of events. But I believe that at midnight the officiating clergy came out of the main doorway and stood at the top of the steps and that all the bells started pealing. The brass band that was assembled beneath then struck up the National Anthem and all the people burst into song. From this point onwards my memory is completely blurred and the ceremony a confusion of hymns, prayers and addresses that were given through microphones and loudspeakers both in Finnish and Swedish and in which I understand a high city official added his voice to that of the Chaplain-in-Chief to the Finnish Army. Yet, if he did, it made singularly little impression on me, but then neither did the fireworks and the flood-lighting, which, I have since been assured, must have enlivened the proceedings. If they did, they passed metaphorically as well as literally over my head, which, I think, proves that they were not as impressive as they might have been, and were probably still suffering from the aftermath of war.

New Year's Day being a holiday, I spent a pleasantly social day with Madge, but on the days that followed she went back to work and I was left largely to my own devices. Nevertheless, she did manage to take time off to visit the Arabia porcelain factory with me.

The Arabia works are said to be the largest of their kind in Europe, and they are undoubtedly a huge concern and one of world-wide repute. By special arrangement, we were shown round by Friedl Kjellberg, one of the most celebrated artists on Arabia's staff, and a sister-in-law of Anna Ekström. We found her at work in the wing of the building that is entirely given up to the studios of the firm's leading artists. Here a greal deal of beautiful pottery is made—pottery that left me with the feeling that the prevailing mastery of form and glaze was well in advance of that painted design. Our guide specialised in glazes, and those which she produced were exquisite. So too was a white egg-shell porcelain that she moulded and decorated with a translucent design, suggestive of the Chinese rice pattern.

But though interesting and original work emanates from the studio wing, the bulk of Arabia's output is mass-produced ware, and of this the production is enormous. Yet only the cheapest varieties could be bought on the Finnish market. All good quality china was—shades of this country!—for export only and, living in Finland, one inevitably asked where it was. Assuredly, it was not in the shops or the homes of my friends where, time and time again, I was struck by the contrast between their beautiful, highly burnished copper coffee kettles and their unattractive coffee cups.

Wandering from workshop to workshop, however, it was not the dearth of high-grade china that impressed itself upon me—

for after all it was made in plenty for the export market—but rather that the high-grade china too was unexpectedly lacking in charm. I particularly remember noticing this, because I had set out with a hope that, as a foreigner, I might be allowed to buy and send home some of the coffee cups that were destined for abroad. But I never even got as far as asking if I might, because I did not see any that I wanted to buy. The reason for this is, I believe, to be found in the rapid development of the Finnish china industry, which has, to all intents and purposes, been fully industrialised since birth. It is without background; no highly developed artistic tradition preceded the era of mass production. When Arabia was founded in 1874, pottery in Finland was a purely utilitarian peasant craft, and not a very advanced one at that, because, wherever possible, wooden utensils were in use.

Abroad Arabia's reputation rests largely on the fact that its wares are excellent value for money. At home, the firm is so well established that it practically holds the monopoly of the china and earthenware trade. From the Gulf of Finland to the Arctic, Arabia's wares flood the market and the result is frankly monotonous. The same polychrome jugs, fluted bowls and ash-trays fill the shop windows in Helsinki as in Rovaniemi, and very soon I was bored by the sight of them. The factory, however, was far from boring; it was all absorbing, and Madge and I walked for miles and miles without seeing anything like everything.

* * *

As a town Helsinki is not at its best in winter-time. It is damp and inclined to be foggy and though actually warmer than it is in the north, it feels colder. This year the smaller harbours were all ice-bound, but as the weather was not particularly cold the great South Harbour was still unfrozen. In it, the chunks of slate-grey ice that bobbed up and down looked bitterly cold, colder by far than the sheets of snow-clad ice that blocked the other waterways. Wherever I turned, the appearance of the city was dour and chill. The sky was an almost uniform grey and underfoot the roads were so slippery that the speed of the motor traffic appalled me. Yet Helsinki, with all its winter greyness, remains to the young Finn the hub of the Universe—the acme of all that is gay and the one place in which to see life with a capital "L."

As far as I was concerned, my visit though peaceful and pleasantly social was by no means exciting. Nevertheless, I enjoyed myself. For some of the time Heljä was there and together we pottered about the museums and galleries, listened to music and went to the theatre and, in the intervals between these activities, I browsed in the book-shops, visited the Council, gossiped with its personnel and chose out of their catalogue a selection of gramophone records of English music which they promised to lend me and with which I hoped to while away the first club meeting after my return. In this I made a mistake, I should have listened to them before making a selection, for some of them were very well worn indeed. But the outstanding feature of my holiday was the visit that I paid to the new children's clinic, which was constructed between 1942 and 1946 and which owes its existence to the vision and untiring efforts of Professor Arvo Ylppö.

Professor Ylppö is Finland's foremost children's specialist, and in the new children's hospital in Helsinki all his most cherished ideas have found expression. In plan, he will tell you, it resembles an outspread hand with four fingers, each finger containing several superimposed wards and working as a separate unit so as to prevent the spread of infection, the palm being devoted to offices, laboratories, lecture-rooms and the like. The result appears to be such simple, obvious sense that it is hard to appreciate how much thought must have gone into the design.

Every ward faces southwards and gives directly on to a wide balcony, the three stories of each wing being stepped back so that nothing comes between the sunshine and the sick babies who have been put out of doors. And because it follows from this that the higher up the building, the smaller the floor space, the infants are nursed at the top and the bigger children on the lower floors.

I was fortunate in meeting Professor Ylppö; a mutual friend took me to lunch in his house adjoining the hospital. There he greeted us—the smallest man that I have ever met. Perhaps this is the secret of his great love for children; certainly viewed from behind, he would be lost in any group of preparatory schoolboys, as he is not only short, but his frame is very slight. However, what he loses in size he makes up for in personality, and his drive and initiative alone led, in spite of acute wartime shortages, to the realisation of his dream and to the ingenious plan that made its financing possible. At a time when everybody was feeling the pinch, he evolved a scheme for raising money that not only made the building of his hospital a feasible proposition, but which ended by crippling the black market.

Broadly speaking what he did was this: he launched an appeal for funds in the U.S.A. which met with considerable response among Finnish-American citizens and then, instead of having the money transferred to Helsinki, he asked that it should be used in the U.S.A. to buy and ship coffee to Finland. This he did with the connivance of the Finnish Government, who agreed that the coffee should be sold on the open market at a price approaching that which it fetched on the black market—approximately 2,000 marks, or £4, a kilo. Neither the State nor the retailers lost anything by this arrangement, and the excess profits, which amounted to considerably more than the original sum raised in America, all went to the hospital. So successful was this scheme that both sugar and chocolate were subsequently brought into the country in much the same way. The people were naturally pleased that the hospitals should benefit at the expense of the black marketeers and, by the time I left Finland in April, 1948, the procedure had long since ceased to be basically dependent on American charity. With Government connivance, almost unlimited sugar could be bought at a price, and the black market in many products had disappeared. Since then the process has snowballed and been turned to all manner of uses, the last of which was the building of the new school of economics out of nylon stockings, motor cars and luxury goods generally. But this was its swan song; the whole thing was getting out of hand and the Government have been forced to put a stop to it altogether.

After lunch I was taken round the hospital. It was not a very extensive tour, but it was quite sufficient to show just what a children's hospital can be. Every ward was divided into small small soundproof rooms containing from two to six beds, and from each of these rooms a french window opened on to a balcony. These wardlets were easy to supervise, as the partitions between were largely of glass and each one was connected by microphone with a sounding board on the desk of the sister in charge. This served a dual purpose; it made it easy to keep track of the children who were likely to be restless and wakeful without disturbing them unnecessarily, and by means of it and a system of signals any nurse could summon help without leaving her patient. Furthermore, to be able to listen unobserved is said to be often very helpful in the case of psychopathic children.

Professor Ylppö had had three great aims; to minimise the risk of infection, to give the maximum amount of fresh air and sunshine to each child and to provide an all-in training centre for doctors and nurses. His hospital ensures all three. There is fresh air and there is sunshine, and short of housing infectious diseases in separate buildings—an impracticable proposition in Finland, where the climate would necessitate making each building self-sufficient—no greater degree of isolation than having separate wings could be achieved. Moreover, the composite building is ideal for teaching purposes. Under one roof, the students of pediatrics can complete every branch of their training, even to that of preventative medicine, which is catered for by the welfare centre in the main block. And because the treatment of premature babies is the professor's overriding concern, there too he has established a mothers' milk bank for the benefit of the children under his care. Unfortunately, these are the lucky few, for ten out of every 100 births in Finland are said to be premature[1] and among them the mortality rate is 50 per cent. The root cause of this high mortality rate is Finland's geography, which makes efficient health services very difficult to organise and maintain. Nevertheless, a start has been made, as the law now demands that every city and rural community shall keep up at least one child health centre and shall employ a sufficient number of public nurses. The figure designated as sufficient is one nurse for every 4,000 inhabitants, by which the existing shortage may be gauged. Lapland and the remoter parts of northern Finland are visited by mobile child health centres staffed by hardy nurses and doctors who trek from one place to the next by any available means of transport, but more often than not on foot or on skis.

* * *

The morning of the day that I was to leave Helsinki I lost my wallet. I had just been to the bank, and in it were 10,000 marks, my return ticket to Kajaani and my sleeper reservation, not to mention sundry other personal papers. It was some time, however, before I realised I had lost it and when I did I was

[1] For statistical purposes, Professor Ylppö reckons as premature all babies that weigh less than 2,500 grams (roughly 5½ lb.) at birth.

horror-struck. Systematically, I began to retrace my steps until, fortunately for me, I ran it to earth in the General Post Office. It was returned to me by an old man with snow-white hair who told me that he had searched through it in vain for my name and address, but had only been able to find my sleeper reservation. He had, therefore, rung up the railway office to ask where I could be found, but they had been unable to enlighten him, and so, he assured me smiling, he had decided to wait until the evening and take it in person to the train. Impressed beyond words by his kindness and consideration, I thanked him as well as I knew how.

That evening as I lay ruminating in my berth, I wondered not for the first time whether the books I was taking back with me would prove a successful choice. It was not easy to cater for needs, tastes and standards that were so varied. One group in particular needed something to read. It was one composed of factory personnel, and it included their lawyer, Harri Attila, two chemists, Juho Jorma and Kauko Tamminen, a forester, Pauli Simola and an accountant, Eino Juntunen.

They were an amusing quintet, though at the outset I found them a very hard nut to crack. Although they did not appear to know a great deal, they, like everybody else, wanted to talk; but if making conversation by the hour was difficult in a private house, it was doubly difficult in the school building, where the atmosphere always had a paralysing effect upon me. But there was no alternative; the midday hours which I still spent at the mill were insufficient to cater for all the personnel who had been detailed to learn English, so some were obliged to come to school after work in the evening. Partly, I think, it was the sight of five big men wedged into five small wooden desks that I found so disconcerting—they looked so horribly uncomfortable—and partly it was Harri Attila, who threw me out of countenance. He was so extremely precise, he wanted chapter and verse for everything I told him, and in his choice of vocabulary his instinct always led him to the longest of words. He was, in fact, every inch a lawyer. Nor was Kauko Tamminen's attitude calculated to inspire confidence, for every time I even as much as glanced in his direction, his face would pucker up and his mouth twitch disconcertingly with mirth. I am far from complaining, however. The ice once broken, their enthusiasm grew and I very soon found myself, instead of dreading it, positively looking forward to teaching them. They turned up with such clockwork regularity, they were quite disarmingly polite, and even in their hard wooden desks they contrived to look happy.

I believe it was really the Bible stories that did the trick, as from the moment when, quite early on, in desperation I asked them to tell me about the Ark, they never stopped grinning. Largely I think this was because their knowledge, or lack of Biblical knowledge, gave them scope for teasing each other. Be that as it may, the Old Testament was a gold-mine of stories that we had in common, or perhaps I should say to which we had common access, for they certainly had to be dug out from the dim recesses of their minds and shaken free of cobwebs. All things considered, the going was good; between September and Christmas we ran through the stories at the rate of two a week, and very colourful stories they used to produce, even if the tone was often rather out of the ordinary. There was, for instance, the day when I asked them to tell me about "the writing on the wall." The story having been prepared, I waited for someone to begin. Someone did:

"King Belshazzar of Babylon was throwing a party for his wives and his mistresses . . ."

(Shades of *Brush Up* which we were reading concurrently!)

"Concubine is the word we generally use," I put in.

"Why?" said Harri, "My dictionary distinctly says 'mistresses.' "

Kauko's mouth began to twitch ominously.

"Really, I don't know why," I answered, "but it's only in the West that men keep mistresses; in the East they have concubines."

"There is only one word in Finnish," he persisted.

Any minute I felt I should be out of my depth, so I carried on hastily, "Anyway, you can't say 'throwing a party' when you are telling a Bible story—at least, we wouldn't. I know it's in *Brush Up*, but . . ."

Obviously there were certain risks in using *Brush Up* as a text-book. Once I half expected that it would get us expelled from the school premises, and all because the chapter on playing bridge led us to embark on a game. That is to say, I set out to teach my pupils to play cards in English, and bridge in particular, and they ended by teaching me the Finnish variant, a game they call "screw," which is much nearer to whist.

Having bunched four desks together in the middle of the

schoolroom, the fun began. They talked, they argued, they carried out *post mortems*—not always in English—and they explained the rules to me all in a rising crescendo that resounded far and wide and led one of the school staff to poke his head round the door to see what was going on. Knowing the Head's puritanical tendencies, it crossed my mind then that perhaps I might be asked to hold my classes elsewhere, but nothing of the kind happened. All the same, when the party broke up and one of them dutifully remarked: "The Bible, what next?" I murmured in a subdued voice: "You can all tell me about the Tower of Babel."

By Christmas we had finished *Brush Up* and I had begun to feel that the Old Testament might soon pall, so I was bringing them Oscar Wilde's *The Happy Prince and Other Stories*. These stories, which appeal both to the child and the adult, are simplicity itself, beautifully told, spiced with humour and repetitive in language, so that, despite the small choice available, I felt that I could not have done better. That is to say, those were my feelings until the evening when Harri told me that he had just got a new book from England that was most interesting.

"What is it?" I asked with interest.

"*The Intelligent Man's Guide to the Post-war World.*"

I gasped. Close on 1,100 pages of concentrated economics, and I had made him study fairy tales!

* * *

I arrived back at the Freys' to be greeted by a most unusual sight. At the big dining-room table, paper and pencil in hand, sat Sirkka and Kalle looking every bit as intent as Harri doing sums. And sums, I soon discovered, were just what they were doing. The habitually tidy room was strewn with small slips of paper. They were on the sideboard, on the window-sills and on the floor, not to mention the table, on which they were stacked in neat little piles.

"What on earth are you two up to?" I asked, so surprised that I almost forgot to greet them.

They looked up and smiled wanly. "Income tax; you see, it's the new year."

I began to understand. The slips of paper were the counterfoils of all Kalle's receipts for the past year and he was totting up his earnings. On second thoughts, I think it was Sirkka who was doing the addition, while Kalle was busy telling her what to add. I cannot be sure, but either way it was a combined operation that had already been under way for some time and that still took several days more to complete.

When a Finn speaks of income tax he means two things: State tax, which is paid at standard rates all over the country, and municipal tax, which varies in amount from one municipality to another. Between these two the ratio paid by different individuals varies considerably, the lower income groups paying relatively far more to the municipality and the higher ones far more to the State. It is difficult to pin-point with accuracy the lowest incomes to be affected by taxation, because municipal taxes have to be paid on lower incomes than do State taxes. Furthermore, the tax-free allowances granted by the State and the different municipalities do not correspond. Thus, in Kajaani, a single childless individual begins paying taxes to the town when his annual income, after all allowances have been deducted, is over 36,000 marks—approximately £57—but he does not start to pay State tax until his taxable income has reached 69,000 marks, or roughly £110 sterling.

Take, for example, an income of this size, i.e. 69,000 marks; in Kajaani it pays 600 marks to the State and 4,500 marks to the town, making a total the equivalent of almost £8.[1] But on an income of 8,000,000 marks the State tax is nearly 55 per cent of the total, while the municipal tax is only 10 per cent. On incomes that are greater than 8,000,000 marks—incomes so few and far between that no one seems to be able to tell me exactly what they pay—I believe that the rate exacted is a steady percentage. Certainly as far as municipal taxes are concerned, they cease to increase by leaps and bounds and become a regular 10 per cent at the far lower figure of 120,000 marks.

From all this, it can be seen that the rates of taxation are very high; nevertheless, of recent years, this has not been the total sum exacted. In 1945, to pay for the resettling of the Karelian refugees, a capital levy was imposed, the final payments of which are due to be made this year.[2]

* * *

[1] This figure was reached after the fall of the mark, which took place in July, 1949.

[2] 1950.

The first club meeting of the New Year was the one at which I had planned to have the gramophone concert of English music, so, immediately on my return, I set about letting all members know that I had succeeded in borrowing the records from the Council. It was only then that I learned to my horror that the Wednesday in question was Kalle's name-day. Of course, I should not have been taken unawares, but as, in my experience, no regular club evening had as yet fallen on a popular name-day, this particular contingency had never arisen before. The day was almost on us and already it was too late to do anything about it. Yet, from the moment when someone remarked to me, "Oh, but didn't you know it's Kalle's name-day?" I knew that the meeting was doomed, since all the Kalles, Karls, Kaarlos and Kaarles celebrate their name-day together, for all are variations of the same name. Unlike a birthday, there can be no glossing it over; the name in question is blazoned beneath the date on quite half the calendars in the country.

About the attendant celebrations there is a great sameness and an atmosphere at once formal and dated. At about seven in the evening coffee and cakes are put out and the central figure and his, or her, family await the arrival of their friends.[1] In the course of my year in Kajaani, I attended quite a lot of these functions and in the main they were stereotyped and dull. Perhaps this is natural, for the very publicity of the occasion makes picking and choosing among friends and relations impossible. Convention rules the day; all must be invited, and even people who normally gave very successful parties were apt to lapse on name-days into a formality as unvaried as the form of entertainment.

Only about twelve people turned up to the club meeting, and their coming was, I am sure, purely out of consideration for me. Anyway, they were twelve more than I had expected, for most of them had to visit two or three houses that evening. Consequently, there was a general understanding that all should leave early. This they did, though scarcely early enough, for the gramophone was not of the best and the records when unpacked turned out to be very old indeed. Perhaps, I mused as I listened, I was lucky that the audience was a small one, for the concert was palpably not one of my happier inspirations, even if the programme—bar a few typing errors—did look all

[1] Some people have name-day parties in the afternoon as well as in the evening.

right on paper. It included works of Purcell, Elgar, Sullivan, Delius, Vaughan Williams and others, but the only one for whom the company showed any real appreciation was Elgar. As for Delius, he was altogether too much for them, and in the very middle of "On Hearing the First Cuckoo in Spring," I distinctly remember Gretel remarking loud and clear, "Where's the cuckoo? I can't hear it. What's this got to do with a cuckoo, anyway?" just as if she was expecting something in the nature of Haydn's Toy Symphony. Although we laughed a lot, no one could have called the evening a musical success, so we packed up early and went in a body to join the celebrations at the Freys.

* * *

By February the days were drawing out and there was warmth in the sunshine—the season for ski-ing had arrived. To the Finns the month is known as the "Pearl-moon" because then—at any rate in theory—the eaves begin to drip, but I myself felt that the name would be even more appropriate to March, when it often seemed that the brighter the day the more I needed my umbrella. However, by mid-February, the sun was shining brightly almost every day; Eero helped me to buy some skis and whenever possible at week-ends I went ski-ing in the forest with my friends.

It was ski-ing after my heart, for the going was easy and there was plenty of opportunity to look about. Everywhere the snow this year was abnormally thick—so thick that the foresters feared for the young trees, which were at times bent double under the weight of their load. Over all there hung an immense stillness; a hushed silence that was broken only now and again by the soft rustle and thud of falling snow or the sudden piercing war-whoops of the young bloods who were belting along the trails and wanted amblers like me to make way for them. Certainly there was little room to pass or to ski two abreast except where the trails followed the wide cuttings that had been cleared to prevent the spread of the forest fires that are a constant source of potential danger to the country. Their occurrence is so serious a matter that every able-bodied man in the district must help to fight them whatever his age or walk in life. The alarm once given, the police round up all the available man-power and in the process they close all public buildings and places of entertainment. But as I ski-ed through the forest nothing could have seemed more remote than such an emergency. The air was clear and cold, the silence absolute and overhead the sky above the trails shone with all the blueness of the Himalayan poppy. I loved the forest in winter-time; weighed down by snow, the upstanding trees attained an Atlas-like majesty, while the young ones developed a new grace as they bowed before them like sprung bows. Even the Finns moved along the trails with a rhythm that contrasted sharply with their normally heavy gait.

To them, of course, ski-ing is no more a sport than riding is to a cowboy. Yet just as in the west of America everybody rides for the love of it, whether or not it is part of his day's work, so in Finland everyone, with greater or lesser dexterity, skis for the love of it as soon as the weather is warm enough to make it enjoyable, and with the opening of the season for recreational ski-ing, trails of varying length are marked out through the forest. These trails are not marked Indian fashion with an axe, but indicated quite simply by tying paper streamers to the trees so that the skier follows yellow, pink or pale blue strips of paper through the forest; it is almost as if the wood spirits had been holding an astonishingly mundane carnival the night before and forgotten to clear up after themselves. These streamers last a surprisingly long time in the dense and largely windproof forest.

Halfway along the trails, which are often circuitous, there is usually a hut—no Alpine chalet with hot drinks on tap, but a bare room containing only a table, a pencil and an exercise book in which all the passing skiers sign their names. The marked-out trails being limited in number, the object of the young skiers seems to be to get their names into all the books as often as possible, and thus prowess, or at any rate, enthusiasm, is a matter of common knowledge among them.

Towards the end of February, the children get what is known as the ski-ing holiday, when all the schools shut down for about ten days so that they can take advantage of the weather. It is about this time that most of the big ski-ing events take place. These, however, with the exception of the jumping, are not spectacular, for no one can follow the cross-country skiers as they make their way with maps and compasses from point to point through the forest.

About this time the Kajaani O.Y. held its annual sports meeting for its personnel, a light-hearted affair that apparently did not include long-distance ski-ing. Toini, Pauli and I went together—Pauli with intent to compete, Toini and I purely as onlookers.

I found the proceedings somewhat confused and rather lacking in excitement because there was very rarely a straight finish. Everyone was timed off and back and the stop-watch reigned supreme. Moreover, to make things doubly hard to follow, two or three races always seemed to be taking place at the same time and competitors and spectators were almost all dressed alike. Who was coming? Who was going? I had not the faintest idea, and only the confident voice of the Personnel Manager booming from a loudspeaker appeared to me in any way to control the goings on. Veterans disappeared into the forest in one direction, children of the workers in another, while groups of intermediate ages and differing sexes set out on other courses. Toini did her best to clarify the changing situation, but without success; I remained mystified and soon gave up trying to follow what was happening. Instead, I gravitated towards a hollow that had been scooped in the snow and in which a huge fire of tree trunks was burning. There Toini soon joined me, for it was chilly standing about and the warmth of the fire was very welcome.

There was no jumping contest—I imagine because the workers could scarcely be expected to be in sufficiently good training, although, at one time or another, many of them must have indulged in the sport, for built-up wooden ski-jumps are the characteristic adjuncts of all towns of any size and small improvised practice jumps are numberless. Outside Kajaani on the road to the mill there was one of these small jumps where every afternoon, as I trudged back from the factory, I used to watch the youth of the town practising. Here boys of all sizes would congregate, some of them very small indeed, for they all begin to ski almost as soon as they can walk.

Even Torsti, who was barely four years old, had his own little pair of skis. I have good reason to know this, for we went ski-ing together one Sunday morning. Actually it was Harri who instigated the expedition; he burst into my room when I was writing to ask me to go out ski-ing with him. As usual, I failed to grasp what was expected of me, so he dragged me off to Kalle, who soon put me wise. I looked at Harri; his eyes were alight with mischief and I strongly suspected that, knowing how shaky I was on skis, he had dark designs for my future.

But wherever he meant to lead me and whatever devilry he may have had up his sleeve, I shall never know, for Torsti effectually spiked his guns by clamouring to come too.

So we set out, all three of us, for a piece of waste land that was only a couple of hundred yards away. In summer it was a wide, dusty hollow set in a thinning suburb, but in winter-time it made very passable nursery slopes. To reach it the road led down a steepish hill and across the main road to the factory. Intrinsically, this area had little to recommend it; yet it is the one spot in Kajaani that impressed me above all others. Every evening on my way to school, I used to walk past it at just the moment when, in the late autumn and early spring, the sun would set. Then night after night the sky, the snow, the scattered dwellings, the railway sidings and the thin line of the distant forest would be lit with a flamboyancy that no one short of a Turner would ever hope to emulate.

This Sunday morning, my problem was to get Torsti down the hill as far as the nursery slopes because he insisted on ski-ing all the way. I never knew a small boy to have so much determination. Nothing would persuade him to walk down the road and let me carry his skis; he put them on at the front door and off he went. In his well-padded outdoor clothes, he was almost as round as he was high, and, because he was so small, it was considered dangerous for him to have fixed bindings, so he had only toe-straps to keep his skis in place. Poor Torsti, once on the incline he fell so often that he was soon barely distinguishable from a snow ball. He lost his skis and his sticks and on one occasion a soft felt boot as well, yet he remained completely undaunted—ski to the bottom he would. When I say that we spent the whole morning getting to the nursery slopes and back, it is no more than the truth but Torsti never once lost heart or, what is even more amazing, his temper. It was only at the bitter end when we were struggling home up the hill to lunch that he consented to let me carry his skis. And even then, on reaching the top, he once more insisted on putting them on to shuffle the odd twenty yards home. For a four-year-old, it was a truly remarkable performance.

Meanwhile, the unfortunate Harri had been done out of his expedition, but he had, none the less, spent a very happy morning disporting himself all over the slopes, for, like all Finnish children, he had learned to ski as a matter of course. In this they have no choice; as soon as the weather is fine enough, all elementary schoolchildren are taken out regularly twice a week and taught to ski whether they like it or not.

* * *

Towards the middle of February, I went to address the English Club in Oulu. This was the return visit that I had promised Stella that I would make, and although I looked forward greatly to meeting her and seeing Oulu, I have to admit that I went with a sinking heart for, not being at all used to public speaking, I felt horribly nervous. However, I was buoyed up by the knowledge that, so far at least, the Finns I had come across had not shown themselves very critical and had, in fact, had a reassuring way of assuming, whenever they felt bored or did not understand, that the fault lay in their English, instead of leaping to the all too probable conclusion that the lecturer was neither as coherent nor as interesting as he, or she, might have been. This was a most comforting thought, and to it I added the satisfying knowledge that however uninspired I might be as a speaker, the photos of my travels that I intended showing on the epidiascope were beautiful. So, as my train chugged slowly down towards the coast, I hoped profoundly that the epidiascope was in working order. But Stella I knew was efficient—she would never have chosen a popular name-day for a concert—so I was not really very anxious on that score.

The seaport of Oulu has a population of 38,000 and lies four miles up the river from the open sea. Lapp towns apart, it was almost the only Finnish town where I saw positive signs of bomb damage, and these I saw as soon as I stepped out of the train, as directly opposite the station a large area of the town had been completely flattened. In all the other towns where I had been, the damaged buildings had either been made good or so thoroughly cleared up that they were not immediately noticeable. This was so even in Helsinki, where only the shell of the pre-war Soviet Embassy remained to testify to the work of the Russian bombers. True, the Soviet Embassy is now housed in fine new premises, but the charred remains of the old one still stand, an example of poetic justice that the Finns delight in showing to all visitors.

Around Oulu the country is pancake flat, and the town itself is another of those small places whose layout is suggestive of a chess-board. Its principal charm lies in the river, which is very wide and full of islands and whose swirling water was, at least when I saw it, a remarkable shade of jade green. Here in Oulu, the great lake system, over whose upper reaches Kajaani Castle once mounted guard and down whose waters the once-famous tar boats used to ply, finally empties itself into the sea. From the town three great bridges span the river—that is to say, the road travels from the city to the north bank by way of two islands. These bridges are well worth seeing, and as Stella and I strolled across them the flatness of the ice and snow beneath us and the small, busy people wandering about on it, held much that made me think of Holland. But not so the bridges themselves; about them there was nothing of the orderly Dutch, for one of them was the most dangerous-looking structure of its kind that I have ever seen. It looked ripe for collapse at any minute, for the road, which led from one side to the other, literally undulated, and crossing by car was like riding on a switchback. I watched apprehensively while the buses continued to ply backwards and forwards fully loaded. It looked to me a very moot point whether the new bridge that was being built parallel with the old one would be finished in time. Higher up the river, a large new power station—one of the ten new plants destined to replace those lost in Karelia—was being constructed. It was scheduled to be completed by 1950. Luckily, the new bridge was not such a long-term project. Six weeks later, when I passed through Oulu, it had already been opened and the old one was being demolished.

I spent two nights in the best hotel in Oulu. It overlooked a small park and would have been very pleasant had not a wireless blared ceaselessly through a loudspeaker on the main landing. There was no escaping it; its noise penetrated into every part of the building, my bedroom not excepted, and when, just short of midnight, I eventually dropped off to sleep, it was still playing. That this should have been so is perhaps surprising, for the wireless did not then enjoy great popularity in Finland, largely because it was a political organ under Communist control. But by now it may well be that it has more devotees, for its Communist Director-General, Mme. Hella Wuolijoki, lost her seat in the Diet in the July, 1948, election, and in the following October the Diet transferred the control of the Broadcasting Company to a board of members elected no longer by the Government in power, but by the whole assembly.

The afternoon before the meeting was a beautiful one and

Stella and I went for a walk beside the river, crossing it to the north shore by way of a railway bridge on the outskirts of the town. The river, though narrower here, must have run more gently, for it was well and truly frozen the whole way across. Beneath us on the ice a detachment of Finnish soldiers was wading through the soft snow on the surface without any attempt at precision. It was not a smart turn-out:[1] their long, grey military greatcoats were suggestive of the German, but there was nothing of the highly disciplined robot about the men wearing them. Individualists to a man, Finnish soldiers are not greatly concerned with appearances. Stubborn, tough and brave to the point of foolhardiness, the only reproach—if reproach it can be called—that I ever heard levelled at them was that they were apt to throw away their lives defying all orders to withdraw.

That evening Stella took me to dinner with an Englishman, employed by one of the big local mills, and his Finnish wife. She was a remarkable woman, in that she was quite unlike any other Finnish woman I ever met. With her two children, she had spent the war years in England somewhere in the Midlands, where she had acquired very fluent English and the local accent. This accent in itself was rather surprising coming from a Finn, but it was as nothing to her vocabulary, which she had undoubtedly gleaned from her small son. At any rate, when the moment came to go into dinner, instead of politely indicating the way to the dining-room and saying, "Please, please," as most Finnish hostesses do, she rose to her feet and without more ado said, "Come on, chaps. Grub." I could not have been more pleased; the atmosphere of her home was so friendly and informal that my nerves all but vanished, and I arrived at the meeting in an unusually self-confident frame of mind. This was my undoing; I disgraced myself by talking for twice as long as any self-respecting lecturer has any right to talk, and have been feeling deeply contrite ever since.

* * *

Back in Kajaani the burning question in the Frey household was: What next? Kalle's appointment at the hospital was coming to an end and he had to set about finding a new one. This necessitated several journeys to Helsinki, for in Finland—

[1] In contrast with this somewhat colourless display, it is amusing to note that when William of Orange landed at Torbay, he had with him "200 Finlanders in bearskins, with black armour and broad flaming swords."

as I had learned to my cost the previous summer—it is impossible to arrange anything of moment without first going to the capital. Once there, a visit to the State Medical Department resulted in his being offered the post of Chief Surgeon at the hospital of Ylivieska, a small town about six hours' journey from Kajaani, on the Ostrobothnian Plain. Dubiously, for his hopes were not high, he set out to see what it was like, as, apart from the poor conditions said to be prevailing in the hospital there, both he and Sirkka were naturally sociable and neither of them anticipated much in the way of social life in Ylivieska, which was not only a much smaller town than Kajaani, but also a Pietist and therefore a Puritan stronghold.

Kalle returned from Ylivieska shaking his head. He had found the hospital totally inadequate to the needs of the district and altogether lacking in up-to-date medical facilities. Moreover, it was in the hands of a man who should have retired long since and it was evident that the townspeople as a whole were unconcerned about the state of affairs, the general run of Pietist community being conservative rather than progressive.

Should he accept? The matter was discussed at length and once again, this time accompanied by Sirkka, he went to visit the town. In the end he decided to undertake the job, but only on condition that the State agreed to build and equip a new hospital in Ylivieska that accorded to his specifications. At this, he was asked to estimate his needs, and there followed several more trips to Helsinki, during which he visited medical stores and compiled a list of necessary equipment, the cost of which ran into millions of marks.

"I shall never get all I have asked for," he repeated half-hopefully on more than one occasion, as if to reassure both himself and his family, and then added: "And if I don't, I shan't accept the appointment." But he was wrong, and almost before he knew where he was, he found himself committed to taking over the hospital at Ylivieska later in the summer. From his point of view, it was not so bad, for the revolutionising of the medical life of the district held considerable interest for him, but from Sirkka's angle there was little to recommend it, except that a large and pleasant house went with the job; a house, however, that lacked indoor sanitation and running water.

There, exactly a year after they moved in, I went to stay

with them, by which time the foundations of the new hospital had already been completed.

As for Ylivieska, it is a dull little town set in the middle of open farmland from which the forest has receded until it has become a mere background for the wide fields studded with small isolated hay-barns. These hay-barns are perhaps the most characteristic feature of the district, for they pop up here, there and everywhere, breaking the surface of the harvest like an archipelago of small islands. Yet plain as Ylivieska is, due to the prevailing Pietist influence, it has a more definite character than most small Finnish towns.

The Pietism that is found in Finland to-day cannot be traced directly back to the original movement which arose in Germany in the late seventeenth century, although this movement did reach Finland shortly afterwards by the somewhat roundabout way of Siberia.[1] There, on arrival, it is true that it took root, but its florescence was short-lived, and it died a natural death many years before Paavo Ruotsalainen inaugurated, in the late nineteenth century, the movement that now goes by the name of Pietism. Yet, as with the older movement, the basis of present-day Pietism is a fight for pure religion at the expense of doctrine. Nevertheless, its adherents are not Dissenters, but remain within the orbit of the Lutheran Church.

To-day there are some 50,000 Pietists in the country. Their headquarters are at Lapua in southern Ostrobothnia, and there, too, the strongest concentration of them is found. But though most heavily concentrated in this area, their activities are widespread and every summer in a different locality they hold a large open-air meeting.

Strict Pietists are easily distinguishable by their clothes. The women wear long, full skirts and tunics of unrelieved black and cover their heads with deep black head-cloths. The men part their hair in the centre and wear it in a long square cut bob, while their heavy cloth coats have three short slits up the back. This fashion dates from the time of Charles XII and the Great Wrath, and is the one that must have been favoured by the founders of the original movement in Finland.

Superficially the Pietists have much in common with the Quakers, but fundamentally they are poles apart, for pacifism

[1] At that time German Pietist missionaries were allowed to work among the prisoners of war in Siberia, among whom were a number of Finnish officers who had been taken prisoner when Charles XII was defeated in 1709. Subsequently, these men were released and, returning to Finland, brought Pietism with them.

plays no part in their doctrine. Their way of life, however, is not outwardly very different. Smoking is almost their only indulgence, and they look askance on pretty well all forms of worldly entertainment. The drinking of alcohol is altogether taboo and so too are acting, dancing and going to the cinema. Some Pietists even go so far as to refrain from planting flowers in their garden. For recreation, they depend entirely on religious meetings, and whether the celebration is in honour of a birthday, a christening, a wedding or a funeral it follows the same pattern.

The first close-up I had of them was when I went to church with Kalle on Sunday morning. From early dawn, or so it seemed to me, the bells had been ringing, but in fact they did not begin until 9 a.m., when they rang for ten minutes in order to wake the congregation. Again at 9.30 they pealed out to summon the organist, and at 9.45 to greet the Vicar as he arrived at church in rather the same way as an admiral is piped on board his ship. Still later, they rang out to welcome the congregation.

The service was an extremely long one and the huge church only about a third full, though I have no doubt that all who could come were present. Although not rigidly so, most of the men in the congregation were segregated from the women, but what struck me most was that the small children—and by small I mean any between eighteen months and six years old—who were, as a matter of course, brought by one or both of their parents, behaved as quietly as little mice. As I watched them and the age-long sermon flowed solemnly over my head—as it undoubtedly did over the children's also—I recalled quite clearly the Sunday afternoon on which I was forcibly removed from Children's Service bawling at the top of my voice, though just why I set up such a shindy escapes me altogether. No little Finns, I felt sure, would ever disgrace themselves like that, and once again I marvelled at their stolidity.

After the service was over Kalle and I climbed up the church tower and looked out over the countryside. The belfry was square and its windows faced north, south, east and west. Being Sunday, all were wide open, but on week-days they are shuttered unless there happens to be a funeral. Then as the funeral bell tolls, the shutters of the window which faces in the direction of the deceased's home are thrown wide open. Of the two bells that hang there, one tolls for men and the other for women. They ring for five minutes if the funeral is that of a child under five years old, for half an hour if the individual is over fifty, and between those ages the peal may last anything from ten to twenty-five minutes, according to the age of the person being buried and the wishes of the family.

Far below us, in the churchyard, stood the 1939–44 War Memorial—the statue of a young soldier on guard, designed by the sculptor to face the east and now tactfully reversed. This, it was not hard to guess, was the unkindest cut of all. Yet what on reflection I still find strange is the mental rigidity that failed to circumvent this mortification by choosing a subject equally suitable and less blatantly controversial.

* * *

That Sunday after lunch, we all went on an expedition to the seaside beyond Kalajoki. This was no mean undertaking, as Kalajoki was some twenty-five miles away and the party consisted of five adults and four children armed with picnic and bathing paraphernalia, for Martta and Kaisu's successor came with us and also my goddaughter Maaret, now thirteen months old. To take us all, Kalle had hired the ambulance, as Ylivieska, which had so little medical equipment compared with Kajaani, had in this respect stolen a march upon her, and the local garage proprietor numbered an ambulance among his assets. Into it we all piled, to be disgorged later in a forest clearing about a quarter of an hour's walk from the beach.

From a copse of burnished pines, the soft, powdery dunes fell steeply downwards to a wide sweep of firm, yellow sand that stretched away to the south as far as the eye could see; and beyond the sand lay the Baltic, a shimmering expanse of gilded turquoise. The fringes of the soft, dry sand were bespattered with clumps of keen-bladed blue-grey grass that petered out as the sand grew hard and firm, and down by the sea a shallow lagoon was separated from the Baltic by a low, rippling sandbank. It was an ideal spot for the children, for the water in the pool had been sun-warmed. To all intents and purposes, we were alone on the beach, and there we spent a blissful afternoon from which we returned towards evening drugged with sunshine.

* * *

The following evening, at my own request, Sirkka took me to a Pietist gathering. This was easy to organise because, in the district round Ylivieska, there is a meeting almost every night of the year in one farmhouse or another. It was to a birthday party that we went, or, more accurately, for the word "party" is hardly applicable, to a meeting in celebration of a birthday. It took place in a low wooden farmhouse several miles outside the town, and to it we bicycled. On arrival, we leant our bicycles against a tree among a lot of others and went inside. The porch led straight into the *pirtti*, or large farmhouse kitchen, where some seventy people were already assembled and overflowing into the next room. For the most part, they were sitting on benches that were roughly constructed of planks stretched across sawn tree stumps, and one and all were busily drinking coffee and eating biscuits. Already the room was hot and the faces of the men above their old-fashioned tightly buttoned coats were looking very pink and shiny. Beside one wall was a long table on which refreshments had been set out and in the far corner of the kitchen was a massive white-washed oven. Overhead a single powerful but unshaded electric bulb cast an uncompromising light on the assembled company and etched with detailed precision every line and wrinkle on the faces of the elders. All generations were there, but it was from the presence of the rubicund old men and wrinkled black-kerchiefed old women that the scene drew its warmth and colour; they might have sprung straight from the brush of a Dutch old master.

Suddenly a high-pitched, quavering voice struck up a hymn tune. The Vicar and the curate put down their coffee cups and took their places on two empty chairs facing the crowd, and then everyone burst into song; the main business of the evening had started.

Over by the sink, two young girls in pale grey frocks and white aprons went on quietly with the washing up. Demure beyond belief, they must both have been in their teens. The long fair plaits of the younger one hung down her back; those of her sister were neatly braided round her head. When they had finished washing all the coffee cups, they sat down beside the oven to listen, one on a stool with her chin cupped in her hands, the other on the floor at her feet. Sitting quietly there, they made a charming picture; they were so young, so pretty and so very serious.

When the hymn came to an end, the Vicar addressed the meeting. His address lasted for about a quarter of an hour, after which there was another hymn. It was then the curate's turn to speak, and his job was to pick up and amplify the theme inaugurated by the Vicar. These sermons were entirely impromptu and alternated with hymns throughout the whole evening. I believe they had three turns each—and, listening to them, it struck me with great force that, without a natural gift of the gab, it would be all but impossible to be a Pietist minister. These two, however, were at no loss for words, or, I imagine, for ideas, though what these ideas were I, of course, cannot say. I only know that the curate spoke with a continuous tremulo in his voice and that, with each word that fell from his lips, I half expected him to drop a tear.

As usual, the children were as good as gold, the only one to be noticeably restive being the small grandson of the house, who escaped from his mother on several occasions and finally wormed his way through to the front of the audience where he stood, the picture of wide-eyed surprise, looking up at the Vicar, whose tones were rising in the final crescendo that invariably indicated his peroration. As the Vicar's last words thundered out, the small boy raised his hand, and with a look of complete bewilderment, very solemnly put one finger in his mouth.

After the final hymn, there was more coffee-drinking and everyone partook of birthday cake. The heat in the crowded room was now intense, as very few windows were open, and for a long time I had been feeling sorry for the perspiring, overclad farmers and their families. A thunderstorm was brewing. It broke just as the party was coming to an end. It was almost too dramatic, too like the crack of doom, and as it crashed overhead, I was overcome by a deep sense of unreality that was only washed away by the downpour through which we had to pedal home, which was all too wet and all too real.

Although predominant in Ylivieska, the Pietists have not the monopoly of revivalism in Finland. They have a rival in the Laestadian sect, whose founder, Lars Levi Laestadius, a Lapp on his mother's side, lived from 1800 to 1861. Laestadius himself was a clergyman, who lived and worked in the area round Tornio, and still to-day his followers are most thickly concentrated in the north. The essence of their creed is that the soul is reborn after public confession and, at their meetings, in the ecstasy of rebirth, they are said to jump up and down, to sing, to develop cramps, and to make very strange noises. So strange are these noises that they have been onomatopoeically nicknamed the *Hihulilaisuus*. But this is all hearsay. I never consciously met a Laestadian, and I never had the opportunity of attending one of their meetings, but I know that most Lapps belong to the Laestadian Church and that they are as strict in their religious observances as their scattered circumstances permit. Among them, the Koltta Lapps, for whom I have a sneaking sympathy, are the exception. Having lived for years close to the Russian border, they belong to the Orthodox Church and of them Agnes Rothery writes: "They dance and frolic, and take no thought for the future, and trust to the saints to forgive them their sins."

One way and another, religious ecstasy seems always to have played a part in the life of the Finn, as from time immemorial their *shamans* are reputed to have beaten drums and thrown themselves into trances in order to learn the "Word of Origin" before weaving it into a spell. It seems therefore to be part of their temperament, and there is hardly ever a time, even nowadays, when some religious prodigy, usually a young girl, is not making a stir in the country.

One appeared in Kajaani only a month after I left. She was a kitchenmaid from the seminary, who, one night, startled her room-mates by starting to preach in her sleep. This became a nightly occurrence and very soon it was the talk of the town. Loudspeakers were rigged outside the house, and crowds came from far and near to hear her. As may well be imagined, the whole performance was suspect, so on one occasion the minister asked both Kalle and Aarre Uoti to be present in the room while she was preaching, and both of them testify to the fact that while speaking she felt nothing at all and did not react to pain in any way. The procedure was invariably the same: the girl opened with a text and closed by announcing the date and the hour at which she would preach next; a timetable to which she adhered with clockwork regularity. I cannot, of course, speak for what she said, but I did hear the theory put forward that she reproduced fairly faithfully sermons that she heard in the institution where she was educated. Be that as it may, one thing is certain: she was no isolated phenomenon in Finland.

* * *

Day after day, the February sun shone and in its growing warmth life once more began to stir, but the Finns were not destined to be able to give themselves up whole-heartedly to enjoying the spring, for beneath the surface there was a persistent rumbling. They might have been living on the slopes of Vesuvius, and when on February 23rd the eruption came, the Finns learned with more dismay than surprise that President Paasikivi had received a letter from Stalin inviting him to open negotiations for a pact of friendship and mutual assistance similar to those which the Soviet Union had recently concluded with Roumania and Hungary. Consternation was widespread; for a while there was talk of little else and rumours of all kinds were rife. In the Diet, the Democratic Unionists alone advocated whole-hearted acceptance of the proposal; the Agrarian and Progressive parties were in favour of declining, while the Social Democrats and the Swedish People's Party felt refusal to be impossible. There was thus a nominal, if half-hearted, majority in the Diet in favour of opening negotiations, so the President set about appointing an all-party delegation to go to Moscow.

Meanwhile, on the surface at any rate, life in Kajaani continued unmoved by the pending crisis, and early in March some members of the club set about producing a play. The one chosen was entitled *Red Sky at Night*; it lasted for about forty minutes, had a cast of three men and three women and, despite its somewhat suggestive title, had nothing to do with Communism. Gretel, Airi, Hilkka, Yrjö, Kalle and Eero agreed to act, and all six of them threw themselves into their parts with vigour and enthusiasm that I found very gratifying.

My hopes for the play were thus very high as I set about nursing their pronunciation, but it soon became apparent that I was no producer, so I asked Sävy Tähtinen to come to my rescue, as I knew that she had had considerable experience. This turned out to be an excellent move, as, although handicapped by her lack of English, she really knew what she was doing and worked wonders with the cast, and I very soon found myself being gently but firmly pushed aside with the assurance that the play no longer had anything to do with me as it was to be a surprise for the farewell party that the club were planning to give me in April when my year was up. So I gratefully washed my hands of the whole thing, and waited to see the results.

Towards the end of the month—on March 20th, to be exact—the Finnish delegation, headed by the Prime Minister, left for Moscow. Once again political excitement boiled up. Everywhere the country was gripped by a feverish anxiety, and the President, being well aware how averse the people were to relinquishing one iota of their neutrality or accepting any military commitments whatsoever, took the opportunity of giving the nation his personal assurance that the Diet, in conformity with the Constitution, would have to ratify any treaty that was signed by the delegation in Moscow before it could become valid.

The negotiations in Moscow were protracted; the Russians rejected the Finnish proposals, and two of the delegates were recalled to Helsinki for consultation. A new draft was submitted as a basis for negotiation, and with it Paasikivi wrote a personal letter to Stalin, informing him that he did not think that the Diet would ratify any treaty that laid unlimited military obligations on his country.

Easter fell while the negotiations were in full swing, and once again the school closed down and the children had a holiday. Heljä and I arranged to go for a week's ski-ing to Lapland, the Headmaster having very kindly made this possible by granting Heljä a few extra days' leave.

So early one morning, arrayed in trousers and carrying our skis, sticks and bulging rucksacks, we set out for Sirkka, a small village that lay between Kittila and Sarkijärvi on the self-same road that Mike and I had travelled from Rovaniemi to Muonio.

The first stage of our journey northwards took us to Oulu, where we had to change trains. There Stella met us and we had a hasty meal before catching our connection to Rovaniemi, which we reached in the small hours of the morning. Leaving our skis at the station, we started off on foot. Some relations of Heljä's had promised to put us up for the night, and our problem was to find them. Not that we thought of it as a problem as we set out, for our directions seemed more than adequate. From the station, we were to follow the main road into the town until we came to a clump of birch trees; there we were to turn left and go on walking till we passed some glass-houses, beyond which we should see a door with a light burning outside it. This was our destination. "Clear enough," we thought, until finding some wispy little birches—hardly worthy of the name, it is true—we turned too early, and were soon well and truly lost. All Rovaniemi was asleep; our very footsteps in the snow sounded muffled and hushed. There was no sign of a greenhouse, nobody to ask, no visible street names, no numbers on the houses, and, worst of all, over almost every door, like nightlights keeping watch over the sleeping town, a light burned. We felt just as the forty thieves, searching for the solitary chalk cross on Ali Baba's door, must have felt when they discovered that Morgiana had bamboozled them by marking every door in the district. Then, just as we were resigning ourselves to retracing our steps to the station and starting out all over again, we met a man who put us on the right road. After that it was plain sailing; we received a warm welcome, hot drinks and sandwiches and soon fell thankfully into bed.

Next morning, as we made our way into the centre of the town, I could not but be struck by the great strides in rebuilding that had been made since my last visit, and by how much pleasanter Rovaniemi was without the summer dust. As before, our bus started from the main square, but it left later in the morning and we did not reach our destination until about five in the afternoon.

At Sirkka, we were dropped outside the village Post Office, and from there we walked about a quarter of a mile down the road before finding our lodgings. They proved to be in a small box-like wooden building that housed a combined draper's and stationer's shop as well as an astonishing number of guests.

Although the house was tiny, there must have been quite ten people staying in it, and Heljä and I spent a lot of time wondering where the owners managed to sleep them all. But wherever they were tucked away at night, we knew full well where they ate, for we all had our meals together in a minute little room that was, I believe, the proprietor's bedroom. When everyone was at table, no one could possibly have squeezed round the backs of the chairs, and all dishes were perforce passed from hand to hand.

No preparations had been made for our arrival, and we had to wait fully half an hour while our room was made ready and some food prepared. While waiting, we sat in the kitchen and watched the washing up, which was in progress, the regular evening meal being already over. Doing the dishes was, it was soon apparent, a lengthy business. All the water had to be carried from the well and heated over the stove, with the not unnatural result that strict economy was observed at the expense of hygiene.

Our meal, when it came, was of reindeer meat, which in one way or another—the alternatives were little more than "hot" or "cold"—we ate twice a day all the time we were there. I neither liked nor disliked it; vaguely, possibly because of its colour, it reminded me of corned beef, and I reacted to it in much the same way; that is to say, I ate from hunger rather than greed and filled up generously on the bread, milk, porridge and potatoes of which the rest of the meal consisted. The routine of the house was simple; we were fed at 10 a.m. before we went ski-ing, and again on our return at about 5 p.m. In the early morning, coffee, which we ourselves supplied, was made for us.

Upstairs, Heljä and I shared a surprisingly big room that contained a brick stove and was filled, to the exclusion of almost all other furniture, by four beds. But if beds were two a penny, sheets obviously were not, as for economy's sake two beds had been ranged alongside each other so that one under sheet would be made to do for both of us. It was stretched across both beds, and as this left nothing over to tuck in, it was pinned in place with large safety-pins. Above this we had separate covers, for in Finland no one ever tucks in the top bedclothes, all beds being of the kind we call "nautical." As it was dark from 7 p.m. onwards, the whole arrangement was highly unsatisfactory, because, there being nowhere to sit, we were driven early to bed, and there being a candle shortage, we had only one candle in our room. If we were both to read, we had to share it, and if we were to share it, it had to be between us. With the beds as they were, this was highly dangerous, but luckily for us we had not expected to be provided with anything but paper sheets and so had brought our own. All that we had to do was to pull the beds apart and using one of our own sheets, remake them. Then, with the solitary candle ensconced on the chair between us, we whiled away the long hours of darkness reading.

Our first morning was beautifully sunny, and having drunk our coffee and dressed, we made our way across the yard to the *sauna* to wash, and then spent a long time pottering about in the sunshine waxing skis and fixing bindings.

How utterly unlike a conventional winter sports resort it was! There were mountains, it is true, but there were no valleys, no mountain railways, no ski-lifts, no hope of finding refreshment *en route*, no smart ski-ing outfits, no foreign visitors—save me—

and no need to see a soul if you left the beaten tracks. Finally, last but not least, I realised with some apprehension—for I remembered the tales with which Grania and I had been regaled at Koli—that there was no doctor nearer than Kittila, some twenty miles away. As for transport, beyond the daily bus and a few horse sleighs, there were only reindeer-drawn *pulkkas*. Guided only by a halter, the reindeer that pull these small boat-like sleighs seem to move at once forwards and sidewards in a strange, crab-like motion behind which the *pulkkas* skid happily all over the road.

It is putting it mildly to say that Sirkka struck me as out of the ordinary as a ski-ing resort, for the surrounding country was flat except where the *tunturis* reared themselves like giant sugar-loaves, iced on top and ringed by a dark line of forest—dark because the surrounding belt of trees had long since been stripped of its snowy mantle by the Arctic wind sweeping across the plain. Yet all winter sports centres in Lapland are somewhat similar, all being situated near to one or other of the *tunturis* up which everybody climbs. The nearest one to Sirkka rejoiced in the astonishingly Semitic sounding name of Levitunturi, and it was up Levi that we started off on our first morning.

We had not been gone long before I had discovered that climbing on skis in Lapland was hard work; nobody ever used skins, so for someone like me, who as often as not slipped back two steps for every one forward, it was a most exacting progress. Heljä's patience was phenomenal. She must have wasted hours just waiting for me as I puffed up the mountain in her wake, growing hotter and hotter with every step. On the first morning when I was halfway through the trees, I took off my gloves and put them into the sack that she was carrying—a harmless enough action, but one that I lived to regret. Poor Heljä, all the extra bits of exertion always fell to her share, and as usual it was she who was carrying the sack containing our sweaters, the wax and some sandwiches with which we had thoughtfully provided ourselves. Even so, she was well ahead of me, and out of my sight when she came out into the open above the trees.

Here the hillside curved upwards from the hollow where she was standing in a great inverted semicircle, and scattered over the slopes above her quite a number of skiers were practising. Seeing this, she took off the sack, left it under a tree and went on to join them. A little later, I too emerged into the open, but by a slightly different route, so I failed to see the sack which she had abandoned and continued climbing until, about half an hour later, I reached the top of the *tunturi*. As I breasted the summit, I was greeted by an icy wind that seemed to come straight from the North Pole, and I yelled to Heljä for my gloves. Only then did I learn that she had left the sack in the hollow below, knowing full well that we should be practising all day in the vicinity and thinking, reasonably enough, that I should see it in passing. What she had not bargained for was my taking a short-cut—one of those many short-cuts that end up by being so much longer than the proper way.

I only gave a cursory glance at the view, for my hands, which a few minutes before had been damp with heat, were now freezing and growing steadily more and more painful with every minute that passed. It was more than I could bear; I turned and made full tilt for the sack that Heljä pointed out to me lying under a tree in the hollow.

The result was disastrous; the Arctic wind had whipped the snow, which in the woods had been fine and powdery, into a treacherous crust that rippled up the mountainside. I started on a steep traverse, gathered momentum, lost control, and very soon was falling over and over to the bottom of the slope that had just taken me half an hour to climb. I fell the whole way down to the bottom, losing both my sticks and one ski in the process. I got up feeling sick and winded, retrieved my lost ski, which was mercifully within reach, and limped in a daze towards the sack. Things might have been worse, but even so it was for me a minor catastrophe, as I gave my knee a very nasty wrench in falling, the pain of which lasted throughout the whole of our stay. None too brave at the best of times, I now became shockingly timorous and unashamedly addicted to searching for easy ways down. High up, where I could see where I was going, it was bad enough, but low down among the trees it was even worse. What with the tree trunks and the undergrowth, I was in perpetual trouble, and once or twice as I lay inextricably embedded in the soft snow—for in the shelter of the forest it was soft—I saw animal tracks and my mind at once ran to those six wolves said to have been killed at Kilpisjärvi the previous summer. High up or low down, it was a choice of evils.

Yet in spite of my troubles, we had some lovely days on the

mountain, which we climbed by various routes and on which we generally found a surprising number of people, considering how deserted the village always seemed to be. And how professional most of them were, as they raced up and down the slopes, twisting and turning and hardly ever falling. So much of their country being flat, I was amazed at their proficiency, because not only was the going steep, but the snow was so very tricky. It was far too difficult for me, so it was fortunate that the weather as a whole was good and the sunshine high up on the *tunturi* well worth a good many bumps and bruises; and so too, was the almost aerial panorama that we could see from the summit of Levi stretching north, south, east and west far away into the distance.

After several fine days, the weather broke and we woke one morning to find that the wind was blowing at gale force. Nevertheless, we set out as usual in the hopes that the leeward slopes of Levi would be sheltered, but if they were it was only relative. Undaunted, however, we battled on until we reached the summit, where we found that it was impossible to stand upright. Moreover, up there on the hilltop, the snow was blowing so hard that it stung like sand and blinded us completely. Heljä suggested that we should return the way we had come, but that meant ski-ing along the mountainside above a steep cliff that was altogether too sheer for my liking. It was one thing to climb up that way, but quite another to ski down. So, putting on our dark glasses to protect our eyes from the stinging snow, we crawled over the top and made our way as best we could to the hollow where I had first come to grief, and then sank downwards through the trees. It was easy to see how the small pines that had struggled upwards beyond their fellows had become at once so sturdy and so warped. Pekka Halonen's trees, Heljä always called them, because they feature in so many of his pictures, but they were more than that; to me at least, they seemed to embody the whole indomitable spirit of Lapland.

We got back smarting and buffeted and made a bee-line for the *sauna*, which, no matter how much the worse for wear we might feel, offered unfailing compensation. Heljä and I had one every evening, and nothing could have been more comforting to stiff and weary limbs than to relax in its warmth. It was heaven to sink back in a blissful lassitude and let the hot steam soak into one's very being, and then by means of a little soap and a bucket of ice-cold water to emerge a short while later clean, rejuvenated and ready for sleep.

Yet in spite of the comfort to be derived from the *sauna*, I could not but feel sorry for the inhabitants of Lapland when I thought of the children in the village school doing their lessons for weeks together by candlelight, and of the old people struggling out in all weathers to the *sauna* and the lavatory. No wonder that the people go mad with joy in summer-time.

We left Sirkka on Easter Monday in a bus that was even more crowded than the one in which we had come. In Rovaniemi Heljä remained to spend the day with her relations, while I travelled straight through to Oulu, where I planned to stay a couple of nights.

* * *

Two days later, when I returned to Kajaani, the thaw had set in in earnest and the roads were running with slush. It was all very different from the snowy scene that had greeted me on my arrival almost exactly a year before.

This time the town was bubbling over with rumours. It was now a fortnight since the delegation had left for Moscow, and still there was no news and, as a result, my last days in Kajaani were coloured by the undercurrent of anxiety that flowed through the minds of all. There were startling stories in circulation about Russian territorial demands; this or that port was to be relinquished, Lapland was in danger of total annexation now that the railway line from Kemijärvi to the Russian border had been completed, and there was a real fear that the young men might be conscripted into the Soviet Army. In all, it was a crop of rumours of unparalleled fertility and a wave of people anxious to leave the country were caught and held on the Swedish frontier. Constant demands for the extradition of this and that person, alleged to be a Soviet citizen and generally a hapless Esthonian, had long been a thorn in the flesh; it was inevitable that some should think it time to clear out.

On April 6th, the terms of the treaty were broadcast to the nation. Irmeli and I were spending the evening with the Ehos when the news came through, and we stayed on late to listen. As Eero turned on the wireless, a great hush fell on the room. Understanding nothing, I could read little in the faces of my companions, so I waited on tenterhooks for the voice to stop speaking. At length it ceased and someone turned off the wireless. "Well?" I inquired, hardly daring to ask.

"It's not so bad as we expected."

A great wave of relief surged over me; until that moment I had not realised just how bound up with these people my feelings had become.

All over the country, the terms of the treaty were hailed with relief; they were not nearly so drastic as had been rumoured. Finland had undertaken to defend herself against any attack aimed at her or at the Soviet Union over her territory by Germany or any other power associated with her. If necessary the Soviet Union would render her assistance, but only—and in this the terms differed from those of the Hungarian and Rumanian treaties—after talks between the two nations had taken place. Finnish forces were to be used only within their own territory and Finland would be allowed to retain her freedom of action in foreign affairs. Both nations undertook to respect their mutual sovereignty and integrity and not to interfere in the internal affairs of one another. The pact was to last for ten years.

For the time being the evil hour had been averted, not but that everyone knew who would decide what was, or was not, a threat of aggression and that no power in Finland could prevent the Soviet armies from coming to her aid. But as this had been common knowledge for a long time, the situation did not seem to have worsened much. Nevertheless, it remained a fact that the treaty had been signed against the wishes of the majority and was just one more example of the unhappy plight of small nations.

* * *

By now my year was up, and in less than a week I was to leave for home. Preparations for the farewell party the club was giving me were in full swing. The actors were rehearsing vigorously and I alone was idle. In theory, everything was to be a surprise; in practice, all that was going on was an open secret, but that did not stop all my offers of help from being firmly rejected. "Go away," was the general refrain. "If you must do something, why not start ironing your best evening dress."

On the morning of the great day I woke early, and as I lay in bed the thought flashed through my mind: "To-night there will be speeches and I'll probably be presented with something and it will be up to me to say a few words. Whatever shall I say?"

I got up, collected a pencil and paper and made a few notes while I drank my coffee, muttering to myself as I did so, "Not too long, now. Remember Oulu." When I had finished, I arranged my ideas into what I thought was a coherent whole and memorised them, but even as I did it I realised that when the moment came I should probably put everything quite differently. Only one thing was certain; I must, at all costs, express the gratitude I felt.

Later in the morning, I ran into Heljä and coerced her into accompanying me to the nursery garden and helping me to buy some flowers to give to the players after the show. I was doomed to disappointment; in the whole place there were only eight daffodils.

"*Voi, voi*," I said disconsolately. "That's only one daffodil each and two for Sävy."

"Well, what's wrong with that?" Heljä rejoined. "This isn't England; no one will think it at all funny."

But I couldn't bring myself to give them one flower each; I was still too English for that, so I decided that Sävy should have the lot. After all, she was the producer, and she had taken a great weight off my shoulders.

About 7.30 p.m. the guests began to assemble, and when all had arrived, it was a most impressive gathering. Well over eighty people were present, as many English-speaking members had brought their non-English-speaking husbands and wives with them. Moreover, the sight of everyone in evening dress was very festive.

The private sitting-room that was normally reserved for the firm's guests had been turned into a stage and the dining-room into an auditorium, a simple arrangement, for at the best of times they were only separated by a curtain. Every seat in the room was full and quite a crowd were standing at the back. I sat beside Toini, ravishing in her white wedding dress, that she was wearing for the first time since her marriage. Under Yrjö's direction, wonders had been worked with the lighting, which, considering that the play dealt with the supernatural, was in itself a great achievement, for the lights went on and off innumerable times. And not only was Yrjö responsible for all the lighting effects, but I learned later that Sävy had insisted on his undertaking all the noises off as well, which for one of so dreamy a temperament must have entailed quite an effort. There were no programmes; instead, Heljä made a short explanatory speech before the curtain rose.

The play went without a hitch and I felt both pleased and proud of the performance, though it is questionable what right I had to be proud considering how little I had to do with it. There was a genuinely professional touch about it, and Kalle, in the leading role, displayed a mine of hitherto hidden talent and confessed to me afterwards that his youthful ambitions had all been towards the stage. There was no doubt at all as to the success of the entertainment, or the fact that the actors themselves enjoyed it. I think it was Hilkka who said to me rather wistfully later in the evening, "Now you are going away, there will be no more plays, and it was such fun." But she was wrong, for the following Christmas saw the club staging another one.

After the performance, the flowers were presented, and while the local photographer took some pictures everybody drank coffee and partook of very good refreshments. Then Airi, Sävy, Irmeli, Kirsti, and Hilkka sang some English part-songs which they had banded together to learn. It was delightfully done, and, as I listened, I realised, with full force and some chagrin, just what I could have made of club evenings if I had been musical.

After the singing came the speeches; that is to say Yrjö, shy and charming as ever, rose to his feet and thanked me very warmly for all that I had done, said a lot of pleasantly gratifying things and presented me, in the name of the club, with the most beautiful porcelain bowl of duck's egg blue crackle glaze, the work of Anna's sister-in-law, Friedl Kjellberg. It was filled to overflowing with daffodils and narcissi. Now I knew why I had not been able to get any flowers earlier in the day. Never since the end of the summer had I seen flowers in anything like such profusion.

Then, all at once, it was my turn to speak and, strange to say, it was all so easy. I, who all my life have been overcome by diffidence at the thought of public speaking, especially impromptu speaking, suddenly found that I did not mind at all; that I was surrounded by an aura of goodwill, and that all I had to say I meant so sincerely that it overflowed and bubbled out. These people were my friends; they were not at all critical.

I had only to say thank you—thank you for everything, and thank you above all for taking me into your homes and making me feel one of you.

As I sat down, Terttu Salo, my youngest pupil, rose to her feet, and read aloud to the assembled company a poem which she had written. To me, this was the surprise of the evening for, apart from all other considerations, I did not realise, as I undoubtedly should have done, that she knew so much English. Here it is:

"Miss Diana, now you go from here,
You were with us only, only one year.
It is too short time, now the sun set down
Our teacher—oh, she has gone.

"Many times you said, like this, 'Don't, don't say *No*.
That's wrong, quite wrong, you cannot say so.'
The language is very difficult to us,
But we said, 'All is well, what the teacher does.'

"We were many times very, very lazy
And I was every evening little sleepy.
The teacher said always try, try again
Write and read, read and write and so on every day.[1]

"Now, we must say, 'Goodbye,' our teacher dear,
But the memory is always, always so clear.
Some day, perhaps, you come back to here.
Welcome, welcome, our teacher dear."

Barely had she finished than Heljä was on her feet. "Everyone is being so awfully polite to you to-night," she smiled, "I'm afraid you'll go back to England with a swollen head. So I have written you a rather rude poem—you know we Finns have no manners!

"Our Diana so dear,
Who no danger does fear,
Said one day to me
'Before going away
I will one week still stay
Let us go to the hills to ski.'

[1] This is poetic licence; I hardly ever made my pupils write anything.

"So she took her rucksack
And she started to pack
It with things that you need when you ski.
Trousers, blouses and cap
And a *Huge* Lapland map.
'I am ready to start,' quoth she.

"Day and night, night and day
She went on her way
On foot and by road and by rail.
She had *Sisu*; she was tough,
At least tough enough
To reach Sirkka both hearty and hale.

"But climbing hill Levi
The snow felt so heavy
She muttered, 'I feel fit to drop.
It would be a fine gift
If the club sent a lift
To carry me up to the top.'

"After struggling high up,
Which was tea, not her cup,
She halted a moment to pant and to puff.
Then, with head in the sky,
'I'll see Lapland and—die,'
She cried out and—*voi—huiii—buff*.

"She was brave, I must say
For she climbed every day
To the top of that terrible hill,
With a hurt painful knee
And a loose-coming ski . . .
To fall down as did Jack and Jill.

"We're relieved she came back
With her full-packed rucksack,
We are glad she is with us to-day,
So I ask you to say,
To her three times *hei hei*
And wish her good luck as she goes on her way
HEI—HEI—HEI!"

The audience was in a responsive mood; they "Heied" lustily, drinks appeared and very soon everybody started to dance.

After a while Bertel Ekström came over towards me, followed by Ville Nurminen, Kauko Tamminen, Juho Jorma and Aune Perttunen.

"Come wiz uz," he said. "We 'ave zumzing to zhow you."

I do not understand how it comes about that I have not yet mentioned Bertel, because he always amused me so much. He was the soul of good nature and quite one of my most regular pupils; he rarely missed a lesson and as rarely prepared one. He did not need to; he spoke English with the greatest of ease, but not for the life of him could he say "th," or for that matter the letter "s." To begin with, I tried hard to do something about it, but I soon gave it up as a bad job. Ensconced in a big armchair in the corner of the library, he was perfectly happy with things as they were. There he sat and smiled, and every time I asked him the meaning of a word or a phrase he would reply beaming: "It iz ze zame. We zay it in Zwedish."

To-night he was beaming even more benevolently than usual as he and his companions swept me away from the crowded dance floor and into the pantry, where they proudly displayed a row of well-filled glasses of brandy. We drank a toast—several, in fact—and then with arms linked round each other, they sang "Tipperary" the whole way through from one end to the other, which was a great deal more than I could have done. When they had finished and we had had another drink all round, Bertel remarked with a grin:

"Now we will all 'ave a nize kizz."

So we had a "nize kizz" and became quite hysterical. Then, as the last drop of brandy disappeared, pink and gay and beaming, they propelled me back into the main room and started, as on my birthday, to toss me up and down. They kept it up too until someone's legs gave way and we all fell in a heap on the floor and, as a result, I was so bruised that I could not sleep on my right side for several nights afterwards.

* * *

The day before I left Kajaani, Yrjö's brother came out of prison, where he had been sent in 1947 because of his connection with what is generally referred to as "The Concealment of Arms Affair." According to the then Communist Minister of the Interior, Yrjö Leino, "arms had been concealed in practically all communes, the nature and size of these stores indicating the existence of extensive plans to revolt."